Police and

CW00369817

Government

Histories
of Policing
in Australia

Mark Finnane

Melbourne

OXFORD UNIVERSITY PRESS

Oxford   Auckland   New York

OXFORD UNIVERSITY PRESS AUSTRALIA

Oxford New York
Athens Auckland Bangkok Bombay
Calcutta Cape Town Dar es Salaam Delhi
Florence Hong Kong Istanbul Karachi
Kuala Lumpur Madras Madrid Melbourne
Mexico City Nairobi Paris Singapore
Taipei Tokyo Toronto

and associated companies in
Berlin Ibadan

OXFORD is a trade mark of Oxford University Press

National Library of Australia
Cataloguing-in-Publication data:

Finnane, Mark
    Police and government: histories of policing in Australia
    Bibliography
    Includes Index
    ISBN 0 19 553474 3.

    1. Police—Australia—History. 2. Police—Government
    policy—Australia. 3. Law enforcement—Australia—History.
    4. Police power—Australia—History. I. Title.

363.20994

Indexed by Geraldine Suter
Cover photograph from the *Age*, 10 November 1993
Typeset by SRM Production Services, Malaysia
Printed through Bookpac Production Services, Singapore
Published by Oxford University Press,
253 Normanby Road, South Melbourne, Australia

Dedication
To my parents, Patricia and Peter Finnane

Contents

Preface

The path from beginning to end of a book is long and often circuitous, for this one especially. My list of debts is considerable. The book had its origins in a research project begun with Stephen Garton in 1987 on the social history of policing in Queensland: I owe him an important debt for support in getting that project off the ground and for the continuing stimulus of his own work in a variety of related areas. Our intention was to provide a historical account of the processes of arrest and prosecution in a number of police districts in Queensland: the results of that research have been reported in our joint paper, delivered at the Labour History Conference in Sydney in December 1988 and subsequently revised and published in *Labour History* in 1992. The project was supported by a Griffith University Research Grant (1987–9).

I am indebted for the support from research assistance made possible by this grant, and a more recent Australian Research Council Small Grant (1991–92) for a project on the history of imprisonment in Australia. For assistance which has been especially important in its contribution to the substance of this book I owe a special thanks to Julia Reid and Nicole Skeltys. Other research assistance of use in this book over the intervening years was provided by John Houghton, Ross Laurie, Deborah Edwards, Christina Scott, Judy Smith, Martin Smith and Bronwyn Hammond.

The drafting of ideas for a book on Queensland policing took place during the early months of the Fitzgerald Inquiry from July 1987. The Inquiry had a major impact on the direction of my research which turned from what I began to regard as the limited perspective offered by a social history of policing which did not pay enough attention to the history of police organisation and of policing as an occupation. Papers which began to address these issues were offered at the ANZAAS Conference Criminology Section in Sydney in May 1988 and at the Australian and New Zealand Society of Criminology Conference in Sydney in July 1989, in the days immediately following the release of the Fitzgerald Report. Material published at this time in the *Australian and New Zealand Journal of Criminology* has been used, especially in chapters 2 and 8 of this book. I am especially indebted in this context to the continuing encouragement and interest of Sydney colleagues who have done so much to sustain a critical engagement with contemporary policing and criminal justice issues in Australia – David Brown, Russell Hogg, David Dixon, Chris Cunneen and Janet Chan. I think it was over a drink after the 1989 conference that David Brown prompted me to think about the sort of book which has resulted, providing an account of policing in Australia which historicises the subject.

The book might have been completed sooner, but in a different form, if not for my participation in the work of the Royal Commission into Aboriginal Deaths in Custody in 1990. This was a major preoccupation but a most instructive one for a historian of policing in Australia. I am grateful to Sue Sheppard and Richard Hall who worked in the Brisbane office for facilitating my work for the Commission at this time, and to Geoff Eames and Kathy Whimp at the Adelaide national office for their invitation to do some work on the final report. The chapter of this book concerned with the policing of Aborigines in Australia is an all too short address to some of the fundamental historical questions raised by the Royal Commission and deserving substantial future inquiry.

A further vital context of my work over the last few years has been through my role on the management committee of the Prisoners Legal Service Inc. in Brisbane. Knowledge and familiarity with some important features of contemporary criminal justice in what has become my home State of Queensland has been immeasurably assisted by the many contacts and occasions for discussion which that work has involved. Here my greatest debt is to the founding inspiration of the Service and indefatigable worker in the cause of law reform, Tony Woodyatt.

Institutional conditions can help or hinder research and writing. In my case, the Faculty of Humanities at Griffith University has been an impeccable employer. Two periods of sabbatical leave in 1987 (spent in part at the Department of History, University of Queensland) and 1991 and a period of special studies leave in 1993 have been indispensable aids to writing. My research and teaching colleagues, especially in the areas of Studies in Culture and Politics and of Australian Studies, have provided what I believe is a unique culture of interdisciplinary support of historical research in Australia. Part of that culture of support is also provided by the active research work of honours and postgraduate students. In that respect I have been fortunate in being able to read the quality work in policing and socio-legal studies of Jenny Fleming, Ros Kidd, Rob McQueen, Wendy Selby, Anne-Maree Collins, Jan Cattoni, Shirley Hotchkiss and David Moore.

Other colleagues in Australia have helped along the way by sending me material which helped to situate what I was doing. I want to thank Clive Moore, Darren Palmer, David Philips, Sue Davies, Wilfred Prest, Charlie Fox and Ross Homel as well as all those contributors to the volume of writings I edited in 1987, *Policing in Australia: Historical Perspectives.*

During my leave in 1991 I was able also to visit a number of institutions outside Australia to research, present papers, or just discuss my work: special thanks are due to Carolyn Strange, then archivist at the Law Society of Upper Canada, to Wes Pue, then of the University of Manitoba Faculty of Law, John Beattie and staff at the University of Toronto Centre for Criminology, Nick Rogers at York University, Helen Boritch at University of Alberta, Edmonton, Robert Reiner at the London School of Economics, Clive Emsley of the Open University, Jim Walter and staff at the Sir Robert Menzies Centre for Australian Studies in London, Peter Young and staff at the Centre for Criminology at the University of Edinburgh, Jacques Favier and Jean-Paul Barbiche at Université du Havre, Pauric Travers at St Patrick's College, Dublin, and David Dickson at Trinity College, Dublin. If I have a regret about the limits imposed by the length of this book it is that I have not been able to make the work sufficiently comparative, a requirement which appears the more pressing the more one has the opportunity to research outside one's immediate community.

Libraries and archives have been the source of most of the data in this book. I wish to thank especially the staff at Griffith University Library, the Queensland State Archives, the New South Wales State Archives, the Mitchell Library and the University of Queensland Library. For assistance with production of the manuscript at various stages over the years I also owe thanks to the capable support of Karen Yarrow, Janice Mitchell, Honor Lawler and Margaret Reade.

Support from a publisher and their editors, readers and advisers, is vital in bringing a book to completion. I want to thank Jill Lane of OUP, for her strong support of my proposal, as well as Mark Findlay and a number of anonymous referees for their like encouragement, and Bette Moore for her editorial care. David Walker of Deakin University was generous in acknowledging the potential of an earlier proposal to become something other than what was at one stage destined for a series he was editing.

I have an older debt. It only occurred to me at the end of writing that the subject of government and this way of writing about it was modelled for me in the work of Oliver MacDonagh, a former supervisor. The lucidity and economy of analysis of his books on *Ireland* and *Early Victorian Government* are things I cannot match, but I think nevertheless they have been important models: especially in their conviction that history, and writing about it, has a fundamental place in the present.

The love and companionship of Maureen, and the patience and good humour of our children Ingrid, Anna and Julia have doubtless been tested at numerous times during the nights and weekends on which much of this book was written: they know how much I value their support. The book is dedicated to my parents, who provided an upbringing which valued some fundamental social principles, of justice and equality, which policing and other forms of government have too often faltered in addressing.

Mark Finnane,
Griffith University, Brisbane,
November 1993

Introduction

This book is about the history of the present forms of police organisation in Australia. Its rationale is that contemporary arguments about policing in this country could benefit from a good dose of historical medicine. Alternatively, histories of many subjects touching on social order in Australia could benefit from a greater understanding of the specific contexts affecting the work of policing. It is a contribution therefore to the perennial debate about the proper function of police in society, but one which is distinctive by virtue of its attention to some little examined features of Australian policing.

In spite of crime and police being perennial subjects of media interest and entertainment for the masses, it is remarkable how little they have preoccupied academics and researchers. The subject is of considerable historical importance in a country like Australia, yet there was no history of an Australian police force until 1986. The subject has been almost completely absent from the research agendas or teaching of political science or government departments until even more recently. Consult any book on Australian politics and the most that one is likely to find about police will come under the heading of 'special branch'. Schools of law have of necessity had to pay a little more attention to police and policing, and a handful of the most important writings on the legal and constitutional relations of police have been the product of lawyers. Australian sociology has been similarly neglectful, though again the little that has been written about police in Australia has been closely associated with the work of one or two sociologists. For the most part then, this is still a very new subject in Australia.

Even among the most recent writings on contemporary Australian policing, it is rare to find more than a token acknowledgment of the historical conditions which characterise the modern period. Hence, the two most recent general collections on Australian police, *Australian Policing* (1989) and *Policing Australia* (1992) contain no historical commentaries on police or policing.[1]

Some may be inclined to see historical research in this area as essentially arcane in interest. That is a matter for debate. Nevertheless, it is striking that some crucial matters of contemporary policing are ill understood historically. Let us take one matter which is dealt with elsewhere in this book, that of the role and functions of women police. In a recent essay on the subject in Australia (dealing mainly with New South Wales), the early twentieth century development of the role of women police is seen as one which derives from a perception of women's role as nurturing and caring.[2] Apart from the fact that the references supporting this account refer solely to American and British research, the problem with such an account is that it inverts the much more contentious context in which women police were first employed in Australia. The initiative for employment of women police came from feminist social reformers whose primary concern was to guarantee the protection of women who came in contact with the police from being themselves abused. This was the same movement which sought to separate women's prisons from those of men, and which attacked the criminal law as a domain which privileged men's interests. Hence, while it is true that the longer term normalisation of women police as part of police organisation has had to combat restrictive definitions of women's capacities, this early history of women police warrants recognition at a time which demands that police and other government agencies recognise the different sensibilities and requirements of women as victims or offenders.[3]

Contemporary commentary on police is bedevilled also by historical ignorance on matters of significant change. Take a recent press report relating to the power of a government in New South Wales to remove a police commissioner:

> The legislative provision requiring bicameral support for the removal of a Police Commissioner was introduced in 1931 by the then Labor Premier, Mr Jack Lang, and survived an overhaul of the Police Services Act in 1990 by the former Premier, Mr Nick Greiner.[4]

Mr Lang was responsible for many changes in New South Wales government during his two periods as Premier. But this was not one. Indeed Jack Lang was in opposition and explicitly opposed the legislative change referred to. This was introduced by his successor in the office, not in 1931 but in 1934. The context is crucial. Like other police heads before and later, the New South Wales police commissioner (then known as Inspector-General) had displeased the Labor party through his allegedly partisan role in industrial disputes. Its displeasure was publicly known and viewed by the conservative government and the commissioner himself as a threat to the tenure of the office. As the Queensland and Western Australian governments had done before the war — and as the Menzies Commonwealth government was to do in the 1950s with respect to the tenure of the chief of the Australian Security Intelligence Organisation — the New South Wales government sought by legislation in 1933–4 to establish a very substantial impediment to removal of a police commissioner by a new government.[5] The incident illustrates well the political maelstrom in which commissioners have operated. Understanding the longevity of such a context is critical to understanding present conflicts and possible changes in the relations between police and government in Australia.

In spite of the accelerating growth in police research in Australia in the last decade, it appears to me that there are a number of difficulties confronting any attempt to evaluate the impact of policing in this country. They include the following: a tendency to apply the lessons of police research in the United Kingdom or the United States, on the presumption that the organisation of policing in Australia is basically similar; a tendency to argue for particular forms of regulation of police in Australia which fail to take account of the historical circumstances producing the present arrangements; and a fundamental lack of research on the history of legal regulation and, in particular, the history of the criminal justice system.

The themes of the book have been chosen to argue the case for a specific history of policing in Australia. In some areas Australian policing shares a great deal with characteristics in other countries. This is particularly the case, and predictably so, at the most public face of policing, on the street. It is here where discretion is highest and where the actions of police and the policed are organised by factors which have less to do with local political or organisational constraints and most to do with some fundamental features of policing as work.

In other areas I consider that there have been important differences between Australian and American or English policing, most obviously at the macro-level of the constitutional status of police and extent of jurisdiction of particular forces. The burden of the argument here is to identify what these have been and attempt to explain historically why these differences exist. The differences apply particularly to the relations between police and government, where I argue that conventional critiques of the politicisation of policing are historically naive. In regard to corruption, the topic of the moment in debates about police in Australia in the 1970s and 1980s, the historical evidence is much more difficult to gather, for understandable reasons. Nevertheless, the long list of public inquiries bearing on corruption in Australian policing, going back well over one hundred years, is further grist to the mill of the historian seeking to identify what has been specific about Australian policing.

The book develops as a series of themes rather than historical narratives. I have, however, adopted a rubric which groups these themes into certain historical categories useful for distinguishing the different elements of a complex history. The rationale for the three major sections of the book may be explained as follows.

In section one, 'Police and Government — Public Histories', I explore the historical organisation of police forces as important state instrumentalities in Australia. I examine the political conditions which determined that Australian forces were consolidated, centralised bureaucracies, rather than local ones. The effects of these decisions in the middle of the colonial period on the relations between police and government are detailed. So too are the consequences for the organisation of everyday policing of the centralised controls which have characterised Australian government. These are *public* histories because they bear on the most visible face of policing in the political sphere, affecting sometimes the very leadership of the police forces, and occasionally impacting on the government of the day. The contentious role of police (symbolically, instrumentally) in the maintenance of social order is well illustrated in some of the highly charged political episodes which are scattered across the history of Australian policing.

The second section of the book, 'Governing by Police — Social Histories', assesses the historical role of police in social life in Australia. The lineage of some selected functions of police is traced. Priorities of police, measured in terms both of action (by means of arrest and charge as well as informal intervention) and of inaction (by means of limiting police interventions), are assessed historically. In these chapters of *social* history I am concerned above all with understanding the differential impacts of policing in Australia.

The final section of the book, 'Governing the Police — Hidden Histories', covers historical ground which is least common in policing research. The *hidden* histories of policing are those which are perhaps the most politically and organisationally sensitive of all: the histories of indiscipline and of corruption. From the beginnings of the 'new police' in the 1820s and 1830s in Ireland and England, police administrators have been concerned with the production of police officers who would have the capacity to use their extensive powers, even of force or violence, with appropriate discretion and sensitivity to context. The boundary lines which police are required to discern in many areas of police work are matters of value judgment. Hence the perceived need to provide a system capable of producing reliable, competent and honest officers. Hence too the need to provide a form of government of police behaviour which would address the failings of errant police. On both counts the record in Australia has historically been poor. The argument here attempts to explain why. The problems are addressed through historical evidence from official inquiries into corruption and police misconduct as well as through research on police staff files.

Throughout, my intention is twofold. First, the current state of research, which includes a growing number of histories of the State police forces, enables me to outline some of the principal forces and characteristics which shaped contemporary Australian policing. Second, the primary historical data which I bring to the book through study over a number of years of policing in New South Wales, Queensland, and to a lesser extent other States is intended to open up the field for other research. Detailed statistical study of local areas would be immensely valuable additions to our understanding of legal regulation and social order in Australia. The work is time-consuming but fruitful, if done with the right questions. Other aspects of my research might also be developed through comparative studies of other jurisdictions — the study of police discipline on the one hand, or of the history of police unionisation on the other, offer rich areas of work for the future.

Police organisations in the last ten years have been undergoing the most substantial reforms since the 1860s. Previous changes have preserved the fundamental character of centralised and bureaucratic policing intact in Australia. Whether the contemporary moves to a new accountability through police boards or external commissions, towards regionalisation, and to enhance community contact, produce changes in the practice of policing remains to be seen. The evidence in this book may help to establish some benchmarks from which to assess future change.

Police and Government— Public Histories

The political context of colonial history was the most important factor in defining the organisation of policing in Australia. The specific form of policing in Australia, with minimal local political direction, derives from the colonial period. In the middle of the nineteenth century, colonial governments laid the foundations of centralised bureaucratic policing which have continued in substantially the same form to this day.

The consolidation of the various early colonial forces was an outcome of widespread perceptions and criticism of the failure of the earliest policing methods adopted. Typically the early colonial police were locally-based and controlled, with the development in some places of specialised police functions in bodies like the goldfields or water police. However, a watershed of change in social and political relations in the mid-nineteenth century put an end to these arrangements. The emergence of centralised police forces was not inevitable, and there was controversy and political conflict over the desirable form of future policing. But only in Tasmania did a significant degree of local police organisation remain after the 1860s, surviving only to the 1890s.

It is true that some specialised police forces survived the mainland centralisation of the middle of the century. But this specific-function policing also did not survive the end of the century, by which time the Queensland native police were absorbed in the regular police. While the Commonwealth in the twentieth century revived the idea of specific-function policing (in the form of the customs police, and the intelligence and security agencies), there has been only limited sign of its revival at State level.

Neither have there been any significant moves toward a reconstruction of local policing. Calls in recent years for a greater degree of community policing have not been directed toward divesting the State police of their control of this substantial responsibility. Even where there have been some minor experiments in local policing (eg. the Aboriginal community police of Queensland), the experiment has been patchy and resources to support such endeavours limited.

In spite of the strongly centralist character of Australian policing, it is difficult to establish that policing in this country has been generally better or worse than in other places. 'Australian Police Forces', wrote Commonwealth police commissioner Whitrod in 1959, 'have been administered, if not highly efficiently, at least not glaringly inefficiently in the past, and in any case, such assessment must be mainly a matter of opinion.'[1] Comparison of policing efficiency and effectiveness is bedevilled by the statistical hurdles of national and regional differences in laws and police policies, and by the inherent (and always unknowable) nature of the relation of policing to the incidence of crime. As David Bayley notes in a major comparative review of policing, 'variations in police effectiveness over time or space simply cannot be determined'.[2]

The task here is a more limited, but politically important one. If current concerns about the responsibilities and organisation of policing are to be debated in an informed way, attention must be paid to some of the institutional foundations of police organisation in Australia. To what extent does a particular administrative apparatus of policing, historically formed in a particular space and time, make police forces more or less intractable in relation to contemporary demands for a change in policing? Such is the rationale for the preoccupations of these introductory chapters on the relations between police and government.

CHAPTER 1

A 'New Police' in Australia

In contrast to police in England, America or Canada, most police in Australia are characterised by their organisation on a State-wide jurisdiction.[3] Like the Irish constabulary, which provided many of the early personnel and some of the organisational principles of police in Australia, the colonial police were, in general, administered from the capitals of the colonies. This important fact defined the conditions under which policing in Australia has operated only weakly as a community resource rather than a state imposition.

What were the factors which produced in Australia a centralised, bureaucratically organised police substantially autonomous of political control? The early developments were dominated by the colonial condition of settlement in Australia. Social conditions, anxieties about the new societies as well as the prevailing forms of government were all intimately involved. The inter-relation of these factors was played out differently in the various colonies. For most of the colonies, however, the crucial developments were at mid-century during the attainment of colonial self-government. As Table 1 indicates, to understand the colonial formation of Australian policing we must understand above all what occurred in the mid–nineteenth century.

Table 1 Formation of the Australian colonial police

State	Year of centralisation	Statute
New South Wales	1862	Police Act
Victoria	1853	Police Act
Queensland	1863	Police Act
South Australia	1844	Police Act
Western Australia	1861	Police Ordinance
Tasmania	1898	Police Regulation Act

THE IDEA OF THE POLICE

Histories of police provide two quite different accounts of the formation of modern police. The first says that crime is a perennial problem, that it has been accelerated by the conditions of modern life, especially by industrialism and urbanisation and that police forces were created as a response to rising crime. In this view policing is essentially a good thing, and police forces represent the successful achievement by the modern state of a means of social control in the absence of the norms and social bonds of traditional community life.

The second account suggests that modern police forces are marked by the conditions of their emergence in societies socially divided, above all by class. Police forces are not socially neutral instruments of a general social will for order, but are the creation of specific interests seeking to maintain their conditions of privilege in an unequal society. Hence, police inevitably function to protect the interests of the dominant class in society.[4]

In Australia, the former position was taken by the author of the first substantial work on police. In *The Australian Police Forces*, published in 1960, a Victorian police public relations officer, G. M. O'Brien, reviewed briefly the formation and subsequent history of each of the State police forces. For O'Brien, the 'police force is, in the democratic communities of the British Commonwealth, society's shield and safeguard', a bulwark against anarchy as he put it.[5] More recently, the historian of the Victoria Police, Robert Haldane, has presented a view of that force which, while not seeking to hide many unsavoury elements of its history, presents it primarily as the police which the people deserved.[6] In its rhetorical context such a claim is perhaps unexceptional. Yet its view of 'the people' is too generalised and unhistorical in its presumption of the capacity of the general will to influence decisively the shape and functions of institutions like the police. Such accounts also adopt a teleology of police development whereby all that has happened in the past may always be explained by the history of progress. When a police historian writes that in 1853 'the nexus between Justices and local Constables was severed, thereby bringing Western Australia's police organisation into the nineteenth century',[7] the meaning of police history is reduced to a positive progression from antiquity to modernity.

By contrast, radical critics of the police in Australia, while rarely devoting extended treatment to the history of the police, have viewed the police as inevitably, and usually wilfully, the agents of an oppressive state. Thus it was one of the greatest signs of the treacherous nature of the convicts, according to Humphrey McQueen, that some so willingly played the role of policeman. In their structuralist account of Australian history, Connell and Irving see the police as a state apparatus which played a central role in organising the development of Australian capitalism and the consent of the working classes. In the view of Andrew Moore, historian of the 'secret armies' which were a feature of inter-war political history, there is 'a special relationship which exists between police forces and the capitalist class', intensified at times of crisis.[8] The history of policing in Australia as in other societies suggests much to confirm such views of the importance of the police to the interests of the powerful within government and outside it.

Nevertheless, in their attention primarily to the functions of police (expression of the social will to order or protection of class interests), neither of these views is sufficient to understand the conditions under which police developed in Australia. Since Australian police forces were formed in precisely that period which helped define what the modern idea of police should be, we need to attend to the development of that idea and the contexts of its generation.

When the first European settlers arrived at Botany Bay in 1788, they did not bring with them the rudiments of a police force. What did arrive was some consciousness of the role of 'the constable'.[9] The security of the settlement was primarily the responsibility of the military, sent with the First Fleet. But within a short period of time there was already a proposal, from within convict ranks even, for the appointment of a constable who would assist in the prevention of theft and assault in the settlement of Sydney. The proposal arose in a context which would have been conscious of the demands for reform of the police which had been emerging since the middle of the eighteenth century.

These demands arose in the major urban centres of the British Isles. In the largest, London, the magistrates John and Henry Fielding had initiated the major English police experiment of the eighteenth century—the Bow Street runners. In the second largest, Dublin, the first town or city police Act of Britain or Ireland had created the Dublin Metropolitan Police in 1786. In spite of the later preoccupation of historians of police with a distinction between the 'civilian' style policing of London and the paramilitary style of Irish policing (allegedly highly influential in colonial contexts), the impetus to police reform in the late eighteenth and early nineteenth centuries was strongly urban, preventive and 'civil'.[10]

What characterised the demands for police reform from this time was above all the suggestion for a paid and permanent police. Insofar as there existed a police before this time, it was voluntaristic, and locally-organised. The much vaunted 'English constable' was an ancient office, subject to the direction of local magistrates or justices of the peace. By the late eighteenth century, the effectiveness of the office was being attacked.[11]

The idea of police reform, as it developed in early nineteenth-century England, was diverse in objective. When some spoke of a new police they conceived of an agency which would bring about order not just through increasing the certainty of apprehension, but by extending the regulation of social life. Hence Patrick Colquhoun advocated in 1803 a police for London which would encompass a wide range of duties. An organised police would make possible a better society because it would bring under notice an extraordinary range of irregularities which characterised the unwieldy metropolis of London.

In these ideas Colquhoun was evoking a concept of police which was more familiar on the continent of Europe. There, especially in Germany, the articulation of a method of statecraft had included a general theory of the administration of society by a centralised 'police'. In this context 'police' was something more than its institutional embodiment: it summed up the possibility of a government of social life for the well-being of the whole population.[12] In the social reform England of the 1830s, the generalised potential of police received a powerful push from the ambitions of the social reformer and bureaucratic architect, Edwin Chadwick, who extended the concept of regulation of urban life in ways which suggested the continuing importance of a broad-ranging concept of police.[13] In later police histories this broader notion of police was suppressed, in spite of the significant number of non-crime functions of police which continued in the nineteenth century and later.[14]

While such an all-encompassing notion of the idea of 'police' takes us some distance from the particular development of police in Britain, Ireland or Australia, its significance lies in it marking one end of a spectrum of possibilities for the scope of policing. Indeed, we will see that in the sometimes peculiar circumstances of colonial settlement, police took on functions which have all the marks of being part of the exercise of government broadly conceived.

To this idea of police—one which stressed the contributions which a well administered constabulary might make to the general welfare of society—another and more familiar one was added. This stressed the role of police in the control of public disorder. In England, and especially in Ireland, social protest and dissent in the early nineteenth century prompted numerous proposals for a permanent police which could maintain the peace. In the former, local resistance to the demands of central government limited the speedy adoption of a permanent police to London (1829), only slowly spreading to other cities, towns and boroughs in the following three decades. In Ireland, with a weaker local government base, the central government based in Dublin Castle framed initiatives for the establishment of a regular constabulary, from 1814 on, with a view to enforcing a minimum standard of order in the heavily populated and unruly countryside. The formation of the Irish constabulary as a nationwide permanent police in 1836 represented a determination to establish conditions of order in a society which was already, in the words of one of its historians, a 'social laboratory'.[15]

Disorder itself was not a unified subject of concern. The violence of early nineteenth-century Ireland, with agrarian crimes sharing a sometimes invisible boundary with political protest, was disorder of quite a different kind to that of urban crime which preoccupied many of the theorists of English policing. The functions of the peace preservation forces in Ireland, which preceded the Irish constabulary, were reactive: the outbreak of trouble in a disturbed district would lead to the dispatch of a unit of armed police to quell the trouble. Much was hoped, however, of the urban police in terms of their preventive function—regular patrolling would limit the incidence of crime. As time went on these two principles converged. The Irish constabulary, with its rural barracks and patrols which went out from them, was comparable in many respects to the urban police whose early days were marked by a good deal of hostility in various centres in the British Isles.[16]

In the context which most influenced Australian policing, the idea of police thus emerges as one which is complex in composition. It encompassed ideas of good government at one extreme, justifying non-crime functions which police have often had to assume even if under protest. In the form more familiar to us today the police would act as a more effective means of controlling crime through detection of criminals and prevention of criminal acts. At the other end of the spectrum, the police would act as the ultimate guarantors of social and political order through the control of dissent and protest.

How influential were these ideas of policing in the early colonial period in Australia? And what were the institutional means of their transmission? That is, to what extent were the ideas which found embodiment in the new police in Britain and Ireland reproduced or transformed in the colonial context? We know (potentially at least) a good deal about ideas of policing in the colonial period because they were important matters of political debate. Moreover, the specifically British and Irish dominance of colonial culture, regenerated by migration in every decade of the nineteenth century, meant that colonial ideas about police and criminal justice shared an immediacy with those being considered in the United Kingdom.

Hence, in considering the police arrangements in New South Wales in 1856, the Board appointed by the colonial secretary favoured 'a general system of trained Police', one which was explicitly modelled on the new police forces in the British Isles. The model, it is fair to say, was somewhat fuzzy in its definition but the mid-century appreciation of the innovative character of police developments in Britain and Ireland is evident in the Board's summary of the rationale for the police:

> The principle involved in the system on which the Irish, the London Metropolitan, and the various bodies of the new Rural Police in the counties of Great Britain have been formed, which is now partially in existence here ... we understand to consist in this:—That the Executive Police should be subject to an uniformity of discipline and ultimate direction throughout large tracts of country and, to a certain extent, throughout an entire territory.[17]

While favouring a separation of 'judicial and executive functions', the Board reserved its opinion on the relation between the magistracy and police, a subject of considerable contention in these decades. A matter of interest in the Board's statement of the principle of the new police, is the clear equation of the Irish and various British police forces, by contrast with the tendency of later commentators to distinguish between these two forces. The core of the police, in the Board's view, was its uniform discipline and direction under a governing authority.

Hence the pattern, familiar to Australian historians, of deference to ideas from 'Home' is repeated in policing matters. Yet it was evident to these colonial politicians that colonial circumstance required colonial solutions. A failing of the existing police Act was, said the Board, 'the machinery established therein not having been suitable for adapting a general system of trained Police to the peculiar circumstances of this Colony'.[18] Thus deference to imperial example did not mean indifference to local contexts. The shape of policing organisation was an outcome, not just of ideas, but of state formation and social conditions in the settlements.

THE COLONIAL STATE

Australian police forces are today distinguished by a particular relation to government which can be traced in its legal form to statutes of the mid-nineteenth century. The colonial Acts creating police forces specified that the police were to be headed by a single responsible officer, variously titled commissioner, chief commissioner or inspector-general, who was to administer the police subject to the direction of the colonial secretary or other responsible minister.

These colonial legislatures required that the police were to be controlled from the centre of political power, rather than by local authorities. Correlatively, the police in each colony was to be a single, unified body. Policing was a function for which the state, rather than local communities, took responsibility. The control of all police by a single officer made for hierarchical, and increasingly bureaucratic organisations. The police statutes reflected political choices perhaps appropriate to early colonial society but not for ever after. In these, as in many other matters of government in Australia, however, the institutional frameworks determined at an early stage proved remarkably resilient.

Such choices about administration of the police also imply exclusions. A decision to vest authority in a single commissioner subject to the direction of the colonial secretary excluded for the most part the magistracy and judiciary from an oversight of policing practices. It excluded too the participation or supervisory role of locally elected or representative officials. In consequence, the commissioner became the most important figure in policing, since few ministers would be in a position to know or be capable of knowing the intricacies of a police organisation.

Yet the tendency to a uniform and centralised pattern of organisation in Australian police forces was not immediately consolidated. The process of centralisation of colonial police in Australia involved the attrition of at least three important institutional arrangements of the earliest periods of colonial policing in Australia. First, the early system of magistrate control of police was passed over in favour of control by executive government through the police commissioner. Second, local forces, and thereby the possibility of local control, were eliminated. Third, the process required a suppression of specialised police, those who had previously operated under a strictly limited remit. In sum, the story was one of the substantial accretion of state executive power in Australia in the matter of policing.

Who should control the police? The matter was, at one level, scarcely a subject for contention. The police were established at the instance of the governing authorities. In New South Wales, the governors from Captain Phillip on were authorised to appoint constables and in 1810 Macquarie appointed a permanent police for Sydney under a superintendent and 'Police Magistrate', D'Arcy Wentworth. There began a mode of organisation of policing which was strongly determined by government direction. Victoria and Queensland, as off-shoots of this jurisdiction, shared with it a police directed by government.

In South Australia, policing was again organised at the instance of the governor from the earliest stages of settlement. Reluctance of free settlers (indeed the 'greatest repugnance' in the governor's words) to assume the office of constable led to Governor Hindmarsh requesting Colonial Office approval for establishing a police force.[19] When South Australia some decades later assumed responsibility for the Northern Territory, its policing responsibilities were carried out through a sub-inspector answerable (in theory) to the commissioner in Adelaide.[20] In Western Australia, the responsibility for policing was immediately assumed by the Lieutenant Governor, Captain James Stirling, who appointed justices who were to be responsible for constables appointed on a part-time basis. The rule of initially strong state control is confirmed by the case of Tasmania, which was at first governed by a network of police magistrates responsible directly to Governor Arthur. Only later did decentralisation mark Tasmania off briefly from the rest of the country.[21]

For all of the Australian colonies, therefore, the control of police was from the earliest moment vested in the governor. Yet the path from the governor's prerogative in the appointment of constables or police magistrates to the enactment of legislation authorising centralised police forces under single police heads with substantial autonomy was not inevitable. It was fought out in often contentious circumstances.

This was so because governors did not retain absolute authority in colonies which were growing at a sometimes furious pace. Most obviously was this the case in the 1850s. But the changing mix of population in a place like New South Wales produced social conflict between old and new settlers and between emancipated convicts and free settlers in particular. The justices of the peace, originally appointed by governors as a means of securing order in the infant colonies, sought power in their own right and in some places opposed the pretensions and power of the government-directed police magistrates. Colonial politics consisted for much of the period before self-government in struggles between what was often seen as the autocratic power of governors and the aspirations of civilian justices to a power of their own.

This politics impacted on the history of policing through the issue of control of the police. The appointment of police constables subject to the direction of magistrates was a common feature of early police organisation. The distinction between policing and judicial functions as separate offices was blurred at this time. Hence, the superintendence of police was frequently in the hands of government-appointed police magistrates whose tasks were also those of adjudicating in the summary courts.[22]

It was this arrangement which was fundamentally altered by the re-organisation of policing at mid-century and later. The establishment of administrative control by an officer such as a commissioner rather than by a local magistrate was a clear direction of government to separate judicial and policing functions. Vestiges of the former role of magistrates were retained to a limited degree in disciplinary proceedings: in Victoria, for example, the *Police Act* of 1853 empowered local magistrates to 'discipline police in their locality by hearing summary cases of complaints against the police'.[23] In Queensland, the legislation went somewhat further than this, at least for the first six years, when police magistrates were given responsibility as inspectors of police for their districts, in spite of the primary control being exercised by the commissioner in Brisbane. The result was profound administrative confusion, with evidence that magistrates were responsible for the policing of their districts, but not able to control the movement of police in and out of them, at the behest of the commissioner in Brisbane. In spite of support from Darling Downs squatters and their political friends for the role of the magistrates in policing, the appointment of police magistrates as inspectors was brought to an end in 1870. Thereafter the magistrates' role contracted to that of hearing charges against police in disciplinary matters.[24]

The matter of judicial versus bureaucratic control of the police was linked in some ways to the issue of local control through municipal government of police. As we have seen, police in Australia were not some outgrowth of community innovation — they were a state-authorised imposition. Nevertheless, the expansion of police was often a response to local demands for security, whether against Aborigines, or against bushrangers, gold robbers and stock thieves as well as disorder in rural towns. Prior to the consolidation of police at mid-century, the mechanism of response to such requests for local protection was extension of the *Towns Police Act* to particular locales. Under such an arrangement in New South Wales, police constables were appointed by and responsible to local magistrates. The development of a structure of local government in the 1840s provided an opportunity for true local political control of policing arrangements. As Palmer explains, the attempts of Governor Gipps in 1842 to establish district councils entailed a shift from central to at least part local funding of police. But even where this ambition succeeded in winning local support, as in the incorporation of Melbourne, the difficulty of raising local rates proved an enormous stumbling block. Moreover, the political elite in the legislative council rebuffed Gipps' attempt to require half the cost of police to be raised by local government.[25]

Outside New South Wales (and perforce Victoria and Queensland before separation), other attempts to establish local responsibility for police were exerted by the governing authorities. In South Australia, this extended to an adaptation of English county police legislation of 1840 requiring a contribution to police costs for foot patrols in local police districts. The continuation of this legislation in South Australia was motivated by desires both of government to exercise economy in police expenditure, and of police administrators to secure a buffer against constant demands for retrenchment as the colony faced difficult financial circumstances.[26] The arrangement was of a kind with that which later developed in Canada, with some local governments (at city and provincial level) contracting with the Royal Canadian Mounted Police for the provision of police services. But it fell short of that to the degree that it was only a partial recuperation of costs incurred in gazetted police districts, and the costs of commissioned officers were by statute excluded from the process, being solely the responsibility of the colonial government. And it was well short of the potential for local control embodied in English police affairs in the later nineteenth century: the governing statute in South Australia was concerned only with means of recuperating the cost of foot constables in any police district, and provided no provision by which local government might direct or influence local police activities. The commissioner's authority was preserved intact in such arrangements. Local funding remained in place until the relevant rating provisions were repealed in 1938. By this stage local contribution had contracted to just over eleven per cent of the police budget.[27]

Only in Tasmania was there a sustained attempt to localise police administration in ways which went beyond financial considerations. Indeed the mid-century movement from local to central control which we have been tracing was reversed in Tasmania. There it was that from 1856 to 1898 policing was organised on a municipal basis. The degree to which this arrangement was intended as a means of exhorting local responsibility for police affairs was evident at the outset in a royal commission on the public service. This transfer from central to local responsibility was evidently a response in part to the distaste for the previous system of government controlled police magistrates, associated with Tasmania's convict regime.[28] The decentralisation of police, initiated by legislation of 1858 (for Hobart and Launceston) and 1865 (extended to other municipalities), was endorsed by the royal commission of 1857 as a means of inducing 'a habit of general action for a collective good among a people who, hitherto, have looked to the Government to take action even in matters more immediately affecting local interests'.[29]

The experiment with municipal policing lasted four decades. Central direction, however, was far from absent. The appointment of an inspector-general provided a means of monitoring police forces in the different localities, establishing general rules for the guidance of police, but adapting them as necessary to the particular circumstances of a municipality. That office was from 1867 also responsible for the Territorial Police, appointed in non-municipal districts. In municipalities, appointment and maintenance of police services was mandatory, but also from 1867 it was possible for a municipality to surrender control of its police to the government. For reasons which do not appear ever to have been satisfactorily explored, the system of municipal police began to break down in the following decade. Attempts in 1877 by the colonial secretary to move towards centralisation were stemmed by municipal opposition, but a Parliamentary committee of 1886 strongly endorsed the arguments in its favour, in spite of some significant minority support from witnesses for the virtues of municipal control. 'Divided authority' between police of the territorial and municipal regimes was regarded as impeding the efficient pursuit of offenders. Even so, the desire for retention of some degree of local control was evident in the 1886 Parliamentary recommendations. Yet when centralisation came, in 1899, there was no statutory remnant of the old system, and Tasmania conformed to the Australian model of single administration police forces in a State jurisdiction.[30] A royal commission reviewing the new arrangements in 1906 found no reason to comment on the loss of municipal control, noting among other matters that about 5,000 pounds had been saved by centralisation, with a substantial reduction in the number of senior police as compared to the old local system[31] of a territorial and 21 municipal police forces.

A final consequence of the reorganisation of policing in the colonial period was the amalgamation of specialised police forces. This was closely related to the process described above, with a presumption that unified and central control must mean the elimination of specialist units. Such a development did not entail a constraint on the previous tasks of specialised forces. In New South Wales, the haphazard expansion of the colony's policing resources in the period after Macquarie saw no less than 'six separate forces independently controlled' by the 1840s: the Sydney police, the mounted police, the Sydney water police, a rural constabulary controlled by the rural magistracy, a border police responsible to the commissioners of crown lands, and the native police.[32] What appeared to later observers as the chaotic nature of police administration implied by these multiple forces is confirmed by the difficulties in securing a general responsibility for police located in one office. Thus the Bigge commission in 1820 had recommended an 'appointment of an officer to take charge of the police of the colony as a whole'.[33] Yet the first appointment to such a position, Captain F. N. Rossi as 'Principal Superintendent of Police at New South Wales', was, according to the historian of the police in New South Wales at this period, never more than head of the Sydney police, since he also had to perform duties on the magistrates' bench.[34] The emergence of the Sydney police as a distinct administrative entity was eventually confirmed by statute in 1833, in a measure which prescribed the responsibility of police for a broad range of municipal governing duties.

The complex history of the various police forces in New South Wales up to the 1850s has been told in a number of places. The point at issue here is the effect of centralisation in 1862. This was not only a matter of administrative nicety, but marked the consolidation of settlement. Only a few years before, the New South Wales Parliament had felt it necessary to endorse the continuance of the native police on the grounds that the process of settlement at the colony's extremes still required something other than a regular police force. The implication, scarcely disguised in this and other official mandates for the work of the native police, was that its duties were somewhat outside the bounds of legally accountable policing. As the 1856 Board of Inquiry had it:

> It would be probably impracticable to maintain a police force of a more regular kind, adequate to the maintenance of proper relations with the indigenous tribes.

The nature of this police force in fact precluded 'amalgamation with the other police, and so do its uses'.[35] In the event, however, New South Wales was saved the trouble of amalgamation of the native police as by this time they were serving the 'Northern Districts', and were transferred to Queensland jurisdiction after separation of the northern colony in 1859. The exceptional nature of the native police was confirmed by the lengthy period which it survived as a separate entity in Queensland till the end of the century.

With the exception of the native police, then, centralisation meant the incorporation of other policing entities within the administration of the head of the police department in each colony. Henceforth, specialised police duties such as gold escort, or control of bushranging, would be carried out by the colonial police, with the rewards and ignominy that came with success or failure in such activity becoming a part of the political context of policing, affecting among other matters, the relations between governments, ministers and police department heads.

How significant were police as an arm of public administration in the colonial state in Australia? The varying ratios of police to population, or the comparison of police with other public service employment, suggests the changing priorities of government over time. The long term trends in police to population ratios are summarised in Table 2. In spite of different starting points in terms of chronology and relative police strength, it is worth noting the similarity of the trends between colonies/States. South Australia, Australia's most concentric region, dominated by the role of Adelaide and its hinterland, is the exception to the u-shaped curve of these trends. Its ratios were already low in the 1860s and only increased notably after the 1940s, along with those of other States.

Table 2   Police to population ratios: Australia, 1861–1981

Year	NSW	Vic	Qld	SA	WA	Tas
1861	265.8	247.9	516.3	120.6	na	na
1871	166.8	137.6	358.0	102.4	na	na
1881	160.3	124.0	309.6	131.3	na	na
1891	148.2	134.1	239.8	120.7	399.1	na
1901	158.9	122.8	173.6	99.5	271.0	na
1911	153.5	124.3	152.9	116.1	165.4	148.5
1921	131.4	113	140.9	119.3	151.2	123
1931	142.7	117.1	140.5	128.9	131.4	112.7
1941	133.0	120.4	152.6	146.4	126.8	115.6
1951	133.9	126.5	190.4	147.0	150.3	127.7
1961	138.0	137.5	172.7	150.9	155.9	146.1
1971	160.6	144.6	169.9	174.1	161.6	164.7
1981	182.0	208.0	179.5	247.8	205.4	210.1
						231.4

Source: S. K. Mukherjee et al, *Source Book of Australian Criminal and Social Statistics, 1804–1988*,
AIC, Canberra, 1988.

This data suggests something about linear trends in police employment. But how important was policing as a government function in the colonial context and after? An answer to this question has already been implied by the suggestion that policing was one of the earliest functions of the colonial state. The enormous variety of administrative functions which police assumed in the course of the refinement of the colonial apparatus of government was another indicator of their significance. More concrete measures might include the importance of police expenditure in colonial budgets and their relative significance as employers of labour.

In the 1890s for example, comparison of numbers of police with numbers of state school teachers suggests a varying commitment from colony to colony to the two major functions of policing and education. Interpreting that commitment, however, is complicated by the different stages of settlement which each colony had reached. As Table 3 suggests, the older colonies had a proportionately greater commitment to education compared to those regions which still had a substantial frontier element in their policing administration. This is confirmed by the above comparison of police to population ratios for the different colonies in the nineteenth century. As settlement consolidated and the heavy personnel requirements of the frontier diminished, policing gave way to other government services in importance. By 1900, vital state services such as education provided very substantial employment for teachers.

Table 3   Colonial government employees, 1900

Colony	Police	Teachers
New South Wales	2106	5063
Victoria	1480	4687
Queensland	880	2217
South Australia	363	1259
Western Australia	519	583
Tasmania	250	612

Source: Australians: Historical Statistics, Fairfax, Syme and Weldon, 1988, pp. 306, 333–337. These figures do not include workers in the private sector for either education or police.

The relative importance of police as an area of public service employment, however, was to remain stable or increase after this. The three big employee cohorts in New South Wales at the beginning of the twentieth century, for example, were education, railways and police. Railways, of central importance to the maintenance of the colonial economy and of colonial revenue, employed 3,446 staff in 1905 in New South Wales, at a time when there were already 2,310 police in the State. Teachers continued to dominate government employment, with 5,577 personnel.[36]

Over the twentieth century the number of police employees per capita has increased markedly. The general decline in per capita employment of police which is evident in Table 2 lasted to the Second World War. Indeed, the low point of police employment in Australia was in the period after World War One. The reason was a combination of low labour supply together with government economies. A consequence may have been reduced attention to reported crime and preventive patrolling, leading in turn to low rates of prosecution in the 1920s, a phenomenon of the period.[37]

From the 1940s however, and especially from the 1970s, there has been a substantial increase in the proportion of police to population in Australia. Haldane has observed that one reason for the post-war increase was a change in police working hours.[38] The reduction in the average working week in 1948 was accompanied by an expansion in police numbers in Victoria to compensate for the reduced availability of police. In other States, post-war conditions limited the availability of recruits, restricting the introduction of a forty-hour week in Queensland.[39] Other changes in awards and conditions over the course of the twentieth century meant a convergence of police working conditions with those of other Australian workers, including substantial improvements in leave. A proper appreciation of changing police personnel provision over long periods of time has to take careful account of this context. Increasing the numbers of police employed has not always meant a simple increase in numbers of police available on the streets or for crime investigation.

SETTLEMENT AND POLICING IN AUSTRALIA

Australian historians have been inclined to attribute great significance to the convict origins of settlement in a number of the States in accounting for the later formation of social attitudes and behaviour towards police. Without addressing the generality of the *convict* influence, we can be confident of at least one thing: namely, that the conditions of early colonial settlement were very significantly related to the prominence of the question of policing in debates over government and authority during the first part of the nineteenth century.[40]

In this respect, the Australian colonies were scarcely unique. The establishment of authoritative police forces in other parts of the Empire was closely related to the main forms of social conflict and ideas about the state of political order. Two striking examples of this are to be found in quite different places, Ireland and Canada. The former example has been discussed earlier. In Canada, the foundation of the north-west mounted police provided a striking contrast to Australian examples. Indeed, it has been argued by a historian of the Prairies, Gerald Friesen, that 'the force is central to an understanding of western Canada and, by extension, of Canada as a whole.'[41]

The peculiar role of the mounties, a *national* force of a kind which was never contemplated in the quite different conditions of Australian settlement, was in fact forged in circumstances somewhat similar to those affecting the Australian and New Zealand police. That is, the issue of the colonial and imperial response to the status of the indigenous peoples of these colonies was central. But the mounties appeared as a national force in this context, to make possible the orderly extension of the Canadian federation. While some of the Australasian forces were created similarly to deal with the threat of indigenous resistance, for example in New Zealand and to some extent in South Australia, other colonial police were formed in contexts which were more generally related to the concerns of good order, peace-keeping and government, within the boundaries of settlement. While Australian colonies had their own mounties, their frontier police, their native troopers, there is little in Australia of the extraordinary positive image and connection to national well-being, which the heritage of the mounties delivers in Canada.[42]

Reviewing the development of the new police in New South Wales compared to England and North America, Michael Sturma has argued that the urban conditions which have been seen as so significant for the emergence of police in the latter two cases were far from dominant in the colonies.[43] A range of settlement conditions obtained in Australia. These include the phenomena of convict society in New South Wales, Tasmania and Western Australia; the significant resistance to settlement which prompted the formation of the native police in some colonies; the urban disorder of the 1840s during a period of economic contraction and political conflict; and the impact of the goldrushes in Victoria and New South Wales.

Convictism played its role in the early development of police forces in Australasia. But its significance cannot be exaggerated. New Zealand and South Australia had no convicts to speak of, while Victoria's convict inhabitants were of limited importance in the colony's development. After the 1840s, only Western Australia received convicts. In Tasmania and New South Wales (which lost its northern settlements in the separation of Queensland in 1859), convictism was central to the early history of policing. Yet other factors in colonial settlement quickly took over from convictism in shaping colonial institutions. Moreover, as recent historical debates about the nature of convict society demonstrate, there is only limited agreement about what convictism means as a determining element in Australian colonial institutions.[44]

Little significance should be attached to the fact that many of the early police were themselves convicts or ex-convicts. Given the subsequent history of policing as a career in Australia, the historical judgments which link public attitudes to police in Australia to the convict personnel of the force are highly speculative, and fail to acknowledge the evidence of later consent to policing.[45] What is more relevant is that the perceived need of government to control movements of convicts and ex-convicts of 'doubtful character' early contributed to the state appointment of police magistrates and constables, notably in Tasmania and New South Wales. Where conditions were not conducive to settlement, then the colonial authorities themselves directed special police forces, such as the mounted or border police in New South Wales, to keep order beyond the reach of the magistrates.[46]

Convictism extended its influence beyond the convict colonies to the degree that the non-convict colonies, such as New Zealand and South Australia, early sought protection from escaped convicts and immigrant ex-convicts through establishing police to capture them or impede their entry.[47] A degree of social protectionism developed as respective colonies aspired to construct a society which was free of the taint of convict origins and immune to the potential harms arising from the free movement of those identified as criminals in other colonies. At the close of the century began a rush of legislative assertion of this fear of the contaminating influence of the criminal classes as a number of States enacted an Influx of Criminal Prevention Acts.[48]

The resistance of the original inhabitants of Australia and New Zealand was at least as influential as convictism in the development of policing in the colonies. The history of policing in these years is in part the history of a search for the means by which the Aborigines or Maoris could be accommodated through service in policing. Police work was one of the first means by which indigenous people would become agents of their own dispossession. In some places this service was especially bloody, in others less so. While the history of the native police in Australia is explored later in this book, some comments are necessary here to assess the role of Aboriginal–settler relations in the organisation of colonial policing.

Indigenous resistance stimulated a number of important developments in the colonial police. First, it impelled a centralised police solution to the problem of conflict at the borders of settlement. Conflict between Aborigines and settlers early determined that the policing of those areas which were beyond the pale of settlement should be a matter of colonial government responsibility. This was the case for two reasons.

On the one hand, the governors and the incipient legislative councils faced pressure from settlers to protect them from raids by Aboriginal groups. On the other, government in the colonies, under some pressure from London, was in theory duty-bound to protect indigenous inhabitants from the adverse effects of settlement. The border police and then the native police were expedients developed to adjudicate these conflicting demands. From the beginning this confusing responsibility rendered the policing solution ineffective on the second count and sometimes on the first as well. Notoriously in some districts the native police became themselves the cause and origin of further law and order problems.

Regardless of the failures of the native policing policies, however, their significance can be addressed from other directions. Perhaps most importantly they signified the status of Australia and New Zealand as colonies—places of occupation by European settlers with limited regard for the rights or desires of the occupying inhabitants. From this aspect, the centralising tendencies of native policing policy signify the impossibility of a localised police, with a police controlled and directed by the community of settlers in a limited space. This was an option in Australia, as we have seen, and one which left traces even after the goldrushes in some places. Is it significant that the one place where a localised police survived the centralising tendencies of the mid-century, Tasmania, was the colony in which settlement had by the 1830s almost destroyed the

Aboriginal population? Thereafter the Tasmanians were left only to ponder their convict taint.[49]

But otherwise the particular history of Australian settlement was one in which indigenous resistance perennially posed the question of the responsibility of colonial governments to regulate the conditions of settlement. Magistrates were suspect vehicles of colonial policy towards Aborigines if only because they tended so often to be settlers themselves and therefore burdened with a conflict of interest. Initially they were suspect in any case since they did not possess those semi-military skills requisite for the task of forcible dispossession. Later they were bypassed as native policing was increasingly brought under the more regulated and hierarchical direction of the various government-appointed officers and then by the colonial commissioners of police. By the 1880s, the tasks of native policing were largely those of north and central Australia. The perils of leaving the responsibility too much in local hands was evident in the 1880s in the Kimberleys. There, close relations between squatters and police played a critical role in perpetuating conflict with Aborigines, at a time when in Queensland the tide of policy was beginning to turn, to favour means of mediation, paternalistic as these might be on later reflection.[50]

In such colonial origins was epitomised the antagonistic relation of Australian policing of Aborigines until late in the twentieth century. Law enforcers could envisage the employment of the indigenous population, but always on terms which addressed primarily the security and concerns of the occupying settlers. The fact that some of the indigenous population might obtain advantage from service in the cause of colonial policing helps to explain the meaning it had for them.[51] But it does nothing to disguise the thoroughly subordinated place which was occupied by native troopers and later trackers in the first century of Australian policing—a sign of the more generally subordinated place of Aborigines in Australian society.

Urban contexts have been regarded as a critical element in the formation of police forces in many countries. Australian colonisation was a product of urban development in Britain. The Australian colonies developed and thrived on the export of pastoral production and mineral extraction, feeding the demand from British factories and urban centres. Yet from early in the nineteenth century large sections of the Australian population congregated in the cities and towns of the coastal fringe. Especially they were concentrated in Sydney and Melbourne, other colonial capitals waiting until the 1880s for significant growth. Cities of the nineteenth century were the focus of experiments in government and of discourses about the fabric of social order. These affected profoundly the history of policing, though in colonial Australia not exclusively so, as we have already seen.

Urban order and disorder were implicated in some important police initiatives of the mid-century. The enactment of legislation governing the policing of the Sydney metropolis was the origin of urban policing in many of its most important respects in Australia. Not only were the formal structures of police organisation signalled, but of particular note was the specification of police powers relating to the preservation of public order and municipal regulation. Such powers were transmitted to police as they formed in the other towns of the colonies, being adopted for Melbourne for example in 1838.[52]

When historians speak of the development of policing in the early nineteenth century, it is often in reference to the perceived problems of urban disorder.[53] While there is reason for questioning the *determining* role of this factor in Australian policing, it was far from absent in the years leading up to the mid-century reorganisation of policing. Notably, in Sydney it was a New Year's Day riot in 1850 which led directly to the establishment of a Legislative Council Select Committee which in turn prompted moves towards a centralised New South Wales police, with a sounder administrative structure than had been the case to then. The anxiety over the riot followed a decade in which the condition of Sydney had been a matter of concern for the political elite, with disturbances related to economic conditions and to attempts to reintroduce transportation to the colony. The inefficiency and even mismanagement of the Sydney police in these circumstances prompted demands for police reform which were addressed in the following decade.

The centripetal development of South Australia perhaps ensured that urban concerns were always going to be of particular concern in the development of police there.[54] Urban order was again a matter for attention, though always to be set beside the need to attend to Aboriginal-settler conflict and the problems of bushrangers and intrusive ex-convicts from the other colonies. The importance of a well-disciplined police became evident in 1848 when a riot between police and sailors in Port Adelaide led to the death of a man injured by a police bayonet. Commissioner Dashwood considered the action a failure of police discipline.[55] It was a rare instance of a fatality at police hands in the control of urban disorder in nineteenth-century Australia.

Separating the influence of urban factors from the powerful impact of the gold rushes on the formation of the colonial police is difficult. The colonial police have been tainted in popular memory by a number of seemingly deplorable episodes. The most notorious is their alleged responsibility for provoking the agitation among gold miners leading to the Eureka rebellion. The events of that period, however, do not exhaust the historical meaning of the goldrushes for the history of policing in the Australasian colonies.

In two colonies, Victoria and New South Wales, the gold rushes were centrally involved in determining the political decision to establish a centralised police. In others, especially New Zealand (1860s), Queensland (1870s), and Western Australia (1890s), the responsibility for managing and regulating the gold fields and the associated bullion trade was an important responsibility of the colonial police. South Australia was principally affected insofar as the gold rushes created personnel and administrative problems for the police — problems shared with the other colonies.

Gold discoveries changed colonies irreversibly. Politically and socially they could not be the same after the enormous influxes of population swamped the steadily growing pastoral economies of eastern Australia. Similar effects awaited Western Australia in the 1890s. Police on the goldfields were responsible for managing some of the most difficult and volatile sections of the Australian colonial population in the nineteenth century. The problems of instability and mobility, fanned by rumours of new discoveries, added to the difficulties of regulating a population without social roots in their place of settlement.

Gold was an additional impetus for strong centralised policy. Local regulation would have meant little for a population likely to shift locale at a moment's notice. Labour shortages and heavy flows of goods in and out of each colony provided further perceptions of a need for greater government intervention. From this context flowed the ambition to create a police force which would be capable of exercising substantial authority in the colony. In spite of Eureka, the development in Victoria in the 1850s of a police force with a centralised administrative structure and a set of regulations to sustain its efficiency, was a substantial contribution to the capacity of colonial government to rule in unstable times. It was the Victorian police rules which tended to become the model for the other Australasian police forces. Further, when similar social demands emerged in New Zealand, it was to Victoria that New Zealand authorities turned in their search for commanders and personnel.[56]

Goldfields were the site of other social problems which were implicated in the development of the New South Wales police. At Lambing Flat in 1860, European miners rioted and assaulted Chinese diggers.[57] The event epitomised the racism of the period. It also prompted the New South Wales Premier to move quickly to address the evident incapacity of the goldfields police to act to protect the victims. Hence, the New South Wales police emerged in a new and divided society.

Yet gold was not the only catalyst for the reorganisation of the New South Wales police. As John Hirst has argued, their early history was marked even more critically by the flurry of bushranging which characterised the aftermath of the gold rushes. On Hirst's account, the failure of the police to curb the outbreak of bushranging in the 1860s brought the whole institution of police to a point of disbandment. The problems lay in the inappropriate training and staffing of the New South Wales police. Rather than depend on colonial born bushmen for the policing task, the policy driving the formation of the New South Wales police was to staff it with gentlemen officers from a military or British/Irish policing background, with a constabulary of the same country of origin. Bushranging, the armed robbery of travellers, coaches and rural townships by young bush horsemen, was a social phenomenon for which police from such backgrounds were ill-equipped to deal.

So poorly in fact did the police deal with it that they became the laughing stock of many in the colonial populace empathising with the superior bush skills of the bushrangers. The phenomenon was not restricted to New South Wales. In Victoria, it reached its apogee in the Kelly outbreak in the late 1870s. The repercussions of the police failure to deal effectively with the Kelly gang were felt in Victoria well into the following decade, leading to a reorganised police administration and detective force. Something of the same images of police incompetence confronting mythic rural heroes characterised responses to the stock thieves, the Kenniff brothers, in southern Queensland in the early 1900s.[58]

It is with good reason then that Hirst concludes that the alleged poor reputation of police in Australia, perhaps especially in New South Wales, derives not from their convict origins but from the disastrous performance of police in the bushranging era. The personnel of the colonial police of the later nineteenth century in any case did not have convict origins. And the circumstances under which most forces were consolidated from the 1850s multiplied the social forces which shaped and were affected by police.

CONCLUSION

The new police came to Australia in the 1850s and 1860s at the same time as their consolidation in England, and two decades after their establishment in Ireland. It can be seen from the review of the historical conditions which both constructed and constrained them in Australia that this was nevertheless a distinctive process. There was not a simple transmission of a new institution of government from the metropolis to the periphery of the Empire.

Thus the often-noted influence of the colonial state in Australian settlement eventuated in a policing organisation which was itself highly centralised. Not only in most colonies were all the various police establishments brought together in the one administration, but this administration was then made subject to the powerful authority of a single commissioner, subject *de jure* to the direction of a responsible minister. In Australia, with the temporary exception of Tasmania, the possibility of a significant level of local control of policing was early waived in favour of metropolitan control in each colony. This was the most important long-term consequence of the particular formation of police in the colonies.

While the new police in England and Ireland were conceived and born in circumstances of great social and political conflict and controversy, one could argue that this was much less so in these colonies. The judgment is perhaps a matter of degree. But in the various social contexts which have been outlined above, the traces of later patterns might be seen. The tendency of colonial elites to view with fear or suspicion any sign of lower order resistance produced an expectation of policing as primarily a reactive and, if necessary, repressive force.

The fateful decisions to found the native police in New South Wales and Port Phillip originated a peculiar relation between police and Aborigines which was to endure and be transformed in every generation thereafter. If the police force was an archetypal institution of modern government, then the policing of Aborigines was to become an emblem of all that such government might imply: the bureaucratic transformation of social relations under the ultimate threat of force.

Finally, the mix of contexts described here was brought to its head in conflict over the role of police in the service of government in the 1850s. The goldrushes brought on political and social change of enormous importance to later colonial development. By stimulating policing reform and consolidation in Victoria, they had a major impact on the organisation of policing in other colonies in Australasia. And in so doing, they played a critical role in the colonial state.

CHAPTER 2

Commissioners and Ministers

Although consolidation and centralisation of police characterised most colonial police forces by the 1860s, the colonial organisation of policing did not cease there. The incidence of major police inquiries in Australia between 1883 and 1906 (in Victoria, Tasmania and Queensland) is indicative of the scope of reorganisation of policing at the end of the colonial period. Such an incidence of public inquiries into general police administration was not to be repeated until the 1980s, when first the Lusher (New South Wales, 1981), then Neesham (Victoria, 1986) and Fitzgerald (Queensland, 1989) inquiries, as well as the royal commission into Aboriginal deaths in custody (1987–91) provided the basis for a substantial review of the forms and effects of police organisation. Here we concentrate on some of those characteristics of the organisation of policing at the end of the colonial period and into the first half of the twentieth century which formed the background to more recent crises in the relations between police and government in Australia.

What kinds of administration characterised the Australian police forces? What forms of relation between the police and government prevailed during this era? What impact did police unionism have on the political and administrative organisation of policing in Australia? The years from 1880 to 1930 provide important evidence for answering these questions in Australia. Those years saw the refinement of police organisation, with the development both of specialist agencies and units distinguishing conventional street policing from detective work, and of an increased capacity for intelligence, surveillance and forensic work. This period was marked by the enhancement of the authority and political importance of the role of police commissioner, sustained by judicial and political affirmation of the relative independence and autonomy of police administrations in police affairs.

At the same time, some features of this period challenged a view of police as essentially autonomous, independent keepers of the laws as determined by

Parliament. Political controversy over the nature of police control and account-ability, centred especially on the role of the police commissioner, highlighted the tensions present in the relationship between police and government. From another perspective, the authority of the police commissioner was significantly affected by the development of police unionism, with its postulation of the industrial rights of the police officer. Emerging unionism signified the degree to which police were workers themselves, limiting the claim that they were simply inheritors of the ancient office of constable.

These developments, some of them constructing and affirming police inde-pendence and autonomy, others effectively constraining the authority of the central figure in police administration, the commissioner, can be examined in some detail in this period. We will explore first the role of the commissioner in relation to government and law-making. Second, we will look at the emer-gence of police unionism in its political and industrial context and assess its impact on police administration.

COMMISSIONERS: REFINING THE ROLE

Over time, the role and influence of commissioners[1] on policing has been one of the most contentious public issues in the relations between police and govern-ment in Australia. In order to understand the recent dimensions of this relation we need to chart the changing administrative history of police departments. Such a task requires not only a mapping of the formal departmental arrange-ments, but a commentary on some of the ways in which commissioners defined what was their proper role in the administration of police in their charge.

In what seems to our eyes today the remarkably lean organisation of gov-ernment in the nineteenth and early twentieth century, police departments were nothing more than a sub-department of the major administrative locus of power: typically, the colonial secretary's office. The responsible minister that is, was the colonial secretary or his equivalent (eg. in Queensland, the home secretary). Inevitably this meant that the permanent head of the relevant department, the under-secretary, played a significant role in administrative matters concerning policing.

Regardless of the specific ministerial responsibility for police, the role of commissioner was characterised by a growing recognition of the political con-text in which policing operated. To understand the importance of this recogni-tion, it is essential to appreciate the quite different account of the role of police and ipso facto of police commissioners which has tended to dominate conven-tional discussions of policing in Australia.

In recent years there has been much criticism of the alleged politicisation of the role of police commissioners. Journalists, academics and politicians have alleged that Australian policing in various States has been compromised by the politicisation of police. By this they mean variously that policing decisions have been improperly influenced by government ministers or that police themselves have improperly played a role in policy-making and law-making.[2]

The standard against which these judgments have been made is a well known characterisation of the constitutional position of police in England. Central to this notion is the idea of the original powers of the constable, as an officer delegate of the community dedicated to upholding the law. This is extended to imply that the responsibility of the police, including the police commissioner, is to act as pure defenders of the law, as the saying goes, 'without fear or favour'. According to Peter Sallmann, in a considered critique of the recent role of police commissioners in Australia, police in the recent past have been departing from the 'traditional view' of police as pure and simple instruments of the law, required 'to enforce the law as laid down by Parliament and the courts on behalf of the community'.[3]

Such a notion also underlays many accounts of the role of police under Joh Bjelke-Petersen in Queensland. Hence, Evan Whitton, writing in the aftermath of the Fitzgerald inquiry, described what he regarded as the perversion of the police role in Queensland under the Joh regime. For him, police constituted an arm of authority which should be separated, like the judiciary, from the executive and Parliament.[4] The difficulty with such a view is not only that it misunderstands the constitutional doctrine of the separation of powers (which refers to the Parliament, the executive and judiciary: if the police belong anywhere in this triumvirate, they belong to the executive). It is also indifferent to the historical reality of the development of the police role and function. That reality is somewhat different from the legal and constitutional rhetoric which has been held to define the substance of the police role.

First, the notion of the original powers of the constable has been shown to be of quite recent, rather than 'ancient' origin. In a review of the legal and constitutional position of police in England, published in 1965, Geoffrey Marshall documented the judicial construction of this notion at the end of the nineteenth century. The rhetoric of appeals to ancient English liberties or the common law position of police cannot disguise the quite modern context of the notion, suggesting that we should be mindful of the narrow scope of authority for the claim.

Second, such a notion of the constable's independence, of meek submission to the authority of the law which the police have a simple and untrammelled duty to uphold, flies in the face of the historical realities of modern policing. As the previous chapter has shown, the police in Australia were founded in a specific colonial context which gave them an important *political and administrative* role: guaranteeing the success of settler dispossession of Aboriginal land, sustaining the boundaries of urban order, acting as agents of the state in the collection of taxes, conducting elections, and counting the population.

Hence, police were something other than mere keepers of the peace. But more than this, they subsequently were formed into substantial bureaucratic organisations subservient to the will and direction of the commissioner. The constable's original power, constructed judicially in the later nineteenth century, was being simultaneously negated by the demands of hierarchical submission to the authority of the commissioner.

Moreover, the liberal constitutional notion of the neutrality of the police is challenged historically by important developments of the later nineteenth century in which police commissioners began to play a very significant role in policy formation and law-making. It is this role which suggests above all that modern police have been considerably more than mere instruments of the law or state. They have also been significant players in the construction (and limitation) of state policies of regulation.

Within the colonial inheritance of a centralised police force, responsible to a government minister, commissioners developed a political role along a number of dimensions from the later nineteenth century, if not before. These dimensions included a positive role in law-making, an involvement in shaping the power relations of Australian society in particular ways, and the pursuit of administrative arrangements which would enhance the strategic position of police in intra-governmental relations. Not all police commissioners pursued these objectives to the same degree. And certainly not all shared the same political vision, if by that we mean a desire to see society ordered in a particular way. Some approached the ideal of the dedicated public servant, serving the public interest as best as could be defined at the time. Others were sympathetic to party political strategies of the most reactionary kind.

Taking first the role of police in law-making, the historical record suggests that from the 1890s police departments were capable of substantial influence in the legislative process. This was not by way of electoral influence, as has characterised the more recent ambitions of some police unions.[5] Rather, the police department became a place where significant demands from within government could develop to shape public legislation.

An important example is that of public order legislation. Australian legislation for policing the streets and public places was in the beginning highly derivative of English legislation. The *Towns Police Act* of 1833 in New South Wales, for example, embodied powers which were encapsulated in the English *Vagrant Act* of 1824 and the *Metropolitan Police Act* of 1829. These became the foundation of much of the everyday functions of police in public places, as first Victoria and then Queensland achieved self-government. By the end of the colonial period, however, it is evident that police departments wanted to see significant changes in the nature of these powers.

An illustration of the process is the 1908 reform of the *Police Offences Act* in New South Wales. Amendments to the Act included new provisions regarding prostitution, especially for soliciting, changes to the definition of public order offences which facilitated the proof of offensive behaviour or breaches of the peace, and a broadened scope for bringing charges of vagrancy. The police role in framing these amendments was direct and enthusiastic. While the successful achievement of police demands depended on a conjuncture of interests with other public lobby groups (including temperance organisations and feminist groups), the police had been campaigning actively for a number of years to bring about these reforms, which had already in many cases been implemented in Victoria and South Australia. The nature of this campaign, as Allen has suggested [6] included dramatic changes in the prosecution of prostitution offences, to an extent which she argues acted as a lever in producing desired legislative change.

In the public order area, police response to a rowdy New Year's Eve celebration in 1907 suggested that the occasion was being used to enhance longstanding police demands for law reform. These included the addition of a new charge of disorderly behaviour, a power of arrest for breaches of municipal by-laws, and the introduction of a 'move-on' clause to facilitate control of street crowds. The last was a provision which had been successfully won by South Australian police in 1904. The breadth of these demands was too much even for the sympathetic government of the day, which watered down some of the suggestions while rejecting the 'move on' clause entirely. What is clear, however, is the active role of police, from local station sergeants through to the Inspector-General, Thomas Garvin, in generating reform proposals and constructing a climate which would enhance their likely achievement.[7]

At one level this is scarcely surprising. The police force was by this time a significantly large section of the State's bureaucratic apparatus. If there were some duties (electoral supervision, the collection of statistical and census returns etc.) which were straightforward procedural functions, there were others (the primary ones of keeping the peace, preventing crime or detecting it) which involved police in a complicated set of choices and procedures within the framework of common and statute law. If the law was to be changed in any way to conform with changing political and social contexts, the opinion of those so closely connected with its working was at some stage likely to be sought. What is noteworthy, however, is the degree to which the mobilisation of police opinion in the policy-making process questions the view that the police have in the past simply enforced laws decided elsewhere by others. Rather, for much of the twentieth century, the police have sought to influence public policy in quite direct ways.

Examples from other States suggest that the New South Wales 1908 amendments involved police in ways which were far from unique. Not surprisingly, police initiatives in law reform were almost always in the direction of enhancing police powers or in smoothing the path for successful prosecutions, preferably by bringing criminal offences within the scope of summary jurisdiction. In the early 1900s, in spite of the existence of a general police power to keep order on the streets, police in South Australia consistently failed to maintain order outside betting shops until the commissioner won from the government an amendment allowing them to 'move on' crowds or individuals at will. The Victorian reform of the *Police Offences Act* in 1890 was said by its ministerial advocate to be directly the product of police desires. Achieving those desires was not always easy: as has been shown elsewhere, the Queensland police failed to win amended powers on similar lines to their colleagues in South Australia, Victoria and New South Wales.[8] In spite of the Queensland commissioner's claims that 'the police may be trusted to act with discretion in these matters', the press and Parliament were suspicious of police proposals for enhanced powers including the shift to the commissioner's office of licensing powers and the appointment of special constables.[9]

These examples suggest a process of policy-making and administration in which police were actively and influentially involved in the early decades of this century. During this era the police capacity to influence the political process was enhanced by two developments. One was police unionism, achieved initially against the resistance of most police administrators (most notably and protractedly in Victoria), but quickly developing into a concerted and noisy advocate of police interests. The second was the emergence of police commissioners as vocal public advocates of their department's interests, including matters of law reform. The public advocacy of commissioner Cahill in Queensland, epitomised by his appearance before the bar of the Queensland Legislative Council to defend and explain his Police Offences Bill in 1911, was one example. In Victoria, the same period saw the 'first Chief Commissioner to make statements about the inadequacy of some criminal laws and to suggest legal reforms'.[10] A readiness to comment publicly on law and policy signalled an important development in the political field affecting public policy formation.

Such a development was, however, not free of its hazards for police commissioners. We can take as a final example of the political role of the police chief in this period, the vicissitudes of the career of Captain Frederick Hare, commissioner of police in Western Australia (1900–13). In 1904, the protector of Aborigines in Western Australia, Dr W. E. Roth, delivered a report on the condition of Aborigines in that State. The report was highly critical, among other things, of police administration in its handling of duties involving Aborigines. Hare, as commissioner, took public exception to Roth's report, describing it as informed by the scum and riff-raff of the north. His outburst provoked his suspension by the Labor government under public service Act provisions preventing public servants from public comment. Ten years later, Hare's career was brought to an end in controversial circumstances by another Labor government, this time ostensibly on the grounds of his age. The real reason, claimed by his conservative parliamentary defenders, was because his handling of a major tramway strike a couple of years earlier had antagonised the labour movement. Hare's police career was thus characterised by a readiness to speak out on issues of law and policy (on prostitution, for example, he said the 'necessary evil' should be segregated and so it was, in spite of political pressure to eliminate it[11]) and by his ultimate political vulnerability to a displeased Labor government. In both respects, he epitomised the political nature of the police chief role in this period.

The ambition of police commissioners to take a leading role in the definition of what constituted a desirable social order must be understood against a background of political realignment in Australia, as well as changing contexts of police work in many national jurisdictions. In Australia in particular, the labour movement was demonstrating in most jurisdictions its strength on both the political and industrial fronts. The police role in management of industrial disputation inevitably involved them in political debates and choices which some commissioners at least were only too ready to engage.

But in addition there was the growing sophistication of the police forces as bureaucratic institutions. This was evident in a greater consciousness of training, changes in some of the primary objects of policing with the beginning of motorisation, a development of police technologies in detective work (fingerprinting above all), and in the organisation of surveillance (much of Cahill's period was taken up with ensuring efficient tracking of probationers and released prisoners) and so on. All these developments could be brought together in a greater emphasis on the professional, career-path of the individual police officer. Police commissioners were conscious on the one hand of challenges posed to their authority by the possible rise of new, and unfriendly, political masters. They were preoccupied also with enhancing the status of their departments through exhortations to the impartial and professional tasks of policing. Although the nature of political control of Australian police forces was quite different from that in the United States and Britain, it is evident that the same period around the turn of the century saw the rise in the United States of a movement for police 'professionalism' while in Britain it has been argued that police managerial autonomy was consolidated in the early 1900s.[12] While these developments in both those countries have their own historical contexts, the issue at stake (above all political 'independence' of the police role and correlatively, the responsibility of police administrators to defend and enhance that role, in the public arena if need be) were common with those in Australia.

It is important to remember that these changes took place for the most part without any notable alteration in the statutory form of the relationship between police and government in Australia. When this relationship again became the subject of sustained commentary in Australia in the 1970s, the reference point for discussion was still the statutory model of police commissioner subject to direction of the responsible minister, a relationship which was given its definitive form in the middle of the nineteenth century. That statutory prescription, however, did not eliminate the possibility of a change in the role of commissioner such as the one described above, one in which there was an increasing willingness to speak on public issues and assert a police view of what was necessary to the maintenance of social order.

MINISTERS AND COMMISSIONERS

While the colonial organisation of Australian policing left a legacy of formal ministerial direction of police commissioners, the degree to which the legal form was matched by administrative practice has varied. The historical evidence surveyed above suggests that police commissioners developed a substantial administrative and policy autonomy in spite of legislation usually subjecting them to the direction of the minister. The question remains whether this aspiration to autonomy has ended effective political responsibility for policing.

The nature of relations between minister and commissioner has continued as a matter of interest in public affairs in recent decades. This has been the case not only in Australia. In Britain especially, the 'political' character of policing has been subject to sustained public and academic examination. There the historical trend has seen the gradual erosion of local political direction and accountability of the police as the Home Office increasingly takes charge of co-ordinating and directing the ever decreasing number of local forces.[13] Our outline of the colonial formation of Australian police forces shows why this analysis cannot be immediately translated to this country. Australian police, in the various colonies, were already directed by the local variant of the Home Office in the 1860s. Yet the matter of political direction of police was to resurface in the 1970s and after in a series of often sensational conflicts between minister and commissioner.

In spite of the legislative subjection of the police to government direction, there has long been an ambiguity in understanding the proper domain of ministerial authority and that of the commissioner. When the Dunstan Labor government in South Australia sought to limit the role of police in preventing street demonstrations in Adelaide during the Vietnam war era, police commissioner McKinna considered the government intruding on his own arena of decision and responsibility. The matter was resolved by political direction of the police, but its legacy was a degree of tension between the police and government.[14] As a result of the conflict, an Inquiry by Justice Bright examined the relation between the authority of the commissioner of police and the government of the day. Bright concluded 'that while the government should not interfere in the detailed administration of the law, it should have power to intervene'. Subsequently the *Police Regulations Act* was amended in 1972 'to give power to the government to give directions to the Police Commissioner for the control and management of the police force'.[15] The ambiguity remained however: what should be the areas of responsibility in relation to which the government might give such directions? Bright had recommended that 'a convention should be established … with regard to the limits within which any such direction may properly be given', a convention which should be agreed between the minister and the commissioner.[16] Such a suggestion defined the potential for further disputation between ministers and commissioners who could not agree.

While the 1972 amendment brought South Australia into line with a number of other Australian States, it did not put an end to the aspirations of police commissioners to resist political direction. In circumstances of great political controversy, the Premier, Don Dunstan, dismissed commissioner Harold Salisbury in 1977 after he was found by a royal commission to have failed to disclose matters relating to special branch files in South Australia. Like Queensland police commissioner W. G. Cahill seventy years before him, Salisbury attempted to argue, in the face of clear legislative authority, that the office of commissioner was not responsible to a minister but to 'the Crown — directly to the Queen or her representative in Australia'.[17]

In Queensland during the same period, the political flavour of the government was quite the opposite to that in South Australia. Yet the conflicts were strikingly similar. In the view of the Queensland government of Joh Bjelke-Petersen, commissioner Whitrod was striking an unacceptably independent line in limiting the scale of police response to political demonstrations over the Springbok rugby tour in 1971 and the Vietnam war. When Whitrod finally demonstrated his refusal to accept government cajolery over his initiation of an inquiry into police behaviour in a raid on a coastal hippy community, the government moved to end his career in charge of the Queensland force. More subservient police were sought through the promotion of Inspector Terry Lewis to assistant commissioner against Whitrod's wishes and Lewis quickly succeeded Whitrod after the latter's resignation in protest.[18]

Whitrod's assertion of the independence of the commissioner was of the same order as that of McKinna a few years before him (he had in fact been recommended to the Queensland government by McKinna).[19] In a lecture in 1976 he addressed the Adelaide example directly, drawing from it the moral that an intrusion of government into a commissioner's responsibility in police operations threatened individual freedoms:

> From the police point of view, if the executive, as distinct from parliament, takes to itself the authority to instruct the police when they are not to enforce the law, as in the Adelaide incident, then the rule of law could collapse, and make mockery of each officer's sworn oath to uphold the law.[20]

Whitrod, doubtless reflecting on the experience of six years under a Queensland National Party government, regarded Bright's recommendation of a negotiated agreement between minister and commissioner as idealistic, since the relationship was in real life 'seldom, if ever so, evenly balanced'.[21] The circumstances of the political conflict over Whitrod's leadership of the police were even more complex than this brief account suggests. But the substantial point remains. In periods of social conflict, it appears that the ill-defined boundary in Australia between political responsibility for police and operational autonomy generates potentially destructive divisions between ministers and police commissioners. The laboratory offered by the circumstances of the 1970s shows that this is not simply a matter of reactionary or authoritarian governments attempting to use the police to enhance their control over the populace. Political directions can be, and have been used, both to limit and expand the ambit of police operations: witness the contrast between the directions of the Dunstan and Bjelke-Petersen governments above. When Premier Neville Wran intervened to order the return of an allegedly pornographic painting seized by the New South Wales vice squad, he was not enhancing the power of police but limiting it. The fact that his actions generated great controversy highlights the inevitable political context of policing, in more than one sense.[22]

More sustained examination of the police organisation and its political relations continued in the 1980s. Major inquiries took place in New South Wales (the *Lusher Report*, 1981), Victoria (*Neesham Report*, 1986) and Queensland (*Fitzgerald Report*, 1989). In their consideration of the relations of police and government the record of these inquiries has been patchy. Of these three, only the Fitzgerald inquiry in Queensland went beyond the conventional approach to the issue of police independence. Even so, its solution to the issue ended up potentially confounding the relations of authority for policing.

Each of the inquiries displayed a particular predilection for a thesis of policing which structured its approach. In the case of the Lusher report in New South Wales in 1981, the emphasis was laid on the notion of the original powers of the constable as the basis for police independence. Yet, as was pointed out shortly after by Hogg and Hawker, the notion of police independence deployed in Lusher was ambiguous in its reference. In the first place, the notion of the 'original powers' of the constable, which has a powerful echo in police public commentary on their task (Whitrod being a forceful advocate, for example), is both remarkably recent in case law and quite unable to take account of the reality of modern police work in which police are deployed and governed by policies and rules which are the product of ministerial (government) policy and that of the commissioner. More significantly, its use in Lusher failed to establish the important difference between its implications for the discretionary power of the constable and the relationship between the police leadership and government. As Hogg and Hawker put it, Lusher 'confused and conflated the status of the force and the status of the individual police officer'. The result was simultaneously to understate the degree to which individual police are in reality subject to lawful direction in exercising their 'original powers' and to diminish the authority of the minister in relation to the police force.[23]

The Neesham inquiry in Victoria, reporting in 1986, followed what was by then an increasingly fragile historical view of the police. In a phrase which evokes the influential Peelite conception of the function and role of police, Neesham emphasised that 'the police are the public and the public are the police', drawing on a crucial English legal case to emphasise that the constable was essentially a citizen with a citizen's powers, 'answerable to the law and to the law alone' (the phrase of Lord Denning in the Blackburn case).[24] In its approach to the role of the commissioner the report did not go beyond Lusher, preserving the ambiguity of that position.

The writing of the Fitzgerald report took place in a context which could scarcely avoid the difficulties of any ambiguities surrounding the role of the police commissioner and his subjection to the minister. Clearly powerful ministerial direction had taken place at some levels of Queensland policing. On the other hand, in areas where direction had been wanting, the corruption of police administration had fed on the failure of ministerial responsibility and accountability. The orientation of the Report was evident in its commitment to preserving a clear line of authority between the minister and the commissioner:

> The Minister can and should give directions to the commissioner on any matter concerning the superintendence, management and administration of the Force.
>
> The Minister may even implement policy directives relating to resourcing of the Force and the priorities that should be given to various aspects of police work and will have responsibility for the development and determination of overall policy.[25]

At the same time the accountability of the minister for police was to be strengthened through requiring policy directives from minister to commissioner to be entered in a register, to be tabled in Parliament through the Criminal Justice Commission and its parliamentary committee.

The multiplicity (and potential for ambiguity and conflict) of lines of authority for police work was justified by the need to provide countervailing powers in policing authority and decisions. Nevertheless, the result of this process was one in which there emerged three centres of authority with general responsibility for policing: the minister, the commissioner and the Criminal Justice Commission. The positive side was the affirmation of a formally democratic authority for policing (through both the minister and the Criminal Justice Commission, both accountable to Parliament). However the difficulties which resulted from the implementation of the Fitzgerald recommendations cannot be disguised: three major players with an interest in the policies and outcomes of policing policy and decisions provided enormous potential for administrative and political conflict, of the kind which has been described earlier.[26]

Any attempt to regulate administrative procedures depends ultimately for its effectiveness on the good will of the parties involved. Subsequent history of police–ministerial relations in the various States suggests that there are clear limits to the potential of ever more definitive regulation of administrative affairs. In South Australia, in spite of the clear legislative requirement to the commissioner to take direction from the government, Salisbury chose to resist a legitimate request from the democratically elected government to disclose details of an important area of police work. The resulting conflict brought the dismissal of the commissioner, but also ultimately the end of Don Dunstan as Premier.

Similar fates have awaited other ministers and commissioners who have failed to agree on their respective areas of responsibility. In Queensland, the first commissioner to be appointed in the wake of the Fitzgerald inquiry, Noel Newnham, appears to have faced in his police minister, Terry Mackenroth, an old style political interventionist who from his first days took a highly personalised interest in the running of the police department. When Mackenroth was forced to resign his ministry over allegations of impropriety in personal travel claims, the tensions of his conflict with the police commissioner brought an extraordinary personal and public attack and allegations against Newnham. In spite of ultimately being cleared of these allegations, Newnham found himself in what appeared to be an unsustainable position as commissioner and withdrew his application for a renewed term of office.

Similar highly personalised conflicts between minister and commissioner appeared to characterise police administration in New South Wales during the same period. In 1992 police minister Ted Pickering was forced to resign his post after failing to explain his inattention to police reports regarding the detention and attempted suicide of a youth in a police cell (Angus Rigg). Like Mackenroth, Pickering appears to have developed a highly personal involvement in the everyday business of policing: in the wake of his resignation he told Parliament that he had kept in his office a photograph of a young woman who had died of a drug overdose in King's Cross, a reminder to himself of the responsibilities of police work. In seeking to explain his failure to act in the Angus Rigg case, Pickering had clearly sought to have the police commissioner take the blame. There was talk of whether the government might dismiss the commissioner. The constitutional position was confused in the minds of the responsible players, it being said that the minister had to go because the government could not dismiss the commissioner. This was clearly begging the question. The issue really was whether the minister was able to demonstrate that the commissioner had sought to deceive him, which would constitute grounds for dismissal by Parliament.[27] Behind the details of the incident leading up to Pickering's resignation was evidently a longer period of substantial conflict between the minister and the police commissioner's office.

It is difficult not to conclude that the relationship between police minister and police commissioner will continue to be a contentious one. Reviewing the arrangements in different Australian States, the Queensland Public Service Management Commission concluded in 1993 that 'the experience from all jurisdictions indicates the degree of difficulty involved in defining an appropriate relationship between the Minister and the Police Commissioner'.[28] The division of labour in modern cabinet government has produced ministries with ever closer identification of ministers with important domestic portfolios. A century ago police administration was just a sub-branch of the colonial secretary's office in most colonies. A specific portfolio of police is a quite recent development in most States. Only in Western Australia does it predate the Second World War, with Tasmania the only other State having a separate police ministry before 1960.[29] Today all States have a distinct portfolio, though sometimes linked to other ministerial responsibilities.

The risks for the unwary minister of too close an identification with maladministration, incompetence or corruption in a police force have arguably increased with the development of such specific portfolios. Alternatively, the risks to the efficiency, clarity and fairness of police administration as it impacts on the public also increase if a minister is exercising inappropriate kinds of intervention. In such a context, it is scarcely surprising that in the 1990s increasing attention is being paid to the importance of ethics and of institutional accountability in politics and administration as a means of addressing the shortcomings of a formalistic statement on the relationship between ministers and commissioners.

CONSTABLES OR WORKERS?

A different kind of relationship of police to government was implied by a significant and little analysed development in the early twentieth century. This was the emergence of police unionism. Again, our present understanding of the functions and importance of police unionism have been marked by historical ignorance. Just as political commentary on the role of the police commissioner has proceeded in ignorance of the historical emergence of police autonomy and influence in the political sphere at the turn of the century, so criticism of the political role of police unions in recent years ignores the more complex origins and functions of police unions.

The contexts of the emergence of police unionism in the Australian States were extremely varied. Political culture was crucial. In Victoria, the State most resistant to the attainment of Labor government, conditions were particularly hostile to police unionism, and there alone were police driven to significant industrial action. In Queensland, where Labor was all but unchallenged from 1915 to 1957, unionism was for the most part succoured. But political party complexion was not solely determining. For police unionism was first accepted in South Australia, another conservative State, whereas its formation had to be prompted by a Labor government in New South Wales in 1920.[30]

If conditions for the formation of the police unions varied, so also did their impact. What was common, however, was the substantial alteration in policing relations which the formation of the unions established. By making a range of working conditions, previously the prerogative solely of the commissioner, now the subject of negotiation and even of arbitration by an external body, the authority of the commissioner was significantly qualified.

Fearing such a development, police commissioners and some other functionaries of regulatory institutions (eg. prisons) had resisted the attempts of civil service reformers earlier in the century to bring their offices under the control of the public service: hence the resistance of commissioner Cahill in Queensland to attempts to put him under the control of a departmental under-secretary. Even the introduction of civil service clerks was viewed suspiciously: Cahill warned his minister that it would have a 'disastrous effect on police effectiveness and discipline'.[31] New Zealand, Cahill reported, had recently abolished its civil clerks in policing and New South Wales was about to do so. The notion that criminal justice personnel were different from the general run of public servants was widely shared: in New South Wales, the comptroller general of prisons, Frederick Neitenstein, successfully sought the removal of the prisons department from the provisions of a civil service bill in 1905: prisons, he said, could only be compared to police and a low tone in the officers would lead to disorder in the prisons.[32]

Consequently, the acceptance of a police right to organise for industrial purposes flew in the face of entrenched notions of the peculiarity of the police occupation. Written into early police legislation had been a proscription on police 'combinations' or engagement in political activity. Such an approach was affirmed judicially by the decision of the High Court in *Enever v The King* (1906) that a police constable was not in a master and servant relation to the commissioner owing to the independence of his power as a constable.[33] As much as this decision might have been a legal fiction insofar as it failed to recognise the everyday subjection of the constable to the commissioner, the combined weight of legal opinion and commissioner opposition to the collective assertion of constabulary independence for industrial purposes sustained the barriers to police unionism for a time.

The case for unionism seemed asserted by a quite different judgment of the High Court in the same year as *Enever v the King*. In *Ryder v Foley*, the High Court overturned a Queensland Supreme Court judgment of wrongful dismissal of the constable, Foley. The Queensland judges had considered Foley was denied natural justice in not being allowed a hearing of charges against him. The High Court insisted that police were employed at the pleasure of the crown and that the relevant police statutes had not implied otherwise: police were dismissible at will, effectively of the commissioner, with the approval of the minister as a member of the government.

With the benefit of archival hindsight, we can see the relevance of this decision to a sense of police grievance about their lack of industrial rights. Foley's dismissal had followed a magistrate's inquiry at Charters Towers into a 'combination' of four police, including Foley. Reviewing the papers on the file prior to the High Court appeal by the police department against the Supreme Court decision, the Queensland Crown Solicitor advised the department to keep the papers regarding the magistrate's inquiry out of the High Court altogether. They suggested a 'strong animus' against Foley on the part of the district inspector and, more seriously, that the magistrate had determined his decision on the basis of information from the inspector and access to the police file rather than on the evidence before him.[34] The implication was the denial in fact of natural justice to a serving police officer and the subjection of all police offence to the whim of their police seniors.

Issues covering wages, transfers, and disciplinary matters were all implicated in the developing support in the ranks of police for a collective address of their grievances. However, the progress towards legitimate collective activity was varied. Three different paths were followed in eastern Australia.

In Victoria, the origins were most conflict-ridden. Intractable opposition from the chief commissioner to any suggestion of unionism did not prevent the sympathisers to unionism organising after the First World War. Developing frustration over conditions led in 1923 to the first and only police strike in Australia, resulting not in victory for the aspirant unionists but in an end to their careers as policemen. The outcome was more on the model of English police unionism, with a Victorian Police Association, of muted voice and limited industrial power. The tone is set by the objects of the association, printed on the cover of its journal in the 1920s: 'To conserve and further the interests of the Victoria Police Force; the promotion of good fellowship and social intercourse among its members; the promotion of efficiency and assistance to the administration'.[35] Not surprisingly this was a voluntary association and complaints are frequent in the 1920s of the lack of financial members.

This was quite in contrast with Queensland unionism which also initially faced a recalcitrant commissioner but quickly developed a substantial power as an industrial union. The critical difference from Victoria was the attitude of the government. The Labor government of T. J. Ryan endorsed the formation of the police union from its earliest days in 1915. State arbitration became the umbrella for an early closed shop union: the Queensland union did not face the difficulty of its Victorian counterpart as coverage grew to almost 100 per cent under the aegis of the State industrial award. This was in spite of the resistance of the commissioner, who opposed compulsory unionism, but failed to prevent its application to the cases of the four non-union members in 1920.[36] While in the long run it became a conservative organisation in many respects, the Queensland police union of employees was in its early days, under its radical and long-serving (1917–55) secretary, Hugh Talty, a lively body with a sprinkling of socialist sympathisers.[37]

A middle path was steered in New South Wales where there appears to have been only limited initial enthusiasm among police for collective action to improve their lot. In part this may have been a consequence of better salaries and conditions for police in New South Wales compared to its northern neighbour.[38] Whatever the case, after the initial rejection of the idea of a police union by Labor government minister George Black in 1915 ('a police union would be as inadvisable as a military union'), it was strongly promoted by both the government and the inspector-general in 1920. The New South Wales police association was therefore established free of the political conflict which had beset the efforts of Victorian police, but with a temperament which was somewhat milder than that in Queensland. Most important of all was the lack of access of these police associations in Victoria and New South Wales to industrial arbitration. That was to come in the case of New South Wales only after a judicial inquiry in 1974.[39] Nevertheless the New South Wales association was claiming 89 per cent coverage of the force in 1922, a remarkably high figure for such a body.[40] Attempts by the association to consolidate its coverage were unsuccessful in 1948 when the Labor government, departing from its preferred policy of compulsory unionism, followed the advice of the commissioner of police in rejecting a proposal for compulsory unionism.[41]

Only Western Australian police have shared with the Queensland organisation the name 'union', all other forces in Australia and New Zealand having associations. The difference in nomenclature was more than symbolic in the 1920s but has diminished in significance over time as many police associations have become ardent advocates of a police interest in matters industrial and political. Moreover federation of the police unions (1947 and 1979) in the cross-national Police Federation of Australia and New Zealand has signified the emerging commonality of purpose of police unions over time.[42]

The effects of police unionism on the authority of the commissioner may be seen over time and by theme. Commissioner Whitrod in Queensland may be the most outstanding case of a commissioner whose career was irretrievably damaged by the opposition of the State's police union. But others have shared a less than friendly relationship with the police union. The subject is best pursued here, however, in terms of the identifiable areas of police responsibility which have been altered by the presence and activity of unions.

With their counterparts in the labour movement, the police unions have shared a primary ambition to enhance their members' wages and conditions of service. In addressing the former, there is little doubt that the activity of the police unions has improved the standing of police over the twentieth century. But wages outcomes are also constrained by the priorities of governments and capacities of the economy. It may be a moot point whether improvements in wage levels and other elementary conditions have not just as much been a consequence at times of the difficulty of obtaining police recruits in a competitive labour market.

Within the scope of our interests here, the more striking impact of unions has been on the nature of the commissioner's authority and of the political context of policing more generally. Unions over time have succeeded in persuading governments of the necessity of appeal mechanisms which implicitly limit the freedom of the commissioner to transfer, dismiss, discharge, disrate or otherwise punish or discipline the officers of a police force. As the decision in *Ryder v Foley* had made clear, the authority of the commissioner to dismiss police was untrammelled in the period prior to the First World War. Only Victoria had a clearly spelled out mechanism of appeal against commissioner decisions. Between the wars, however, police unions in a number of States including New South Wales, South Australia and Queensland, sought the introduction of appeal mechanisms which acted as a restraint on the freedom of the commissioner to decide at will what should be done with an errant or troublesome officer.[43]

These appeal mechanisms did not end the concerns of police unions with the disciplinary powers of the commissioner. Indeed, the capacity of the union to determine police policy prior to the exercise of the commissioner's discretion became in the 1970s a measure of the influence of these employee organisations. In almost simultaneous demonstrations of the convergence of the industrial style of different unions, legal and disciplinary action against police implicated in the Beach inquiry in Victoria was limited by police threats of industrial action; and in Queensland, the union precipitated a crisis in the leadership of the police when it sought governmental action to over-rule the decision of commissioner Whitrod merely to hold an inquiry into alleged police misconduct in a raid on a hippy commune at Cedar Bay.[44]

Such interventionism was increasingly evident in the 1980s as police unions sought to influence the outcome of public debates about the relationship between crime and law enforcement. Some instances reached well beyond their impact on the authority of the commissioner to affect government policy generally on crime and criminal law (as in the campaign of New South Wales police to reintroduce the *Summary Offences Act* and in legal action to affirm police independence of ministerial direction),[45] to attempts to curb the capacity of other agencies to inquire into police actions (as in Western Australia where the police union sought to restrain the inquiries of the Royal Commission into Aboriginal Deaths in Custody)[46] and in the highly successful campaign of the Victorian Police Association which succeeded in obtaining the abolition of the Victorian Police Complaints Authority.[47]

These police union activities raised matters of serious concern in criminal justice policy and process. The engagement of police unions in public debate over the direction of criminal justice policy or even over specific matters, such as criminal convictions and sentencing of individuals, has been evident for a long time. A reading of police union journals going back to the 1920s suggests the breadth of union concerns with the wider contexts of policing. The role of the Queensland police union in mobilising support for amendment of the *Vagrancy Act* in the 1920s has been well documented. In the 1950s that union added to its list of objectives the important task of addressing all matters 'pertaining to the rule of law'.[48]

That the Queensland union was not exceptional in its disposition on these matters was evident in South Australia in 1959, during events surrounding the notorious Stuart case. In the midst of a growing controversy over the circumstances of the conviction of an Aborigine, Rupert Max Stuart, for the rape and murder of a nine-year-old girl, the South Australian Police Association issued a statement defending the 'six reputable police officers' who had obtained Stuart's confession. The statement contained numerous factual errors regarding Stuart's previous criminal history and precipitated attacks by lawyers on the association. Stuart's solicitor pointed out that the President of the association was none other than the senior police officer of the six who had interrogated Stuart. The resulting controversy did not restrain the association as the President, Detective-Sergeant Paul Turner, himself began talking to the media. Soon after, just before the Privy Council in London was due to hear Stuart's appeal,

Turner was reported in the Melbourne *Herald* as saying that the crown would produce affidavits regarding Stuart's previous history. Turner's public revelation of crown affidavits in advance of the case became itself the subject of legal and public controversy. Such actions indicated a lack of ethical restraint on the part of Turner himself, as of the association of which he was President. They did not cease with the proceedings of the commission: after the release of its report, Turner made further statements to the press in Sydney about evidence which the commission had decided not to hear. K. S. Inglis, the historian of the case, concludes: 'it was unfortunate enough that the policeman himself saw nothing improper or even imprudent about this last essay in public relations; but it was alarming that his superiors let him make it.'[49]

Such intervention of the police union may be regarded in hindsight, in view of its role in aggravating public concern over the case, as less than wise if the intention was, as Turner claimed, 'the protection of its officers and not with the merits or demerits of the case or with red herrings.'[50] Regardless of that, however, the significance of the episode in the context of our concerns here is that it shows the growing confidence of police unions in their capacity to intervene in public affairs affecting criminal justice.

Is such intervention by police unions a legitimate dimension of their responsibility to their members? An affirmative answer implies few if any restraints on the criminal justice matters which might become the subject of police union activity. An answer in the negative, however, requires that we draw clear distinctions between matters that are part of the industrial conditions of working police officers and those matters, in fact the everyday substance of their work, which are not.

Can these boundaries be drawn? The issues, already touched by the Stuart inquiry, became more and more the subject of critical debate in the 1970s and after. There was little effect of this debate in public policy, however, with it being increasingly evident that police unions were capable of exercising considerable influence on public affairs.

A countervailing voice in public policy was provided by the Fitzgerald report in Queensland. The non-industrial activities of the two police unions (for 'employees' and officers), in demanding 'the right to influence the selection of the Police Commissioner or Minister', were condemned as 'singularly inappropriate' by Fitzgerald. Union interference in disciplinary matters, a twentieth century development affecting the administrative discretion of the commissioner, as has been argued earlier, was not regarded as proper, 'save in any general sense relevant to industrial relations.'[51] The participation of the police unions more generally in debates and political activities affecting the criminal justice system and law reform was not directly the subject of comment. Fitzgerald's implication, however, was clear: the police unions had played a role disproportionate to the ambit of an industrial organisation.

Discussion of the implications of these developments has tended to the view that police unions were intervening meddlesomely and without legitimate claim in areas which required government and public discussion free of the distracting and even threatening presence of police viewpoints. However this view faces some difficulties in the light of changes in the status of police during the twentieth century. These changes included not only the legitimation of police unionisation, a significant enhancement of industrial rights gained by other workers well before the police. They also involved the enhancement of police political rights. Having been denied the franchise in the middle of the nineteenth century at a time when it was being bestowed on most other males in the colonies, the police gradually won the right to vote. That right, conditional as long as police were prevented from participating in political organisations, was itself gradually extended, to the point where police could stand as candidates for election to Australian parliaments.[52]

Having recognised a right to organise industrially and to participate as individual citizens in political affairs, it is difficult to envisage a mechanism whereby police unions could successfully be restrained from political engagements, without compromising the gains which police as citizens have gained over time. A restraint on the political activities of a police union as an organisation is conceivable: but should this union be singled out for attention in this way? Whether it is possible in any case in the aftermath of the 1980s experience to establish a clear distinction between the political and industrial interests on which a police union may legitimately speak is a moot point. In this arena, as in others involving policing, there may simply be no substitute for recognising the perennially political nature of policing. In this context it can be shown that police do not always get their own way nor do they always have only one voice, like any other political interest.[53]

CHAPTER 3

Conflict, Surveillance and Control

The modern history of police in the English-speaking countries has been marked by a political discourse which seeks to limit the possibility of police becoming nothing more than the agents of governmental whim. As is well known, opponents of the introduction of an organised police to England referred derisively to the 'Continental' form of police, which was seen as undermining liberty through the operation of political spies and police tactics unrestrained by law.

We have seen earlier that the colonial police were not the outgrowth of popular desire, but the creation of governing authorities. Debate over the forms of control and organisation was present in the colonies, but it was of limited significance compared to debates in Britain at the same time. Yet few decades in Australian history have been free of claims that the police have been acting as agents of government in ways that were incompatible with liberty and the rule of law. The relations between police and government have therefore a particularly polemical dimension when they touch on the use of police in times of substantial political and social conflict. The charge that the police are the agents of political control has a lengthy history. Some of its dimensions are explored below.

Paradoxically, the possibility that government might divest itself through privatisation of responsibility for a critical public function such as policing attracts equally polemical debate. The presumption of public debates about policing in Australia, as in many countries before the 1980s, was that police tasks were only properly filled by public functionaries, answerable through political and legal processes for their conduct. The knowledge that policing, broadly conceived, is a task involving a private workforce of greater numbers than the public police, has not had a great impact on Australian debates.

Nevertheless, as the leading scholars of this development have emphasised, the modern significance of private policing demands a reconsideration of 'commonsense notions of what policing is'.[1] In particular, suggest Shearing and Stenning, the meaning of policing requires 'reframing' to suggest much more the functions of ordering, rather than simply fighting crime or disorder.[2]

The subjects dealt with in this chapter represent the two ends of a spectrum of debate about the proper role of police in modern societies. If policing is a wholly public function, what should be the restraints on the public police in situations of conflict over what constitutes the public interest, or indeed over what constitutes a minority interest demanding to be heard? If a substantial part of policing, in spite of the existence of public police, is in fact carried out by private agents, then what mechanisms are available, in a society purporting to be governed by the rule of law (itself a notion dependent on the existence of a public sphere), to protect individuals and groups from harmful and intrusive behaviour by private police. These are policy questions which might be raised in addressing the future of policing. However, our concern is primarily historical. We look first at the role of police in the management of industrial and social conflict in Australia, second at the development of an explicitly political police apparatus at Federal and State level, and finally at some aspects of the role of private police in Australian history.

POLICING DISSENT

Much political controversy over police in Australia has originated in the policing of dissent. It might be tempting to refer this controversy to the conventional party political divisions in Australia since the 1890s. Tempting, but not persuasive — the evidence suggests that the willingness of governments to invoke the assistance of police in responding to dissent is not restricted to non-Labor administrations. Indeed, the history of Australia's Federal political police has been significantly enhanced by the contributions of Labor governments.[3] So too, in times of crisis such as depression, war or industrial ferment, Labor governments at both Federal and State level have not shrunk from calling in the aid of police.

When we talk of the policing of dissent and conflict we must, however, distinguish the roles of the ordinary run of State police forces and those of the specialised police, in the form of the State special branches and the Federal political police, especially the Commonwealth Investigation Branch and the Australian Security Intelligence Organisation (ASIO), a creation of the Federal Labor government in the 1940s. Since the specialised police authorities have had explicitly political surveillance functions, their role deserves separate treatment. However, the more general responsibility of police for preserving the peace has authorised police to manage social, political and industrial dissent in Australia's history.

Many times since the 1890s, to go back no further, the police in Australia have been responsible for keeping the peace during times of severe social conflict. The very meaning of keeping the peace has been enhanced or demeaned by police actions and behaviour during incidents. Who decides what keeping the peace means during such periods of extended social and political conflict? What responsibility rests on individual police at the front line or at police headquarters? Understanding this important part of policing history requires more than investigating regulations and rules. What happens on the streets or in other places at such times, and what administrative and judicial mandates or sanctions afterwards result—these are the materials which help us decide what the real functions of police are.

In an influential formulation of the functions of policing, Egon Bittner argued that the fundamental feature of policing was its legitimate use of force. Without a recognition of the degree to which the function of public police rests in the last instance on the expectation that police will act without being resisted, on the basis that in the last resort, force will be used, we cannot distinguish police functions from those of other state agents. Hence an important test of consent to policing (and hence of the legitimacy of the police at a particular place and time) must be the extent to which this ultimate power of police is acknowledged in a way which reduces the police need to use force.[4]

Hence, the use of police in times of social conflict has frequently helped define popular views of the police in Australia. Police themselves have on occasions resorted to the use of force with enthusiasm, on others shown that they were somewhat less than willing to do so. The incidents in which they have been called on to act en masse against collective action include episodes which are in some ways definitive of a certain view of Australian history, a view which represents it as the story of a struggle for liberty and justice against an oppressive social order. Some of the notable examples include:

- the 1890s strikes, of the maritime officers and of the shearers, principally in New South Wales and Queensland, strikes in which the police, aided by the military and by special constables, played a highly controversial role;
- the 1912 general strike in Brisbane, when again the police role was enhanced by the presence of special constables;

- the controversies over conscription and war involvement, and the generalised industrial conflict of 1916–17, which affected a number of States and brought the Commonwealth Government into a significant role in policing for the first time;
- the social and industrial conflict of the Great Depression in which police powers were enhanced in some places to address a number of new challenges to social and political order;
- the social and political dissent of the 1960s and 1970s, whose highpoint was the conflict over Australian involvement in the Vietnam war, but which included protest by Aboriginal groups, a new wave of feminism, and other dissent including much which was focussed on the very issue of public order and police powers generally.

Any historian of Australia could multiply these incidents, especially with reference to the extended conflict between the labour unions and the police over the last 100 years.

In each of the examples mentioned, there was significant challenge to the authority of the government of the day. In some, the extent of that challenge could not be foreseen. However weak may appear the tradition of violent or revolutionary dissent in Australia in retrospect, the passion of conflict to those caught in the middle of it cannot be underestimated. Fears, anxieties and rumours are social as well as psychological phenomena whose effects cannot readily be foretold.

In reviewing the record of police and government in the management of dissent we need to remind ourselves that both sides of any political conflict may be, as Robert Reiner has put it in a different context, 'understandable from both conflicting points of view'.[5] The fact that they are understandable does not imply a necessary absolution of blame or accountability for wrongs done. But determining blame, the preoccupation of much history in this area, does not always help us to understand why something happened and what might be done to avoid it happening again.

What does the history of the policing of conflict and dissent tell us about the functions of the police in Australia during this century? First, we need to note that there is little evidence of a consistently repressive role throughout the last 100 years. Or to refine the judgment, it is evident that some police authorities have sought to avoid open conflict or a resort to force through tactics which were aimed at lowering the temperature of conflict. Sometimes this involved a conscious avoidance of provocation. In the aftermath of the open conflict between police and striking unionists in the 1890s in the eastern States of Australia, it appears that police in both New South Wales and Queensland chose to limit the danger of provoking the ire of unionists in times of industrial strife. Such an approach was consistent with an expectation that police preserve the peace as much as prosecute all known breaches of the law.

Hence, there have been periods when police were concerned to minimise their intervention, either for fear of provoking more general disorder or in the interest of establishing or maintaining legitimacy in the eyes of the public, or of particular communities. Over-zealous interventions in union meetings were the cause of critical comment on the personnel file of a young Queensland police officer who breached this norm in 1911.[6] Sympathy of police for striking unionists near Newcastle in 1905 was scarcely disguised in the critical report of a sub-inspector who considered that the bravado of an American strike-breaker was 'very injudicious in the too open display of his revolver coupled with rather free statements of what he intended to do with it.'[7] More recent examples include the police tactics avoiding direct confrontation with striking unionists evident during the 1985 electricity strike in Queensland. Unashamedly repressive legislation against striking unionists and their supporters was passed by the Bjelke-Petersen government. The latter was forced after some weeks to call in police supervisors to find out why usually compliant police were not enforcing the new legislation against picket lines: police response had been muted, evidently in the light of changed tactics since the damaging confrontations of the 1970s street march era. Under government direction, the police then proceeded to take more active intervention against picket lines, sometimes unwisely since many cases were thrown out of court or led to actions for wrongful arrest.[8]

On the other hand there is ample evidence of forceful intervention which in some cases provoked serious disturbance and in many instances became part of labour and popular folklore about the repressive role of the police. Notably, some of these instances in the folklore involved incidents in which non-police played significant roles. Hence, the restrained role of police in Melbourne in 1890 during the great maritime strike has been overlaid by the memories of the directions of Colonel Tom Price, leading a military contingent in aid of the civil police, to 'fire low and lay them out.'[9] The role of special constables, little more than vigilantes lacking restraint or discipline, both during this period of the 1890s strikes and during the 1912 Brisbane general strike, has equally contributed to the sour memories of police partisanship during some of the major conflicts of Australian history.

The existence both of evidence of restraint and of undisciplined and abusive violence suggests that we need to understand historically what mix of factors determine the character of police response or management of dissent. First, the attitude of the government of the day has been crucial. Indeed, much of the controversy over the role of the police in Australia has centred on those instances in which the police were perceived as having acted at the direction of government. This was the case in the 1890s in both New South Wales and Queensland in response to the shearers' strike. It was so again in the 1960s and 1970s in the response to peace dissent and in the confrontation over the right to march.

The importance of this factor — the conformity of police action to government direction — is validated by the negative case examples of the Dunstan (South Australia) and Bjelke-Petersen (Queensland) governments, each of which wanted the police commissioner to take (in the case of Dunstan, to refrain from) particular action in response to protesters. There is no general rule here, only the central factor that police decision-making invariably takes place in a political context. That context may be one which leaves police commissioners relatively free to determine that action. On occasions it has been one in which an unashamedly political direction has been given to police to respond to dissent in a particular way. Attempts to somehow purify the policing environment of this political context are doomed to failure since the very nature of sustained political or industrial conflict is always going to involve decisions about the degree of intervention warranted.

Second, if the roles and responsibilities of police ministers, premiers and the government generally are a relevant factor, then inevitably so is that of police commissioners. Our examination of the development of their role in chapter 2 suggested that police commissioners in the early part of this century adopted a particular view of their autonomy. Yet, even so, the political perspectives and sympathies of police commissioners have varied enormously. The notable examples of Whitrod and Salisbury suggest the type of somewhat austere commitment to autonomy in the face of enormous political pressure to adopt a specific course of action. Others have appeared variously on the continuum from autonomy to partisan intervention. The complexity of this situation is again illustrated when we look at the role of some of the notoriously conservative commissioners. Urquhart in Queensland, a right-wing ideologue, adopted a position in the Red Flag Riots of 1919 which suited the Labor government of the day which was embattled by forces to its left.[10] Again in Queensland, Lewis, who was perhaps less party political than self-interestedly corrupt, was all too ready to do the government's bidding in the aftermath of a number of years of tension between the police administration under Whitrod and the government of Bjelke-Petersen .

A strong commissioner, acting in a political environment which was less interventionist than that of Queensland, was more likely to have success. Bringing the police force behind a policy of restraint has been the objective of those commissioners who observed the disordering consequences of open confrontation. Referring to the need for all police to conform to the new organisational philosophy, Victorian chief commissioner S. I. Miller noted in 1977 the change in mode of policing demonstrations during the 1970s. According to Miller:

> In demonstration situations, it became apparent that violence escalated violence and that it was preferable, where possible, to avoid confrontation unless violence to persons or substantial damage to property occurred. As a result, the organisational philosophy of restraint was translated into the operational strategy of a minimum visible police presence, commensurate to the task. This device has succeeded in defusing potentially explosive situations.[11]

Such a philosophy and strategy has not always been the preferred path of police leaders, especially where they faced strong pressure from government to act otherwise.

Similarly broader political contexts may have an important role to play in the direction either of restraint or action. During the 1930s depression it is evident that police were under pressure not only from executive governments to take a particular role in the policing of dissent and protest. Local government could be a nagging force calling for police action against the unemployed, as has been documented by Brian Costar in a number of centres in Queensland. So also could private individuals and groups, property-owners seeking redress against the troublesome unemployed. Both government and police of course were not above using the complaints of the general public, however undefined, to justify police repression or removal of troublemakers of an uncomfortable political persuasion.[12]

Finally, what of the situation itself? How much of what happens in the course of these policing responses in political conflicts is governed by the circumstantial contingencies in which the values and dispositions of serving police comes into play? Detailed historical analysis of incidents of conflict in Australia is uncommon. Typically the accounts of police conflict with protesters or strikers are reconstructions of a general context, on the basis of press reports and in some cases police files. The analysis, even of case histories, tends to be of a level which tells us little about the capacities and responses of street-level police in these situations. Exceptions include studies which have tended to conclude that police in the field were often far more restrained than some of their political masters and indeed of some commissioners.[13]

The most sustained examination of the policing of a major public event in Australia — an event which is instructive to the extent that it is not of a conventional political or industrial or even social protest kind — has been in a study of the Bathurst bike races. Police researcher, Chris Cunneen, and his colleagues were able to document the demonstrable deterioration in public order pro-, duced by a policing strategy which was quite the opposite of Miller's 'minimum visible police presence'. In this case, the New South Wales police chose over a number of years to reverse the Eureka strategy and insert a police stockade in the middle of the threatening mob. A change in police strategy, involving a less visible police presence and a greater dependence on the capacity of the bikers' organisations to police themselves in turn eliminated the 'riots'.[14]

Correlatively, recent police incidents in Australia have pointed to the fragility of any moves towards a less activist policing strategy. Significantly, many of these notable incidents of the 1970s and 1980s have involved Aboriginal people, whose degree of disaffection with Australian society has put them in frequent conflict with police. A result in some rural towns, especially in New South Wales and Western Australia, has been substantial over-policing of the streets and resultant escalation of public order incidents. In one or two cases this pattern has also been repeated in incidents in major cities, with a heavy-handed police response to relatively minor public order offences.[15]

The policing of dissent in Australia confirms Bittner's dictum that police function is at its base an exercise of 'legitimate' force. The degree to which a *particular* use of force is legal may in some instances become a matter for legal determination or the subject of public inquiry through a royal commission, as in the aftermath of the 1890 strike in New South Wales or the 1970 Vietnam demonstration in Adelaide. Legitimacy is however primarily a political matter. The historical evidence suggests that some police commissioners, like some governments, have considered that discretion was a better way of preserving the peace and maintaining legitimacy than prosecuting the law to its fullest extent. Other governments, and commissioners, have clearly not been averse to resorting to forceful policing to control dissent in the pursuit of quite partisan ends. In these matters policing can never rid itself of its ultimately political role. But the attainment of political ends, even where they are admirable ones, can be sometimes perverted by the choice of unwise means. Where the political ends themselves are questionable, the means are likely to be even more so. This has frequently been the case in the history of security police in Australia.

IMAGINED ENEMIES OF THE STATE

Political intelligence and surveillance has been an important formal function of police since the First World War. While the amount of policing resource and activity occupied by these functions has been relatively small, the public political significance of the activity has been substantial. No account of the relations of police and government in Australia can overlook the history of these agencies. Moreover, for most of this century, this has been one area in which the Commonwealth has shaped the direction of policing activity.

Under the peace-keeping mandate, police in the nineteenth century had been from time to time involved in surveillance of troublesome political figures and groups. The depression of the 1890s, with its industrial strife and the emerging challenge of socialist and labour movements provided numerous opportunities for police reporting on the activities of perceived subversives and disruptive elements. As a police function, however, this was seen as part of ordinary police duties, on a par with reporting on disturbances of any kind, with a view to limiting their future incidence. The emergence (as in Britain in the context of the Irish Fenian bombing campaigns of the 1880s) of a 'special branch' of police with particular responsibilities for surveillance of radicals or extremist groups, was some decades away.[16]

One advantage of the lack of a specialised function in this arena was the limited possibility of police elements developing their own criteria for defining what counted as subversive activity. Later experience of the activities of the political police in Australia, as in other places, was to suggest the wisdom of those early nineteenth-century critics of the methods of continental police, with their spies and politically suspect activities.

The origin of a separate political police in Australia lies in the First World War. In hindsight, the conditions were ripe for a specialised police, though the emerging role of the Commonwealth government was perhaps not predictable. The three decades before the war had seen an escalating capacity for political conflict between organised labour on the one hand and employers and their sympathisers on the other. The circumstances of the war intensified these conflicts, and divided the labour movement itself. Political conflict between Federal and State (especially the Queensland) governments, reflecting broader political divisions between supporters and opponents of the war and conscription, played a determining role. The Commonwealth had been content to rely on the State police as its agents in seeking information about potential subversive elements in the lead-up to and early years of the war, in tracking down suspect German-born residents of Australia, for example. In 1917, however, in the midst of continuing antagonism over Commonwealth attempts to enforce conscription, the Hughes Nationalist government (formed in the aftermath of the Labor party split in 1916) considered it no longer had in the Queensland police force a reliable ally. Under the direction of the anti-con-

scription Labor government of T. J. Ryan, the Queensland police incurred
Hughes' wrath when he was hit by an egg thrown by a demonstrator in the
southern Queensland town of Warwick.[17] Arguing that the Queensland police
were incapable of protecting Federal politicians, Hughes established a Commonwealth police force to operate in Queensland, a short lived experiment
which did not survive the end of the war.

More consequential were the war-time innovations in counter-espionage
and surveillance. Responding to British demands that Australia establish a
branch of MI5, a counter-espionage bureau was set up. It was replaced after
the war by the establishment within the Federal Attorney-General's department of an investigation branch with responsibility for collecting information
and recommending appropriate measures (e.g. deportation) against foreign-
born suspected communists and socialists. The branch became the base on
which later Commonwealth security agencies were built.

It was not alone in its political surveillance, however. During the inter-war
period, the State police forces operated in a context of substantial social and
political conflict. Tracking of the activities of left-wing unionists and political
figures had been part and parcel of the ordinary duties of State police during
the First World War in particular.[18] Those tasks continued in the inter-war
period, especially with respect to the surveillance of socialists and communists
in the industrial movement and during the social and political conflict of the
Great Depression.[19] These tasks, as much as they had a partisan political context and effects, were nevertheless linked directly to the police mandate for
keeping the peace, as well as addressing Commonwealth intelligence requests
regarding immigrants and aliens, rather than becoming part of a more general
political surveillance of a particular part of the population. That came later as a
consequence of the Commonwealth's intervention.

The Commonwealth government's involvement in political policing took a
new and striking turn in the aftermath of the Second World War. Both domestic and international factors were influential.[20] One was the local challenge to
the dominance of parliamentary Labor in Australia, with the strengthening of
the role and influence of the Australian Communist Party in the union movement. Already before the war the activity of communists and other left-wing
activists had frequently attracted the attention of the State police and of the
Commonwealth authorities. During and after the war, the political position
became more complex. Now it was not the labour movement facing conservative governments, but organised labour facing a Federal Labor government. In
some of the States too Labor governments were faced with the pressure of dis-
affected unions, some led by communists. In the 1890s when government in

Australia had last faced such substantial opposition, the political colours of government had been different. Much of the difficulty of the 1940s was the articulation of a long-standing dispute within the labour movement over the politics of reform or revolution.

The situation was exacerbated by the international situation. Initial wartime gratitude for the role of the Soviet Union in the struggle against Nazism had by 1948 given way to the outbreak of a 'cold war' of the western powers against the threat of communism. The Labor government of Ben Chifley in Canberra was caught in this poisonous atmosphere in ways which began to threaten its independence and survival. Facing the hostility of some major unions on the domestic front, it had to look also to the protection of Australian independence. Here the government faced great pressure from its closest allies, Britain and the United States, to enhance its security apparatus in order to deal with what was seen as Australian vulnerability to communist subversion.

The details of the formation of the Australia Security Intelligence Organisation (ASIO) need not detain us here. What is noteworthy is evidence of a distinct lack of enthusiasm for the idea of an Australian equivalent of MI5, a counter-espionage agency with what was clearly acknowledged at the time as a potential to operate as a political police to the detriment of the well-being of many citizens.[21] In spite of this, the Labor government of Chifley acquired the ignominy of association with what became a notoriously anti-labour special police. This Commonwealth agency, with its brief to contain the threat of communism to Australia, became a vehicle for prosecuting the cold war in Australia.[22]

True to its origins in domestic and international affairs, ASIO's history after 1949 was intimately connected to the course of Australian internal politics as well as occasionally to its external relations. Its most sensational early blooding was in the course of the Petrov affair. ASIO agents were instrumental in the course of events which led to the defection of Soviet diplomat Vladimir Petrov and his wife. The subsequent royal commission tainted Labor leader Dr H. V. Evatt with associations with the Soviet Union. In these and other activities in the 1950s ASIO agents played a politically partisan role, their work being directed primarily at identifying threats to Australian security from the political activism of the left wing of the labour movement. The impact of its work spread from the union and party political spheres into cultural affairs, with the leftist backgrounds of writers and artists being scrutinised to screen them out of eligibility for government funding support.[23]

An essential component of its operations was the curious structure of State support for ASIO's purported national security functions. In the absence of a Commonwealth police (not formed until 1970), ASIO relied on the formation within each State police force of a special branch, by administrative decision of the police commissioners, agreed at their annual meeting in 1948.[24] In operations which were poorly monitored by the respective police commissioners and in some States well disguised from the government, the special branches collected information on a broad range of individuals and groups, most of no demonstrable threat to national security. As described in an official review of South Australian security branch records, these intelligence operations were in the majority directed against 'imagined enemies of the State'. Scrutiny of the records suggested that the wholesale collection of information about 'leftists' had accelerated from the time of the Petrov royal commission in 1953–4. The individual subjects of special branch files included judges, most Labor parliamentarians, many unionists and numerous other politically active people. There were few records relating to the activities of non-Labor or right-wing politicians and activists.[25]

The role of ASIO extended in the 1960s to become an important instrument of government in the divisive conflict over Australia's participation in the Vietnam war. Fears expressed in 1948 over the threat of such an organisation to the freedoms of ordinary citizens[26] were confirmed again by the activities of an Australian political police which was incapable of distinguishing legitimate political dissent from the threats to national security which were formally supposed to constitute its reason for being. In the States themselves, the work of the police special branches was increasingly exposed to public scrutiny by the critics of political policing. As the political composition of government changed, there was growing pressure to reassess the role and accountability of the various police forces and of ASIO insofar as they were concerned with countering political dissent.

Hence, two leading Labor political figures became involved in the conflict over the ambit of political police in Australia. In events which have been discussed in the previous chapter, the South Australian Premier, Don Dunstan, challenged the police commissioner over his withholding of information relating to the activity of the special branch. A subsequent royal commission into the matter of special branch records uncovered evidence of the political bias of police surveillance. Large numbers of Labor politicians, union leaders, and antiVietnam dissidents had become the subject of police intelligence files. The quality of the intelligence itself was poor, much of it being compiled from press reports, and there was little monitoring of the accuracy of information or assessment of security risk involved. Justice White made extensive recommendations for the destruction of irrelevant records and the greater accountability of subsequent intelligence gathering.

The Labor government of Gough Whitlam had earlier been engaged in the first substantial challenge to the prerogative of ASIO. Suspicion that the organisation was withholding security information relating to the activities of the Croatian Ustasha group in Australia prompted an unprecedented and unannounced visit by the Commonwealth Attorney-General, Lionel Murphy, to ASIO headquarters in Melbourne in March 1973. The so-called 'Murphy raid', with the minister assisted by Commonwealth police, led subsequently to a major inquiry into the operations of intelligence and security in Australia by Mr Justice Hope.

The Hope royal commission took three years to report and formed the basis of subsequent legislation. The new Act (Australian Security and Intelligence Organisation Act 1979) provided for greater formal accountability through the responsible minister but also enhanced ASIO's surveillance powers and the protection of its agents. Subsequent reviews of Australian intelligence operations in the 1980s and a further ASIO Act 1986 has created further monitoring of the organisation through a parliamentary committee.[27]

Whether over the course of recent decades there has been a significant restructuring of ASIO's powers remains a matter of dispute. The exposure of some of the sloppier methods of intelligence gathering indulged in by ASIO over the years has led to a new emphasis, as elsewhere in policing, on professionalism and accountable procedures. At the same time, ASIO has retained a degree of secrecy and power which has been criticised as incompatible with the proper functioning of a democratic state.[28]

The corresponding apparent diminution of the role of political police at State level has not been achieved without political conflict over these sensitive policing issues. Resistance of the South Australian police commissioner to the demands of government for more control over the activities of the special branch led, as we have seen, to the dismissal of the commissioner and also contributed to the demise of the Premier. During the 1980s the political distaste for these police activities led to a sustained move against them in a number of States.[29] In Queensland, sensitivity over the activities of the State special branch over the previous two decades appears to have contributed to the pre-emptive destruction of files in the months leading up to the Labor victory in December 1989. In each case, the unpalatable history of political policing in Australia, rarely able to demonstrate a substantial public benefit, was evident. Whether the recent attempts to establish a greater degree of political accountability and more clearly defined responsibilities for police intelligence operations are capable of delivering longer-term compliance of police with these requirements remains an open question.

PRIVATE POLICE

A development of increasing interest in the management of policing in the late twentieth century has been that of private policing. Some critics have seen in it the sign of a state increasingly concerned to divest itself of traditional public responsibilities. More historically minded researchers have suggested either that public policing may be seen as a possibly short-lived episode in the management of social order, or else that private policing has always remained a dimension of policing during the last century and a half of organised State policing.[30]

The limited accounts of private policing in the Australian context are sorely lacking in any historical perspective. Without substantial investigation into the history of private detective and security agencies, for example, it is premature to claim that this development represents a 'broader move involving the transfer of certain responsibilities and powers away from public police forces'.[31] Nevertheless, a historical account of the field of 'private' policing in Australia is likely to show that over time there have been important shifts in the relations between government agencies and private interests.

These changes have been influenced not only by transitions in economic ideologies and policies. It is evident that an expectation by private individuals or groups that governments take responsibility for their security will be at least in some part influenced by the capacity of government to provide policing resources. This was the case in nineteenth century colonies when settlers demanded that their security be guaranteed by police — a demand that stimulated the spread and diversity of police forces, but which was not always able to be met. Besides economic factors, however, there are matters involving legal regulation and social norms which affect the role and responsibility of government for policing. A corollary of this is the likelihood or not of specialised private agencies having a role to play in policing.

Laws made a difference to the possibility of public or private policing. Prior to family law reform in Australia in 1975, for example, the arena of divorce was a civil law matter in which State police had little role to play. The responsibility for investigation rested, sometimes notoriously, on private detective agents. The introduction of no-fault divorce reduces the market for private investigators in an arena such as family law. In areas of economic life where the viability of colonial economies rested on the security of production and sale of mineral wealth in the form of gold, the colonial police were early allocated the responsibility for carrying out guard duty which would later pass to private firms: the gold fields escort duty was an important part of the foundation of colonial police establishments in the 1850s and 1860s.

Social norms and expectations also played their part in fostering the role of public or private police. There is evidence that absence, failures, or perceived inefficiency of the official police could lead to the employment of private police in the colonial period. In the infant settlement of North Brisbane in 1849, the 'lack of police protection led to a night watchman advertising his private services; he quickly attracted fifteen subscribers, at one shilling per week', leading the government to increase the constabulary by two.[32] As today, there was movement between the public and private sectors. Detective-Inspector Christie of the Victorian Police had his first experience as a private detective while working for a businessman. His experience led him to apply to Superintendent Nicholson for employment in the colony's detective force. In the 1870s, while still engaged in private service, he received a major reward offered by a wealthy Victorian whose family jewels had been stolen: the man had previously offered the reward to the colony's police, but expressed his dissatisfaction with them by turning to the private services of Christie. Christie went on to serve as a customs detective as well as in the colonial force.[33]

Other Victorian police crossed the boundary from public to private in the later nineteenth century, sometimes evidently under pressure. Cornelius Crowe, an 'inquiry agent' who was a thorn in the side of commissioner Thomas O'Callaghan in a 1906 royal commission, had been discharged from the Victorian police in 1897. Subsequently he set up a private inquiry agency and night patrol business, in the course of which work he claimed he had uncovered police links with burglary rackets.[34] Crowe's pamphlets publicising his cause were perhaps also a means of boosting publicity for his business, which was advertised on the covers.

The business of private policing was not restricted to the activities of inquiry agents and detectives. Australia may not have had the enormous private police forces employed by major companies which characterised for example the management style of Ford Motors in the USA in the 1920s,[35] but state-sanctioned special purpose police workers were a feature of the management of a number of areas of social and industrial life from the late nineteenth century. The employment of special constables is a well known example: their role in the response to labour strikes in the 1890s and in Brisbane in 1912 was seen as necessary to police control of incipient disorder.[36] But the very designation of special constable points to the ambiguity of the boundary between public and private: these constables were given quite specific police powers under the police Acts. The question of their use of those powers was a subject of contemporary debate, but their legal status is clearly linked to that of public police.[37] In South Australia, for example, local special constables could be appointed in the 1870s in Adelaide suburbs to relieve the pressure on central police personnel resources.[38]

Other agencies were sometimes subject to less identifiable statutory regulation but exercised police powers in their control over individuals for whom they were deemed responsible. This was notably the case with welfare agencies (especially those administering institutions for children and the destitute and aged) and missions (in the case of Aborigines). Again, however, the degree of control was a matter for some State oversight. Many of these agencies in effect were delegated powers of policing over individuals in lieu of the active presence of colonial police. And in a crucial matter, that of the exercise of force, they were in theory dependent on invoking the aid of State police. The growth of State control over these fields of welfare administration in fact led in some cases to a critical response to the wrongful exercise of force by welfare agents: hence the evident active interest of New South Wales State Children's Board chairman, C. K. Mackellar, in the prosecution of abusive guardians of State wards in northern New South Wales around 1915.[39] By the 1920s, much of what had been private welfare in Australia in the colonial period had become State controlled, whether in the areas of child care and control, or Aboriginal administration, or the care of the destitute. The role of the State police in aid of these other State agencies was indispensable.

In this decade, however, it was also noted that police duties were shared by a range of other State and private agents. Hence in 1927 the *Victorian Police Journal* published an item on the phenomenon of 'Private Policemen'. What distinguished police, it was argued, was not the uniform but the powers. From this angle the article went on to identify some of the other occupants of the role of police: water bailiffs, responsible for seizure of goods of debtors on boats; prison warders who possessed the power of arrest; the rail police, a unit of considerable importance in an organisation critical to the functioning and economic viability of modern societies. These were predictable enough categories, assimilable to the powers of special constable. But the article also identified the role of private police in other institutions:

> all the great shops and stores have their private policemen . . . these stores in many cases have a dossier of all the light-fingered persons known to them, complete with photos, and descriptions. The most successful shop policemen, however, are women.

Perhaps it was the very gendered nature of public policing which made women as private police in shopping stores the more unobtrusive and therefore successful. The extent of employment of private police in Australia was not addressed in the article; much of the commentary was drawn from examples such as the use of shop police in Paris. Similarly, drawing attention to another industry making use of its own police, it was noted that the great whisky firms employed these agents to drop into bars to check whether a publican was substituting cheap liquor for the genuine article.[40]

While there is little secondary discussion of the phenomenon in Australia, recent work on the department store has pointed to the gradual development of an organised response to shoplifting, with some big stores employing a detective by 1900. Continuing attention to the problem of store theft by the major retailing organisation in New South Wales led to an enhanced role for private detectives by the 1920s. Reekie concludes that by this time detective schemes, with some stores employing up to six detectives, were replacing the earlier informal reliance on sales staff. The mobility between public and private police is evident in the appointment of a former chief of the New South Wales criminal investigation branch to a major Sydney retailer's executive staff in 1928.[41] Other strategies of private policing included the development of surveillance within the store itself, as the control of employee theft became a priority.

In other areas of the economy, private policing, unregulated and punitive, was part of the workplace. While the enormous specialised private police forces of major industrial enterprises like that of Henry Ford in the USA[42] were less likely in Australia, the mechanisms of private policing were a part of management style in a major Australian corporation like BHP between the wars. The attention of foremen and watchmen in BHP's Port Kembla works in the late 1930s was focussed on the activities of union activists. The insecurity of employment in this large steelworks was maintained by the capricious use of summary punishments awarded by foremen, ranging from dismissal through suspension to downgrading. In the absence of mechanisms of appeal or standards of natural justice which might be expected in public administration, it is scarcely surprising that militant unionism became a favoured vehicle for redressing the harsh policing of these workplaces.[43] The interrelation of private and public policing was also a feature. In 1939–40, twenty-five men employed at the Newcastle steelworks, also run by BHP, were summarily dismissed following advice from the investigation branch of the Commonwealth Attorney-General's department that they were suspected communists endangering the war effort.[44]

The use of private police was not restricted to large companies — it extended to government agencies. During the depression, the favoured means of travelling the long distances necessary for many (mostly men) to get work was to take free rides on a goods train. 'Jumping the rattler' was frequent enough to become itself a specified offence in, for example, Queensland's reformed vagrancy legislation of 1931. Offences in law are nothing without prosecution, however, and police were insufficient in numbers or enthusiasm to pursue the intended targets. One result was the employment by the Queensland railways department, as in other States, of security officers some of whose tactics 'gained them a reputation as "basher gangs".[45]

The little-noticed but continuous history of private police in Australia is evident in the variety of uses indicated above. The post-war expansion of this policing has added significantly to the range and organisation of private policing services. Major security firms have become an integral part of the policing apparatus in Australia, their role and interests being only sporadically noticed in this country from the 1960s. During the decades in which public policing became a focus of common official and academic debate and inquiry, private security and policing attracted less attention. But their growth to levels which were considered to exceed the personnel and budgetary capacity of the public police has been noticed at intervals since the early 1970s.[46] The activities of private agents and security guards became the subject of express legislation from the 1960s, though generally only to the extent of requiring official licensing.[47] Today, as in the past, the levels of accountability and public knowledge of police activities which apply in the sphere of public policing, remain unknown and largely undemanded in the arena of private policing.

In the context of contemporary political agendas for the privatisation of public functions in a broad array of government responsibilities, it is not surprising that private policing is starting to come under some scrutiny. More recent analysis has suggested for example that the shift to private policing is a much more subtle process than entailed in the straightforward employment of private agents and security guards to carry out conventional watch and inquiry functions. Rather, as O'Malley has argued for Australia, the development of the modern insurance industry, with its notions of risk minimisation and cost-spreading, entails an engagement of responsibility on the part of the private citizen for crime prevention.[48] From this perspective, private policing is as much a product and means of changes in forms of government as it is a phenomenon of the growth of the security industry.

Much discussion of private policing is preoccupied with its allegedly problematic relation to the financial interest of major capitalist organisations (whether security firms or insurance companies). This leads some critics into what is the uncomfortable position of defending the prerogatives of the very police forces which under other circumstances are constantly the target of criticism.[49] The attrition of public police functions, however, might be regarded as a positive development, where it empowers communities or individuals, rather than simply subjecting them to yet another layer of rules and impositions. To cite just one example from a later discussion, the development of less harmful and more effective policing in Aboriginal communities in Australia has been seen in many quarters as requiring a greater devolution of police functions into community policing mechanisms. 'Private' justice mechanisms, consisting variously of Aboriginal-controlled police patrols, Aboriginal-run institutions for those on parole or community service, or Aboriginal punishment and social control measures, have all been debated and trialled in Australia in recent years.[50] The evidence of such innovation, significantly qualifying the prerogatives of public police and justice, suggests the possibilities of 'privatising' policing in ways which go beyond corporate gain.

Governing by Police — Social Histories

In the first section we explored some of the contexts of the political organisation of police in Australia. In this section we will examine some of the *effects* of policing on Australian society. The role of police in maintaining certain forms of social order has been a political question for most of the history of organised policing in Australia. This might be a question of limited political significance if in fact police could be shown to act in ways which were neutral socially. Historical and contemporary evidence, however, suggests that this has been far from the case.

Instead, the social impact of policing falls unevenly on particular populations. Some of the reasons for this lie in the way crime and offending are defined. Others relate to the way in which police and criminal justice decision-making is constructed. The priorities of criminal justice agencies, including the police, may change over time. Whatever the reasons, it is well known that policing outcomes, whether measured by those apprehended or not or those protected or not, are socially skewed. In Australia in the last couple of decades, very high rates of arrest of Aborigines for minor offences have signified the role of police in the maintenance of an unequal society. Equally, it has been strongly argued in recent years that the historically low rates of arrest for rape and sexual violence, which on other evidence are offences which have a high rate of incidence in Australian society, indicate the role of police in the maintenance of inequality between the sexes. The priorities attached by both police and governments to the regulation of street offences and the crimes of the poor contrast markedly with the low attention paid to the crimes of the rich and powerful.

Not all these indicators of the uneven impact of policing can be attributed to direct, positive decisions taken by police. To argue that policing contributes to inequality is not to say that inequality is constituted by the police. However, it is necessary to understand *how* police actions towards particular populations and offences have been formed historically by the role of the law and the organisation of police powers and practices. These matters will concern us in the next three chapters.

First, we explore some important themes in the organisation of police work in crime detection, surveillance and prosecution. Particular attention is paid to the development of finger-printing, to the use of informers, and to the practice of obtaining confessional evidence, as aspects of police work which have long and controversial histories. They are some of the means by which crime has been policed. Hence, they also constitute an important dimension of understanding the extent and limits of government by police in Australia.

Second, we will be looking at the history of public order, of keeping the peace, in Australia. What have been the legal and policing constraints in defining the proper concerns of police in the major part of their active work, that of policing the streets, whether for drunks or motorists? To what extent was police activity in the cause of peace preservation and order maintenance oriented to the control of particular populations rather than particular behaviours? That is, what does the historical evidence about the impact of this major part of police arrest and prosecution work tell us about the functions of police in Australian society?

Conversely, keeping the peace has had another set of meanings in the regulation of sexual relations. Like the legal system generally, the police have not been the unambivalent defenders of public or private morality. They have been criticised for inactivity in the policing of rape and sexual offences involving women whether in or out of domestic space. They have been criticised for their zealotry in prosecuting and persecuting homosexuals, or their unaccountable conduct in the policing of prostitution. In each case the historical role of police needs to be understood in terms of the directions of public policy, the actions or failures of other criminal justice agencies, and of the disposition of police themselves. In chapter 5 we explore some of these themes in relation to the policing of domestic violence.

A third concern will be with a history which has a unique status, that of the government of Aborigines. No other population in Australia has had its history so marked by the agency of the police. Understanding the forces which have shaped that history tells us much about how police work, and with what effects, in Australia.

In each of these arenas of activity, the history of the police has been part of the social history of Australia. Policing, that is to say, is not confined in its effects to the arrests of individuals. Rather, through delineating the space of acceptable or legitimate behaviour, policing has acted in identifiable ways to sustain particular kinds of social relations. In some of those contexts police have preserved a privileged status and power which has underlain many of the most controversial practices of policing.

CHAPTER 4

Policing Crime: Detection and Conviction

From the earliest moments of Australian policing, there has been a persistent theme in popular and political definitions of their primary function the police: exist to catch the criminal. Despite being confounded over repeated generations by the complexity of the phenomenon of crime, the police mandate is seen as one in which the defenders of social order, the thin blue line, combat the threat of the criminal. Yet many factors in both legal enactment and police operating procedures contribute to a world in which police target only some practices which can be classed as criminal, while ignoring or remaining indifferent to others. The prevalence of unpoliced anti-social practices and behaviours requires a more complex explanation than, for example, the concept of corruption can contribute. It has to do with the development over a long period of police priorities, constituted both by law and by administrative practices. This chapter documents some aspects of the history of police knowledge and detection of the criminal.

One approach would be to describe and analyse the distinction drawn historically by police between the criminal and the law-abiding population. This distinction is at the heart of the police enterprise, embodied in the earliest rule-books. Another approach is to explore the means of surveillance and detection and their social import. In what ways are these police techniques dependent on other social conditions and how does their deployment affect the relations between police and society? In exploring mainly this second approach, this chapter seeks to suggest that police work in the detection and prosecution of crime has an impact on the relations between police and the policed in ways which cannot be measured simply by the statistics of crimes prosecuted and criminals punished.

THE CRIMINAL CLASSES

If the police catch criminals, who are the people they catch? The foundations of policing in the Australian colonies were associated with perceptions which postulated particular social groups as threats to social order. Hence bushrangers and Aborigines were seen as some of the primary objects of policing. So too in the early colonies, even those colonies without a function in the convict system, convicts and ex-convicts were seen as potential sources of colonial crime.[1]

The centralised police refined these generalised concerns about the classes of people and offences which deserved attention. Police rules and regulations, issued from the commissioner's office, or published in handbooks or guides from the 1840s on, helped to sharpen the focus on the criminal. But was it the criminal or the act of crime which was the target? We need to be conscious of the changes over time in the capacity of police to identify those groups of the population which deserved close attention. These changes must be explained in terms of a developing technology of policing.

Early police rule books or guides, for example, were preoccupied principally with classifying behaviours which were likely occasions for criminal prosecution, demanding arrest. All the same their texts display a presumption that there are ready-made distinctions to be drawn between the class of respectable citizens and those groups, the criminal classes, which need to be carefully watched.[2]

These presumptions about the criminal classes were given statutory force by the enactment of habitual criminal legislation in some colonies, following on English legislation which had been passed in 1869.[3] This empowered police to place discharged prisoners under surveillance, effectively placing them on indefinite probation. A complaint from an ex-prisoner to a South Australian parliamentary inquiry in 1872 indicated the reality of enforcement of this type of legislation under which police could at will search the dwelling of a discharged prisoner on suspicion of receiving stolen goods.[4]

Such legislation, together with the police guides, identified the range of people and behaviours which was the object of police work in criminal investigation. The pragmatic task of policing, however, was to be able either to predict those people likely to breach the boundaries, or to identify those who had already committed crimes. In both tasks, the police were aided by a number of new technologies and practices of policing which were introduced between the 1880s and the Second World War. Contemporary policing has simply refined these important developments.

Preceding the development of any of the technologies of criminal detection, however, was the process of criminal investigation. Already in the colonial period it was becoming a specialised area of police work. Criminal investigation branches were composed of specially assigned police, the detectives, whose work practices distinguished them sharply from general police. Their plain clothes, the lack of regular beat work, the limited accountability for the time spent beyond the surveillance of superior officers—all were factors helping to create a distinctive work culture.

In contrast to the strict bureaucratic regimes which characterised the organisation of the ordinary police, the detective departments could be autonomous and self-governing, if not self-serving, oases. Autonomy without regulation or accountability could over time translate to maladministration, inefficiency and corruption. They were problems which beset the organisation of detective work in Victoria in the 1870s (subject to severe criticism by the Longmore commission in that colony in 1883) and of the Queensland criminal investigation branch in the 1890s, subject to somewhat similar criticism following its failure to solve a number of sensational murders near Brisbane in 1898.[5]

Such problems spilled over into the relations between the two different kinds of police. Tensions between detectives and uniformed men were exacerbated by differences in work norms. In Victoria, the antagonism between detectives and uniformed men had been so great in the 1870s that the Longmore commission was able to cite cases which had failed because of refusal of one group of police to cooperate with another.[6] In South Australia, the animus between the two branches was evident in 1872 in allegations by the general police that they were being spied upon by the detectives.[7]

The work routines of criminal investigation were unpredictable, whereas those of ordinary police were marked out in time blocks for the very purpose of ensuring disciplined policing. Moreover, there were important differences in the milieux in which they worked. While general police were advised to know the doubtful characters on their beats but warned to keep their distance from them, detective police were enjoined to associate with the criminal milieu in order to facilitate the task of crime detection.

In these very differences rested much of the alternate glamour and notoriety attached to criminal investigation. Police autobiography and biographies of police typically deal with sensational crime and its detection, rather than the humdrum of police work.[8] The *Australian Police Journal*, the first professional police journal in the country, commencing publication in 1946, quickly became dominated by the writings of crime investigators, documenting techniques of investigation and triumphant stories of detection and subsequent conviction of offenders. Popular journalism of course has long sustained this police view of what constitutes the highest achievement in policing.

In such a context has developed a variety of police strategies and techniques which aid the work of investigation. The significance of these is not merely that they refine or facilitate the work of crime detection, but that they have frequently had a broader impact on the society being policed. That is, police work is not simply a matter of reacting to events which must be set right — rather, policing itself is an active agent in the creation of particular social relations which characterise crime as a social event — a behaviour which involves offence, reporting or observation, and a policing response.

This may be seen in the development of various strategies of detection and information-seeking. Perhaps most notorious, and at the same time central to the way police obtain knowledge of certain kinds of (mainly property) crime, is the use of informers. For the entire history of crime investigation, the cultivation of informers has been considered essential to the maintenance of police knowledge of the criminal world. Not surprisingly, the cultivation of close relations between police and informers has resulted in ambiguities about the objectives and means of police work, ambiguities which tip over into the police cultivation of crime itself in notorious instances.[9]

The cultivation of informers was at the heart of controversy over the performance of the Victorian detective force in the 1880s. Inquiring into the efficiency of the police in the aftermath of the Kelly outbreak, the Longmore commission concluded that 'the employment of criminals seems to be the distinguishing characteristic of the system pursued by Victorian detectives in recovering stolen property and bringing offenders to justice'.[10]

The system of using informers known as 'fiz-gigs' ('paid to start the prey which the expectant detective captures without trouble or inconvenience') was one which was justified only in extraordinary circumstances, but had, according to the commission, become a common practice in the Victorian detective force. The commission regarded the widespread use of fiz-gigs as variously 'un-English', 'dishonourable' and opposed to 'fair play'. The portentous language of its criticism should not be allowed to detract from the finding that this branch of police was a 'standing menace to the community' and a 'nursery of crime'. Detectives, far from prosecuting and preventing crime, were engendering it.[11] In the process they had acted with demonstrable harm towards people who had not committed an offence.

Criticism of this system of police-work which placed such great emphasis on the securing of convictions at almost any cost has continued at sporadic intervals, suggesting the continuity of these police practices and the difficulty of reforming them. A concern to monitor the use of informers is evident in New South Wales, where up to 1932, payment of informers required the approval of the colonial secretary—about 40 were on the payroll at that time.[12] Contrary to Haldane's interpretation, they were not an atavistic survival of the convict days,[13] but a dimension of police detection which would continue to prove useful in the years ahead.

Hence, as recently as the beginning of 1993, the Independent Commission Against Corruption in New South Wales found that police had regularly used prison informers to obtain convictions against certain individuals: the rewards for the information, ranging from monetary ones to reduction in sentences, early release or dropping of serious charges, mirrored exactly the modes described in evidence before the Longmore commission in the 1880s.[14]

Equally notorious has been the recent involvement of Queensland police in a large-scale operation intended to undermine car-theft rackets. Armed with an indemnity against prosecution for a criminal figure involved in car-stealing, police working on 'Operation Trident' attempted to target those involved in the disposal of stolen cars and parts. Some police themselves became involved in the racket, purchasing or selling stolen items, with consequent serious harm to the unknowing victim-owners of the stolen vehicles.[15]

The persistence of the police use of informers over such a long period of time prompts the question of what factors in the organisation of policing support it. Such factors have differed little in recent times from those which existed in the 1880s. Judicial sanction of the use of informer evidence, even where it verges on entrapment, makes it possible for cases to be developed on the basis of such support, encouraging police resort to its use. A corollary of this explanation is the important limits on police which the judiciary might exercise: it was an adverse judgment of the Supreme Court which led to a disclosure of 'Operation Trident' in Queensland.

Most importantly, however, police departments emphasise the importance of conviction, and police culture has helped prioritise crime detection as a critical focus of police work. Hence, in spite of the occasional exhortation stressing the dangerousness of the use of informers,[16] the practical instruction of police came to emphasise the importance of cultivating informers as a source of police knowledge of crime and the criminal classes. Outlining his 'Advice to Detectives' in 1948, Ex-Chief-Supt. T. Wickham of the New South Wales Police, noted that:

> Any Detective who knows his business has his own little coterie of INFORMERS. In fact, he is not much of a Detective if he has not . . . INFORMERS are personal assets to the Detective and he should, for quite apparent reasons, closely guard their secrets

and keep their identity hidden, even from other Detectives, unless there is some good reason to do otherwise.[17]

Wickham's advice, published in the pages of the *Australian Police Journal*, stressed the potential use of all the powers available to police. These included a full exercise of police discretion in the prosecution of offences. The inducements which might be made to potential informers are implied in this advice:

Police generally can also lend valuable assistance by a sensible and equitable interpretation of those difficult laws we have to administer. I refer of course to traffic and liquor laws particularly. If we exercise care in this respect we will avoid making enemies of decent citizens who inadvertently commit minor breaches of these Acts. There are, of course, some Acts which should be used to their fullest extent. For instance, the consorting clause of the Vagrancy Act is one that can be used to great advantage by an astute Detective to assist him in his work against criminals and reputed criminals. But the exercise of great care is required in order not to abuse it and give cause for serious complaints by decent citizens who might be found associating innocently or legitimately with criminals.[18]

From this perspective, the task of the detective and of police generally was the maintenance of a distinction between the decent citizen and the criminal which would help the police in their task of prosecuting crime. The ease with which the latter objective can become the end justifying almost any means subsequently became legendary in repeated official inquiries in the 1970s and beyond. A brief examination of the use of informers suggests how this means of securing a knowledge of the criminal classes has been embedded in police work.

IDENTIFYING THE OFFENDER

An implication of the discussion of the long history of the use of informers is that other modes of investigation and surveillance developed alongside the informer system, rather than replacing it. They included technical innovations, such as fingerprinting, electronic communication, from radio and telephone through to computers, and a battery of forensic tests which continue to have a controversial application in the courts but play an essential role in police investigation.[19]

Many of these developments were technologies which depended on the organisational characteristics of the police department, with its capacity for communication and for record-keeping. Each of the new detection techniques was ultimately dependent on the efficiency of the department in which it was operating. Moreover, some of the most significant developments in crime surveillance and investigation were essentially administrative devices, an extension of the capacity of the police force as a bureaucratic institution to keep records and registers of the movement of particular parts of the population. In addition, the Australian police forces developed over the twentieth century modes of linkage and communication which compensated for the division of most police tasks between State jurisdictions.

Fingerprinting is the best known technology of detection founded during this period. Its introduction to Australian policing was rapid, a product of the capacity for diffusion of policing technologies and information which developed internationally at the turn of the century. A meeting of the State commissioners of police in 1903 agreed on the establishment of a uniform system of fingerprint identification.[20] By 1906, the Queensland police were systematically collecting the fingerprints of known 'bad characters under arrest'.[21] Over the next few decades, all Australian forces cooperated in the exchange of fingerprint data, with the New South Wales police becoming the central agency for collection.

The acceptance of fingerprinting as an aspect of policing and criminal investigation required certain historical conditions. These included the development of the science itself, its legitimation by the judiciary and by legislation, its development as an aspect of police administration, and its articulation to other methods of surveillance and detection. From such a perspective fingerprinting can be seen to represent the broader development of criminal investigation as police work in the twentieth century.

The introduction of fingerprinting accompanied the development in the late nineteenth century of new sciences such as biometrics and eugenics. These sciences postulated patterns in human inheritance knowable through their traces in the physical attributes of individuals. Their importance cannot be underestimated, however much we might decry their links to politically reactionary and ultimately fascist social policies. For whereas in the early nineteenth century, the most influential strains of opinion affecting policing had postulated the existence of certain criminal classes and types (the 'dangerous classes'), by the end of the century, sciences such as eugenics and psychology were beginning to identify individual variation as the basis for understanding human behaviour.[22] Policing preserved both views of the incidence of criminality, relying for example on the hypothesis of the existence of criminal classes for the development of consorting legislation in the inter-war period, and on fingerprinting (and later blood typing, and more recently DNA testing) for the accurate identification of individuals.

The significance of this change from the criminal type to the criminal individual was directly addressed in judicial debates around the accuracy of fingerprinting evidence. Indeed, in 1912, judicial conflict over the status of new scientific postulates was evident in the course of a Victorian Supreme court appeal on just this point. The judges divided over the significance of individual variation as a scientific fact. The chief justice spoke for the nineteenth century view that human beings divided into types, implying that some individuals were similar in physical attributes. 'Nature cared nothing about individuals, but cared everything about types', opined the chief justice. The majority of two judges differed, registering the impact of the new sciences in their defence of fingerprinting as an accurate signifier of an individual, and hence a reliable test of guilt in a criminal case.[23]

Judicial affirmation of the admissibility of fingerprint evidence was just one side of the legitimation of this policing practice. The other was the legislation of conditions under which police might take fingerprints. The matter was crucial to the potential effectiveness of fingerprinting as a means of tracking offenders. Police desired a broad ranging power to fingerprint, certainly broader than was indicated by the initial practice limiting it to convicted offenders on indictable charges. Changing the criteria allowing police to fingerprint was a drawn out process, varying from State to State, as discussed below.

The third condition of police use of fingerprinting was the very capacity of police administration to centralise and communicate information. This capacity was already evident in the nineteenth-century publication by colonial police of a 'Hue and Cry' or police gazette, which documented criminal activities and the movements of released prisoners as well as other surveillance information. In this context, police administrations in Australia enhanced their data collection and data swapping progressively through the twentieth century. The annual conferences of police commissioners provided a level of integration of policing which was absent in the more formal structures of strict State responsibility for most areas of policing.[24] By the inter-war period, regular exchanges of detectives personalised the system of exchange of information which had become an everyday feature of criminal investigation in previous decades.[25]

Finally, fingerprinting relied for its value on record-keeping of as broad a coverage of the offending community as possible. The police force was already equipped with this capacity. Apart from the regular book-keeping in watchhouse records especially, which police departments had already refined, the 1880s had seen the introduction of surveillance of those under probation as first offenders.[26] In Queensland, for example, a photographic register was maintained to ensure police around the colony kept an eye on those placed on probation following their first offence. Photographic records were assuming importance as a means of detection and surveillance, through circulation in each colony's *Police Gazette*.[27]

Police were not alone in their responsibility for this surveillance. By the 1920s the volume of photographic records exchanged between prisons departments and police departments within and between States and countries was very substantial. In 1926, for example, the New South Wales prisons department supplied 730 photographs of criminals (prisoners being released), with the police department subsequently circulating 6,600 copies to other States and New Zealand, and 25,200 to city and country police in New South Wales. In return, the New South Wales police had received 2,394 photographs from other States and New Zealand.[28]

Fingerprint data was subject to the same routines of exchange. By 1955, when the New South Wales fingerprint section was acting as the central bureau for all Australian forces, New South Wales was receiving annually over 68,000 fingerprints from within the State, another 26,000 from other States, and over 600 from other countries. By this stage the volume of recording was so great that New South Wales police decided to discontinue taking prints of people charged with some minor offences. Prints were used not simply for criminal investigation but for regulatory purposes, such as applications for licenses which police were required to vet.[29]

Hence, the diffusion of fingerprinting as a technology of crime detection required a conjunction of historical conditions, including changing scientific knowledges and the organisational capacity resident in the police forces, as well as judicial and political legitimation through case law and legislation. But its historical significance is not restricted to these important conditions of its use. For an important implication of the development of an accurate means of population surveillance and detection was the possibility of universalising its use. Requiring people to give their fingerprints, before they were sentenced on conviction for an offence, was problematic in a common law culture which postulated the innocence of the accused.

In the 1920s and later, the temptation of expanding the net of police observation of the potentially criminal classes overrode earlier caution. In 1931, for example, the Queensland *Vagrants, Gaming and Other Offences Act* gave police discretionary power to fingerprint those charged under the Act, before conviction. The context was the increasing tendency of police to argue that a significant proportion of crime was the product of more or less 'professional' criminals. Hence, the 1935 circular to police advising them to use the Act to fingerprint the 'undesirable type', even where such people had only been arrested on a minor charge, a direction extended in the following year to include those arrested for 'train-jumping'.[30]

Elsewhere, uncertainty over the appropriate use of the power of fingerprinting endured at least into the 1950s. In a 1955 report highly critical of police investigative procedures in Tasmania a former Victorian police chief commissioner, Alexander Duncan, noted 'a difference of opinion in the minds of certain police officers as to police power to take fingerprints of persons in custody'. The government advised the commissioner of police that legislation would be introduced to clarify the matter.[31]

Perhaps the most telling example of the ambition of police to use fingerprinting as a means of general surveillance was an extraordinary move of the Australian police commissioners, initiated at their 1957 conference, to seek Commonwealth approval to fingerprint all immigrants, registering copies at the Australian central fingerprints bureau, maintained by the New South Wales police in Sydney. The proposal followed public and police debate over the criminal activities of immigrants and the commissioners had compiled a list of crimes committed by migrants which was used to back up their case. To its credit, the Commonwealth told Victorian Premier Henry Bolte in 1959 that this proposal would make immigrants into second class citizens. Moreover, the number of migrant criminals was small compared to the 1.3 million migrants who had arrived in Australia since the war.[32]

Fingerprinting did not exhaust the generation of new technologies and procedures for the investigation of crime in the twentieth century. During the inter-war period, the *modus operandi* system of recording data about the activities of criminals and patterns of offending was spread throughout the Australian forces. It was enhanced by the already-noted cooperation of the State forces and the Commonwealth investigation branch through the exchange of information.[33]

On top of organisational and communication changes, other technologies of the twentieth century, such as listening devices and forensic testing of many kinds have been important and often controversial additions to investigative technology. In its capacity to breach legal and cultural norms of privacy, the former has been the subject of substantial dispute, most notoriously in the so-called 'Age-tapes' episode, leading to the prosecution of the High Court Judge, Lionel Murphy, in the 1980s.[34] Forensic science itself, and especially police reliance on it in prosecution, was damaged substantially by the revelations of its misuse in the Lindy Chamberlain saga.[35]

The development of these crime investigation and surveillance techniques are an important part of any history of government by police in Australia. The refinement of record-keeping and the development of large databases of suspect populations undoubtedly contributed to a police capacity to monitor and detect crime. They enabled a targeting of specific individuals who might in the future become suspects in criminal investigation. On the other hand, they broadened the potential for police coverage of the activities of people who were suspect on other grounds. Enough has been said earlier and elsewhere about the history of political policing in Australia. The possibility of extensive surveillance of the politically active population, however, was laid by the development in police departments of techniques and practices for monitoring those suspected of criminal activity.

GETTING A CONVICTION

The establishment of criminal investigation branches in the various forces proceeded under the general mandate of police to detect crime where it had not been prevented. Detection implied prosecution and conviction. Inevitably police would be judged in the public domain of media and Parliament by their success in securing convictions. From the beginning, however, there were anxieties over the way convictions were obtained. They were anxieties which fed not only on the regular instances of police malpractice in the prosecution process, but on jealousy within the police force itself directed towards the successful cop.

The street policeman had to observe the detective building a career on a reputation for catching 'crims'. The majority of police were not involved in the business of catching thieves, rapists or murderers. Even arresting drunks was not an everyday experience for many police, to judge by the annual ratio of arrests to serving officers. In such a context, it is scarcely surprising that some police, engaged in routine duties, observed with rancour the greater acclaim won by detectives in working on more serious crime. Deflecting a question about the preoccupation of detectives with obtaining convictions, inspector-general James Mitchell told a 1918 New South Wales parliamentary inquiry that:

> it is not the first duty of police to secure convictions. The duty of the uniformed branch is prevention. We put men in uniform and they promenade our thoroughfares openly in order to show that they are police officers. The detective branch is on a different footing. After offences have been committed, it is the duty of the detective branch to clear up those offences, and recover property stolen from citizens; therefore the detective who secures the recovery of stolen property, and also secures evidence that leads to a conviction before a jury or other tribunal undoubtedly secures

kudos, as against the man who cannot recover citizens' property, and who cannot secure evidence to gain convictions.[36]

Mitchell's evasion scarcely hides the implication that, without convictions, a detective's employment was meaningless. It was and is this fundamental objective of crime work in policing which again and again has brought the means of achieving convictions under notice for the degree to which they breach the boundaries of legality. This has sometimes required a compliant judiciary to mandate the means in view of the end (conviction of an offender) which is desired.

Crime investigation focussed on results — obtaining convictions for crimes committed. Strict regulation of work routines was inimical to this work. However, without attention to systems of record-keeping and time allocation, it was all too easy for criminal investigation organised in such an unsupervised way to become highly inefficient, oppressive to individuals, or corrupt.

The problems arising from this system have been a matter for public scrutiny from time to time in Australia as elsewhere. Getting a conviction might bring 'kudos', but at what price? While Victoria reviewed its practices extensively in the 1880s, in the aftermath of the Kelly outbreak, and Queensland subjected its criminal investigation branch to intensive inquiry in 1899 in the wake of the unsolved Gatton and other murders, Tasmanian detectives were the subject of a similar inquiry in 1955. The report of Alexander Duncan, formerly Victorian chief commissioner, into the Tasmanian criminal investigation branch, suggests the costs of a commitment to convictions as the primary task of criminal investigation.

Duncan's report followed an earlier inquiry in which detective police had been severely reprimanded for their treatment of a sailor under arrest in Hobart. Duncan found a mode of organisation of the criminal investigation branch which fostered inefficiency and abuse of power. Training was negligible, with the main tasks learned on the job from superior officers. Book-keeping was haphazard: the Tasmanian police were not issued with standard, page-numbered notebooks to record their inquiries in a systematic and accountable way. Neither were there other records considered important by this time such as a register of crimes reported ('felonies and occurrences') or an office register to record officer movements and work routines from day to day.

Duncan considered these organisational defaults to be similar to the mentality operating in the crime section. The primary object was to secure convictions by the fastest possible means. The easiest means of doing so was to obtain confessions. Regardless of the multiplication of investigative technologies and procedures, the practice of the Tasmanian criminal investigation branch was focussed on eliciting a confession. For this purpose, as Duncan described it, a number of officers would be present at the arrest and interrogation of suspects. Without spelling it out, Duncan's clear implication was that the whole operation was designed to intimidate the suspect. All this went against the spirit of the judges' rules, noted Duncan. Moreover, it hindered successful prosecution by neglecting the more painstaking task of collecting credible evidence to sustain a case.[37]

The recurrence of criticisms of the practices and uses of obtaining confessions in crime investigation and prosecution is almost tedious. The multitude of recent instances in a number of jurisdictions in which confessional evidence has been challenged and convictions successfully overturned should not allow us to view the past complacently. Indeed, the incidence of public inquiries and judicial statements regarding these practices over the past century or more encourages the view that these are part of a norm in policing, rather than the corrupt or venal exceptions.[38]

Hence to go back no further than the 1930s, it was the same Alexander Duncan who had critically reviewed the use of the 'third degree' in criminal investigation in Victoria in that decade. The inquiry had been prompted by a condemnation by the State's chief justice, Sir Frederick Mann, of prolonged detention for questioning. Mann claimed to be speaking for all the judges in urging that it was time that prolonged detention and examination of suspects 'be curtailed by law or regulation':

> There is no doubt in my mind, that public policy does require that if we are to maintain the invaluable characteristics of unquestionable fairness in the administration of the criminal law some limitation must be put on this growing evil.[39]

The only historical commentary on this episode argues that the incidence of extorted confessions in Victoria at the time was an indication of retardation of police professionalism in Victorian (and by extension Australian) policing. Overseas, suggests Haldane:

> the combined forces of scientific knowledge and humanist thought were forging a new police professionalism that saw academics, scientists, lawyers and policemen working together to improve the quality of police investigations, while safeguarding the rights of suspects.[40]

Victoria, he adds, lagged behind the 'level of community awareness and debate about the humanist aspects'. This view seems excessively optimistic about the impact of professionalism. It underestimates the degree of subsequent concern about police practices, the long history of complaints about them, and the failure of police 'professionalism' in recent decades to prevent such practices.

Duncan's inquiry accepted the substance of Mann's criticism as it applied to the criminal investigation practices of the Victorian police. According to Haldane, Duncan considered the police methods 'crude', with untrained men left to their own resources:

> Even more troubling were the numerous 'serious allegations made against members of the police force', and the instances of police being successfully sued for damages.[41]

Duncan recommended improvements in training and scientific work for detectives. But longer term experience of the criminal justice system suggests that the issues went well beyond matters of training or professionalism.

Hence, in spite of three or four decades of improved training in criminal investigation, the following years saw not only Duncan's Tasmanian inquiry, with its criticisms of police methods reminiscent of those he had described in Victoria in the 1930s. In New South Wales, a number of challenges to the obtaining and use of confessional evidence developed in the early 1950s. In the first case, McDermott, who had lost an appeal to the High Court against his conviction, in a judgment which established an Australian standard on the issue of confessional evidence, was nevertheless released after a royal commission found his conviction was unsafe (as discussed later).

Then, in 1954, there was a 'spate of challenges to confessions', following two cases, those of Studley-Ruxton and Rigby, which focussed public attention on police conduct. In the former case, the matter was not just one of the use of confessional evidence, however obtained, but of the use of violence in police detention. A royal commission into the Studley-Ruxton case was inconclusive on many of the matters, including a failure to explain some injuries on the person involved: it also noted the frequency of allegations regarding police assault in such circumstances.[42] Reflecting at the end of the decade on some of these circumstances in an article on 'Confessions to Police', the metropolitan crown prosecutor doubted:

> that police as a matter of course or frequently extort or concoct the confessions to which they depose. Yet at seasons, to allege beatings, threats and concoction is so much the vogue that a genuine complaint may fail to win due regard.[43]

Kidston vaguely referred to a group of twenty cases about the year 1954, in two-thirds of which confessions had been challenged but with little success. The case law approach of lawyers to such an issue[44] was incapable of shedding much light on its incidence, but there is little doubt from its recurrence as a public issue in the 1950s and after of the continuing cogency of confessional evidence as a means of getting a conviction. In Victoria in 1965, judicial criticism of police methods led to an official inquiry. The solicitor-general, in an unpublished report to Parliament;

> received complaints of the use of violence and threats by the police in order to obtain confessions and also allegations that confessions had been fabricated. He concluded that these abuses took place 'more often than on occasional or isolated instances.'[45]

This report was contemporaneous with some of the earliest social science research on the operations of the criminal justice system in Australia, that of Elizabeth Eggleston. Her discussion of the report drew attention to its particular relevance to the interrogation of Aborigines. The matter was especially remembered at this time following the most sensational inquiry involving police in the 1950s. In South Australia, Rupert Max Stuart had been found guilty of the rape and murder of a young girl and sentenced to death in 1959. Stuart was an Aboriginal. Evidence was given in the inquiry by anthropologist Ted Strehlow that Stuart's confession, the main evidence against him, could not have been dictated by him, as an Aranda man speaking what Strehlow called Northern Territory English. While the inquiry rejected Strehlow's argument, it concluded that the conviction was sound. But public disquiet over the conduct of police in the case had in the meantime led the government to recommend a pardon for Stuart.[46]

The Stuart case, in spite of the inquiry's conclusion on the issue of the guilty verdict, demonstrated the fragility of the confession as a basis for prosecution of a serious crime. The construction of the confession as a piece of evidence was exposed by the detailed scrutiny of the procedures used to obtain them which the inquiry unfolded.

The problems were of two kinds. First, the 'plain fact is', reported the commissioners, 'that the prosecution was content to rest its case upon the confession, without seeking for the testimony by which it has now been fortified'. This criticism of police dependence on the confession alone was of course exactly the same as that which had been frequently raised before, by Duncan in Tasmania in 1955, and by Longmore in Victoria in 1883. Amplifying the problems of an exclusive reliance on the confession as evidence was the manner in which confessional evidence was obtained.

In Stuart's case, there were two records of a confession. One had resulted from an oral interrogation; another from a question and answer session beside a typewriter. The first was led by a constable who took no notes of the interrogation while it was proceeding, recording his recollection of the questioning a day later after he returned to Adelaide from Ceduna. The inquiry considered this opened up a 'policy question' on which there seemed to be 'two schools of thought':

> There are those who hold that questions and answers should be recorded on the spot, and those who hold that the sight of a note book and a pencil dries up sources of information that might otherwise be fruitful. It is, no doubt, a matter of opinion, or perhaps of policy, which course is to be preferred.

The fact that the inquiry, following a trial and appeals to High Court and Privy Council, was still undecided as to whether procedure in police interrogation was a matter for policy or opinion suggests how weakly such a crucial part of criminal investigation was regulated. This did not prevent the commissioners concluding that the police constable who had conducted, and a day later noted, the oral interrogation was 'speaking incautiously' in claiming at the trial that his account of the oral interrogation was 'word perfect, and, secondly, that the words used in the written confession were what the petitioner had said . . .'.

The inquiry then went on to give a frank account of the way in which the written confession must necessarily have been produced. There was no doubt that Stuart had received:

> . . . more help with the wording of the written confession than [Constable] Jones was prepared to admit. The evidence is that the first part was the result of question and answer reduced to narrative form, and we think that it was conceded that the dates and times were generally the results of questions, for example, 'was that 19th December, 1958?' or 'what was the time when (so and so)?'.[47]

The construction of the confessional evidence could not be more clearly described. The problems in Stuart's case, regardless of the merits of his appeal and protestation of innocence, arose from the fact that, as already noted, 'the prosecution was content to rest its case upon the confession'.

The question arises then, how was it possible that prosecution dependence on a procedure which had for so long been problematic could continue? The answer has much to do with the repeated affirmation by the judiciary of the admissibility of confessional evidence. Judicial discretion to admit this evidence in criminal trials is said to be governed by the need to balance the public interest in gaining conviction of guilty people and the public interest in the protection of the individual from unlawful and unfair treatment.[48] Yet the judicial discretion was likely to be only sparingly exercised to exclude evidence, including confessional evidence, even if improperly obtained. Chief Justice Mann, operating under Victorian statutory provisions, had stressed in 1937 the constraints of the judge in dealing with the conditions under which police had obtained the evidence. The matter in the 1950s was seen as one which turned centrally on whether or not the trial result itself would be fair and just.[49] Except in cases of demonstrable violence by police against detainees, the judgment of the court was essentially about the quality of evidence before the jury, not about the conditions under which it had been obtained.

Pronouncement from the bench, or lack of it, on the admissibility of evidence before the court was ultimately a means of giving police the freedom to pursue to the limit of the law, and beyond it, their desire to obtain a clear statement of guilt, under conditions which beg the meaning of the word 'voluntary'. Regulation of any kind is a two-fold process: it not only constrains but opens up a field of action. The way in which judicial pronouncement affected the discursive norms of policing practice can be shown clearly in an example which antedated Stuart's case.

Writing in the *Australian Police Journal* in 1949, the deputy clerk of the peace in New South Wales addressed the 'Questioning of Persons in Custody'. The article resulted from a recent High Court judgment on confessional evidence which still stands as a guide to the law in Australia. Frederick McDermott had been convicted in 1947 over a murder committed in 1936. Appeals to the New South Wales Supreme Court and the High Court on the admissibility of confessional evidence failed. The judges refused to reject confessional evidence unless there had been a clear breach of the Judges Rules and statutory obligations regarding statements in custody (which were governed in New South Wales by s. 410 of the *Crimes Act*). On the basis of the High Court judgment, which formulated the Australian test for the voluntariness of a confession, Cleland concluded that police had a rather wider power of investigation prior to arrest than had been understood. The police should not have to feel that they had to take a suspect before a magistrate immediately they formed a conclusion to arrest and charge him or her.[50]

Judicial pronouncement, mediated through the advice of another functionary, was here taken to define the proper limits of police practice. Regulation of police practice in fact helped to define more broadly the scope of what police might properly do, at least as interpreted by the deputy clerk of the peace. The High Court had spoken and the decision was relayed by a court official in ways which mandated a police freedom to interrogate in custody.

The legal standard was thus set firmly in place. But questions of justice and police practice nevertheless remained open. Was the verdict safe in this case, which had gone right through the Australian courts and produced a clear affirmation of the voluntariness rule, whatever the problems of making that practical in a policing context? Four years after the High Court rejection of

McDermott's appeal, a royal commission found that the trial had miscarried: McDermott was released. The commission concluded that new evidence which had been uncovered by a newspaper reporter threw doubt on the conviction.[51] The police were unable to sustain their case, after having gained a conviction on the basis of a confession which the High Court had accepted as admissible. The fragility of the confession as a reliable determination of guilt was evident yet again.

One effect of this unresolved feature of police crime work was its re-emergence as a major criminal justice issue in the 1970s. The criticisms by Duncan in Victoria in 1936 and in Tasmania in 1955 of police reliance on too easily obtained confessional evidence were broadened into a more sustained critique — this time from outside police circles — of the phenomenon of the police verbal. The frequency of use of confessional evidence as a basis for conviction was subjected to scrutiny by academic lawyers, criminologists and civil liberties groups. In Queensland in 1977 and again in 1989, major inquiries into the criminal justice system identified the phenomenon of police abuse of the freedom they enjoyed to construct a case oriented less to the marshalling of comprehensive evidence than to securing a quick conviction. The Fitzgerald commission in particular named and analysed the practice of 'verballing' in some detail, aided by the testimony of former licensing branch officer, Jack Herbert.

'Police', concluded Fitzgerald, 'see successful prosecutions as one of the few positive aspects of their work'. This work is, however, faced with continual frustrations in the shape of due process requirements, which police are often ill-prepared to address. Hence:

> steps to redress what is perceived to be an unequal contest are readily open to police officers. Evidence of guilt which is manufactured or falsified or improperly obtained diminishes the effect of the presumption of innocence and such requirements as proof beyond reasonable doubt and unanimous verdicts, and greatly decreases the prospects of acquittal for those whom the police decide are guilty.

In such a context, police reliance on unsigned records of interview and 'confessions' of informers had developed as a 'feature of Queensland criminal trials'. Police were inducted to the process which had become part of the culture of crime work:

> Herbert said that although some police would not verbal, there was usually no need to sound out an unknown police officer to see whether he would give false evidence. It was just accepted. When a person was arrested police would sit down at the typewriter and 'you would make the story up as you went along'.[52]

Herbert's description was disarmingly similar to the allegations which had been made over the course of the previous fifteen years in the campaign against verbals, especially in New South Wales. Videotaping of interviews was regarded by some, including the Australian Law Reform Commission, as a means of addressing this police malpractice in building a case against an accused. However, it could only be so if the readiness of the courts to admit evidence obtained in a variety of circumstances was addressed. By the beginning of this decade, in spite of the numerous incidents in Australia and overseas in which convictions obtained on the basis of confessional evidence had been overturned, it was still uncertain how effective new technology and new regulations regarding police practice would be.[53]

Police work in the solving of crime and the arrest and prosecution of offenders makes up only a small part of their total responsibilities. The significance of such work, however, extends beyond its application in particular cases. Not only does crime work, through its representation in popular journalism, fiction and the media, contribute powerfully to popular views of police, it also contributes substantially to the debates around police powers and law reform which have characterised public perceptions of police in Australian history. Further, if a fundamental characteristic of the police in a rule of law culture is its operation under publicly known and legally accountable rules, then the persistence of questions about the character of police practices in crime work suggests the very fragility of the concept of rule of law in Australia. It is for these reasons that the history of police work in crime detection continues to demand attention in any consideration of the role of police in the process of government in this country.

CHAPTER 5

Keeping The Peace

The historical mission of the new police was a dual one: the control of crime through prevention and detection, and the keeping of public order. In the settler colonies of Australia and New Zealand there was an additional task, the desire to secure the land for free settlers and pastoralists, a topic we explore in the next chapter.

In important ways the first two tasks were interrelated. Crime would be the more effectively prevented by a constant presence of police on the streets, a symbolic statement of order and a guarantee of intimate knowledge of the populace at one and the same time. We have also seen that over time the crime detection role became specialised, concentrated in detective branches armed with a variety of special techniques and knowledges. The bulk of policing work, however, was more mundane. The police patrol, on foot, bicycle, horse or later in a car, accounted for a large component of police duties. Potentially the whole population was the object of surveillance. But the social history of policing is the story of how police targeted particular groups for attention and paid limited attention to others.

This chapter is concerned with two sides of the police task of keeping the peace. Common to both is a shifting boundary which separates the public and the private, the former the business of the police, the latter a domain on which they tread only warily. We are concerned then first with understanding the changing forms of public order policing, and second with exploring the constraints on the policing of the private sphere, as this has been publicly defined. Our task is to understand the conditions under which police work has historically been preoccupied with certain public order offences, drunkenness and traffic offences for example, and on the other has paid highly selective attention to offences involving women. The reasons for these differing levels of attention have much to do not only with legal definitions of offending and political mandates for police priorities, but also with the formation of police themselves, a subject for separate attention in later chapters.

POLICING THE STREETS

A police report of 1927 defines the sort of social distinctions and behaviours which are the stuff of police work on the streets. Asked to respond to the repeated claims of a suburban progress association that the outlying Brisbane suburbs of Northgate and Virginia were beset with larrikinism and robbery, the acting sergeant at Nundah outlined his perception of the social character of his district, identifying those who wanted watching. Like many police in other contexts the sergeant was inclined to downplay the complaints.

The suburbs of Northgate and Virginia, reported the sergeant, were first class localities, with residents in good occupations and having expensive homes. 'There are no places w[h]ere rough and low class people inhabit & there are no professional larrikins'. Indeed, he reported, the behaviour complained of, youths calling out to passers by, was the product of children of some of the residents and was not serious enough to warrant attention. Foot and cycle patrols were used throughout the district but one area was closely attended by police:

> Hendra is also a thickly populated locality where many training stables are situated & jockeys reside which has to be patrolled at night time as frequent as possible together with Clayfield and Eagle Junction portion of Nundah division. A rough class of people reside at Clayfield & Eagle Junction which is an old settled place and where cheaper rents are paid, and where a push known as the Porky push have existed for a long time, but have given no trouble now for some time past owing to bicycle and foot patrols.

In spite of the 'rough' area patrolled, the sergeant insisted that the frequent cycle patrols curbed larrikinism and other trouble.[1]

We may surmise various explanations of the nature of this response. One is that such complaints were in fact of little substance, or not serious enough to warrant police intervention. Another is that police requested by their superiors to respond to public complaints may inevitably feel defensive, justifying the success and efficiency of their own style of local policing through denial of any serious disorder. A third possibility is to take the report at its face value, a working document of policing in which some behaviours and groups are identified for special attention. Whatever the dimension we choose to explore in this particular case, this report illuminates the social distinctions being made in street policing.

Making distinctions of this kind was part of police work. Police rules and training prescribed responsibilities for distinguishing the respectable from the rough, though of course not all the rough were a threat to order. Nevertheless, in the parlance of police, rough areas wanted watching, and the history of peace-keeping is in large part that of the processes by which police watched, intervened, arrested and prosecuted the inhabitants of these areas.[2]

The powers available to police in these duties were considerable and highly discretionary. The chances of successful prosecution of charges laid for public order offences were good, and probably better where a magistrate was in sympathy with a local law and order campaign. In the incident just cited, the police were able to refer to their recent summonsing of 16 youths in the area in the previous three months with all convicted. Police discussion of their activity in controlling larrikinism makes clear the exemplary function served by selected prosecution. Although the sum impression of the files suggests a relatively low level police response to 'larrikinism' in Brisbane over some decades, the prosecutions cited indicate the importance to police of the panoply of police charges, such as obscene or indecent language, offensive behaviour or assaulting police.[3]

What was the origin of these powers and how were they expected to be used? There were two generic sources of police public order powers in Australia: vagrancy statutes and police offences ordinances or statutes. Both were English in origin but with rather different genealogies. The vagrancy statutes were redrawn in the early nineteenth century, but their history dated back to Elizabethan times, with attempts of the early modern English state to control the large numbers of wandering property-less and workless labourers. Reform in the early nineteenth century broadened the scope of the Acts to become a major instrument of regulation of public places.[4]

In their nineteenth century form they also comprised a multi-use instrument directed at various forms of money-making which flourished in the margins of the economy: thieving, gambling, prostitution and so on. Their use by police as a general public order power was also glaringly obvious to some other personnel in the criminal justice system. A governor of Melbourne Gaol in the 1870s noted the ease with which the police invoked the vagrancy Act against those they wished to see off the streets:

> Some fortnight since a miserable looking & evidently stupid man was brought to the Gaol under the common charge used by the Police when they have nothing else to urge against a prisoner, 'Having no visible means of support'. This charge first intended to catch card sharps & such like rogues is now conveniently used for the purpose of obtaining shelter for the destitute who are found lying about homeless by night.[5]

Vagrancy law has been seen by some commentators on colonial history to signify the preferences of a society which is intolerant of outsiders.[6] In truth, its role in colonial societies is much more mundane than this. As an inheritance of English law, it was part of the baggage of policing which came with the organisation of the criminal law and the criminal justice system in the middle of the nineteenth century. The coverage of vagrancy law shaded over into police offences Acts in some jurisdictions. These derived from attempts of the nineteenth century state to govern urban spaces more comprehensively. Typically in the mid-nineteenth century, in the New South Wales form of the towns police Acts for example, the police offences statutes empowered police intervention in all kinds of street or public activities. As particular localities achieved the status of towns by virtue of government proclamation, the police powers which applied in Sydney would be extended to the new areas.

In fact, many of the powers at this time were those which we would regard today as lying in the domain of municipal government by-laws, affecting the kinds of activities which might legitimately be carried on in public places. To recognise this is to note that the nineteenth-century police was an instrument of considerable flexibility in the service of government. Particularly in Australia where notions of local government were weak, the police, acting under central government statutes for the good order of cities and towns, were intimately involved in the delineation of social and economic spaces in these areas as well as in the delivery of mundane government services. Police officers have often felt these to be extraneous duties and annual reports from the nineteenth century on are full of complaints about the burdens of allegedly non-police duties which were held to impede efficiency.[7]

From the perspective of often impecunious governments, the use of the police as general task-workers in the collection of information about the population was undoubtedly justified by the substantial cost of this major public institution in the nineteenth century. These duties at least gave police something to do in places which had limited public order or crime problems. If police were also to do what the manuals said should be done, that is get thoroughly acquainted with their local beats, then the collection of statistics, the serving of notices and orders, the management of petty sessions courts, and the running of elections were means of achieving that objective.

However, this work had to be done with discretion. The heavy-handed copper who was over-intrusive or put away otherwise law-abiding citizens who were committing a minor offence against public order could be an embarrassment to senior police who had to field complaints from aggrieved parties via their local politicians. Having the judgment to know what constituted an offence, and to whom, was part of the task of learning policing. When a constable arrested three men on a charge of disorderly conduct in Charleville in 1899, it was scarcely surprising that the case was dismissed: their offence was that they had been talking loudly after midnight. On the complaint of the men concerned over their arrest in such circumstances, the constable was cautioned for being over zealous.[8] In New South Wales, as in London, the early task of the new police was to treat those of respectable position with consideration: hence in the 1850s those who could afford the standard forty shilling fine after arrest for drunkenness were released as soon as they were sober, relieving them of the humiliation of being paraded with the drunks through the early morning police court.[9]

If we measure policing priorities by volume of arrests and prosecutions then there is a simple contrast between nineteenth and twentieth-century policing. The focus of the nineteenth century was on the social offence of drunkenness. The preoccupation of the twentieth century was rapidly to become motoring offences. Neither task brings prestige or favour to police involved in the work, but the social significance of these two activities was undoubtedly influential in shaping police behaviour at one level.

The priority given to charging drunks and other public order offenders was justified by the mandate of preserving the peace and civilising manners. 'Public decency and decorum are as much objects of police as the protection of property', opined the London *Bell's Weekly Messenger*, in the 1820s.[10] Policing in the nineteenth century meant maintaining order in the cities and towns, providing an encouragement to a process of civilising manners which was as relevant to outback settlements in the bush as it was to Sydney, Toronto or London. Drunkenness was not only a social nuisance, an affront to the changing norms of public decorum, it was also associated significantly in the minds of opinion makers and social reformers with some of the most pressing problems of social life. Drunkenness distracted from work, it was associated with violence in some cases, or more generally with the ongoing problem of poverty and the creation of dependent populations. Temperance movements, which were at times the major political and social movements of the nineteenth century in Australia as in Britain and North America, constituted a recurrent stimulus to police control of public drunkenness. The meaning of drunkenness became not just a matter of personal worth, a sign of a lack of control—its public exhibition became a constant reminder of an ever-present threat to the strength of a society. Late in the century, the language of moral decay gave way to a perception of drunkenness as a threat to racial vitality.[11]

Whether the concern was moral or medical, the authority for police action rested in the public order provisions of towns police Acts, liquor legislation and vagrancy Acts. Being drunk in a public place, being drunk and disorderly, drinking at the wrong place at the wrong time, were all occasions for the enormous proportion of police time given to watching and detaining drunks. The other side of the matter was the protection of the drunk person: detention was also a protection against those who preyed on the drunk. Hence the two-fold attention to drunkenness of police sergeant Michael Broderick, stationed at Longreach in western Queensland from 1894: his vigilance was, he said, exercised against the 'spielers and loafers' who 'rob drunken Bushmen'.[12]

In the nineteenth century, drunkenness was generally the most important of a number of public order charges which made up the bulk of police and magistrate's daily business. This was the case in all jurisdictions. For example, in New South Wales in 1881 where there was a relatively high ratio of police to population of 1 to 266, there were 18.8 charges of drunkenness per officer, making up a clear majority of the 34.4 charges on all offences per officer in that year. In South Australia at the same time, with an even higher police/population ratio (at 121), the number of drunkenness charges was somewhat less significant as a proportion of police work, but the combination of drunkenness and other good order charges was still responsible for about two-thirds of charges laid.[13] Far less was policing concerned with tracking murderers and taking thieves.

The chances of a policeman being involved in the more exciting business of crime detection was in any case very low. Some of this work was becoming specialised, the responsibility of detective officers, who were of course dependent to some degree on general police. But a comparison of colonies (Table 4) suggests a per officer rate of at most five or six charges per annum for offences against the person or property in the 1880s.

Table 4 Charges per police officer, offences against person and property, 1881

	NSW	Vic	Qld	SA	WA
Person	1.9	2.0	2.0	2.5	3.6
Property	3.6	3.4	1.7	3.0	3.1

Source: Data drawn from Mukherjee, Source Book. Tasmanian figures are not available owing to localised nature of police jurisdictions as this time.

What was the norm a century later? The likelihood of an officer being involved in charging for an offence against the person had actually declined by 1971 in all States (Table 5). Some increase is on the other hand noticeable for property offences, but still the likelihood of the average police officer being involved in this work leading to an arrest was no more than once in every two months. The great bulk of police charges heard in the Magistrates Court by 1971 was no longer even associated with drunkenness or good order offences, although these remained significant.

Table 5   Charges per police officer, by offence, 1971

	NSW	Vic	Qld	SA	WA	Tas
Drunk	8.0	na	10.0	5.0	9.7	1.1
Good order	11.6	2.2	10.9	7.3	14.1	3.0
Person	1.7	1.7	.5	.9	1.4	1.3
Property	6.7	7.5	3.1	4.1	12.1	7.5
All offences	56.9	61.6	36.7	69.2	60.8	51.5

Source: Data drawn from Mukherjee, *Source Book*; Victorian data does not enable comparison of minor offences.

On an Australia-wide basis, of the 52 charges per police officer heard in magistrates' courts by this time, 36 of them would be for 'petty offences', eight for good order, six for property and just over one for offences against the person. Inconsistencies in recording data make it difficult to compare States with confidence, as the table suggests. But the evidently mundane nature of policing duties is indisputable whichever way one looks at these figures. What the table leaves unsaid but implied is that the bulk of police work, measured by charges laid, was by 1970 in a category which had not existed to any great degree at the turn of the century: the regulation of traffic.

Are we to imply from this that the volume of these tasks is evidence of an over-intrusive state, bent on extracting revenue from the petty offender under the guise of keeping public order? The sight of the modern police officer routinely booking offending drivers for turning against a sign or parking in a restricted zone brings frequent complaints. Nevertheless, in terms of two long-term mandates of policing, the prevention and detection of offences and the keeping of public order, it is clear that the routine character of policing of traffic has substantial justification.

The most striking evidence of its justification is the extraordinary amount of harm which has been caused by the modern car. The brutal fact of twentieth century urban and rural life in Australia has been the extremely high risk of death or serious injury on the roads, particularly when compared with the low risk of homicide or manslaughter from other causes. Figures compiled on an Australia-wide basis (Table 6) suggest the exponential growth of mortality in car accidents from the 1920s.

Table 6 Death by homicide and car accidents, Australia, 1925–1985

Year	Homicide	Car accidents
1925	83	517
1935	106	1,060
1945	77	754
1955	139	2,168
1965	162	3,163
1975	224	3,788
1985	314	3,007

Source: Data drawn from Mukherjee, *Source Book*, pp. 645–650.

Already in the early 1920s, with only a low rate of car ownership, deaths from car accidents were four and five times the rate of homicide in Australia. By the 1960s, more people were dying on Australian roads every two months than the total of Australian soldiers killed in the six years of combat in Vietnam. None of this is to take account of the further enormous impact of serious injury on the roads.

The loss of life and injury incurred by the motor vehicle was an early concern of police. The passion for statistical documentation of crime which had developed in some nineteenth-century police forces was transposed to the new task of analysing the incidence and causes of traffic accidents. Death and injury, whether culpable or accidental, did not exhaust the police interest in the management of traffic.

Hence there was for some time uncertainty about who should be responsible for the order-keeping function of traffic direction in city centres. By 1915, however, the Western Australia police commissioner was calling for that State to be brought in line with the majority of others in placing all licensing and regulations associated with motor vehicles under police jurisdiction.[14] In the absence of municipal capacity for policing, it generally fell to police to take on the task. Often they faced intransigent opposition from motor vehicle interests like the automobile associations which painted the police initiatives as meddlesome and interfering with the much fancied civil liberties of drivers.[15] Speed controls introduced and policed from before the First World War soon became the source of much police work and revenue collection, contributing to the great growth in regulatory offences as the century wore on.

City order was also the function of police, through their direction of traffic. It was a task which had preceded the arrival of motorised transport, being seen as an essential part of policing duties from the towns police Acts on.[16] In addition to keeping order at intersections and monitoring pedestrian behaviour, the police initiated moves for more regulated parking. The very design of urban streets became an issue as the contradictions grew between the nineteenth-century layout of the cities and the twentieth-century transformation in their use by the car. So quickly had the car impacted on policing that the Western Australian commissioner considered in 1925 that 'the control of traffic has now become so interwoven with ordinary police duties that it is impossible to separate them'.[17] It was by this time affecting staffing levels and was to remain so. The seriousness of the road death impact of the car raised the possibility of an unlimited expansion of police efforts in response.

The public order problems posed by the car led in time to innovation in policing mechanisms and the functioning of the courts. Police regulatory powers were expanded by the establishment of speed limits and controls over parking. But these were only modifications of powers which had already been well in place in the previous century. It was no great step from prosecuting for the offence of 'furious riding' on a horse to that of charging a driver with exceeding the speed limit. But two important changes in the decades after the Second World War signified a different kind of relation of police to the policed.

The first was the adoption of a system of legal regulation without court appearance which became known as 'on-the-spot' fines. The change was necessitated by the huge volume of work which the laying of police charges and preparation of cases entailed in the course of traffic regulation. Only a small proportion of offenders bothered to defend the charge in any case. The result was a routinisation of the vast majority of traffic offences.

A more controversial innovation was the introduction of random breath testing (RBT). This roads equivalent of a stop and search power was the first time police had been given a general power to surveil the population without having reason to suspect an offence. As an innovation, it was a victory for the cause of proactive policing. The underlying rationale was of course prevention of road accidents by reducing the number of alcohol-impaired drivers on the road. Its introduction, however, shares with a number of other governmental interventions in the twentieth century the influence of a collectivist ideal of the common good. Sociological interpretations of the introduction of drink-driving laws have emphasised the figure of the 'killer drunk' as the moral target of legislation and policing strategies.[18] Like that earlier target of police and moral interventions, the habitual drunk, the 'killer drunk' was a figure of the social imagination. Similarly it has been argued by Emsley that the social construction of the figure of the 'road hog' strongly influenced the course of law and policing of motor traffic in Britain in the early twentieth century.[19] According to Homel, the dominance of the image of the offending drinking driver has in some jurisdictions impeded the development of rational social policy aimed at reducing the risk of harm caused by the mix of drinking and driving.[20]

From a different angle, whatever the perverted course of this area of crime prevention in particular jurisdictions, a view of the history of modern government might set the development of strategies of random breath testing in the context of administrative modes which share much with public health strategies having as their aim the reduction of risk behaviour.[21] Admittedly this strategy through its use of penalties and a deterrent rationale differs from some aspects of public health, but the randomness of the strategy (if we ignore the issue of targeted police activity) shares with health screening the object of reducing a population's risk through identifying risky individuals. The conventional common law requirement of evidence of a reasonable intention as a basis for judging guilt was waived by the adoption of a concept of the risk to self and others posed by drinking. The threat of random breath-testing would simultaneously act as a deterrent to would-be drivers and a means of removing those undeterred from roads, for a shorter or longer period of time.

Not surprisingly, there was considerable resistance from some quarters to the introduction of RBT. The police commissioners were discussing the uses of the breathalyser in their conferences in the 1950s. But it was not until 1968 that it was used in New South Wales and only in the late 1970s that RBT was introduced in Victoria and then progressively in other States. Political resistance of the kind which had marked its introduction in Britain, with much anxiety over civil liberties, characterised its adoption in Australia. Indeed resistance to the introduction of RBT became something of a political standard for conservative Queensland Premier, Joh Bjelke-Petersen, who held out until 1986 before conceding a modified form of breath testing programme.[22]

In terms of its impact as a policing strategy, the effect of RBT has at least two dimensions. One is that there is evidence, in spite of its 'randomness', of drink-driving law being socially skewed in its policing. Homel and others have pointed to the disparities between the distribution of drink-driving behaviour and drink-driving prosecutions, with young men being particular targets of the latter, in spite of the much broader spread of drink-driving behaviour in all age groups and (though to a much lesser extent) across sexes. Other evidence suggests that RBT has been especially targeted on specific places or suburbs: Homel's research notes the predictable targeting of the Bathurst bike races at Easter,[23] but other evidence, as in Wood's research in Hobart, suggests also the more mundane and less visible differences between random testing in different socio-economic areas. From this perspective, the reaction of a Queensland officer to the opportunity presented by the introduction of a similar scheme in Queensland in 1986, takes on new meaning: saturation policing through the 'Reduce Impaired Driving' campaign 'was an attempt to clean-up the "lawlessness" in the Woodridge region'.[24]

Secondly, RBT was considered to have had some significant effect in reducing fatalities, though this effect could not only be explained by the specific process of police stopping, testing and arresting offending drivers, with subsequent prosecutions. Other deterrent agents may have worked, including the size of accompanying publicity campaigns, which appeared to Homel to explain much of the difference in impact of RBT between New South Wales (successful) and Victoria and South Australia (much less so).[25]

If the phrase 'governing by police' has any meaning in Australia, then the policing of public order has a large claim to centrality in that mode of government. Yet the patchwork of examples of quite opposite policing strategies illustrated here suggests that this government is uneven in its social impact. Like other modes of government (welfare especially, education, even health) the effect of policing through this state instrumentality constantly has the effect of demarcating the worthy from the deplorable, the respectable from the rough, the good from the bad. Police, no less than other state functionaries, have played their part in reproducing inequalities, or even in enhancing them.

Police are not generally aware that they play such a role as the social distinctions which the law articulates and produces become very quickly the basis of moralising judgments about the worth of those they police. The question is whether policing can surpass such a heritage of class and social distinctions to respond to citizen needs in a more democratic society. In the everyday examples of the policing of drunkenness and of motor traffic we can find evidence of both good and bad policing strategies.

In these mundane tasks, which have nevertheless important social rationales, good policing might have as its target the reduction in risk of harm to individuals, whether 'offenders' or other parties. Bad policing on the other hand amplifies the usually minimal harms caused by drunkenness or traffic violations. It does so when policing results in aggravation of police-citizen relations through poor management or selective concentration on particular groups or individuals. The difficult but necessary task of police authorities is to ensure that policing of these everyday infractions of social order meet standards of prevention of crime or offending behaviour dangerous to self or other, without causing more harm than good.[26]

Domestic violence: public or private?

By virtue of their role as keepers of the peace and agents for the detection and prosecution of crime, police were considered the guardians of a public domain. But how was the public domain defined? What actions and relations were legitimately the concern of the public and what should be left alone? The answers changed over time. So did the methods of policing related to these answers.

A telling example is the area of violence within the family. The term domestic violence is a modern concept for behaviours which are clearly ancient and have differing cultural meanings and significance.[27] The legitimacy, if not the practice, of acts of physical punishment, whether exercised by legal authority or between individuals, has been undermined in many modern cultures. In setting limits to violence, however, the state and policing authorities, themselves the agents of violence in particular settings, have contributed to the definition of a sometimes hazy boundary between public and private. From the earliest statements of the rules of the new police in the nineteenth century, the response and responsibility of police in cases of domestic conflict were severely limited.

Not only were police warned generally, for example, not to be meddlesome or over-zealous in any of their dealings with the public. Specific instructions directed police to avoid intervention in domestic quarrels. As the Queensland Police Manual put it in 1876:

> The police are not to interfere unnecessarily between a man and his wife who are quarrelling, unless it is absolutely necessary to prevent serious violence to either party or public disturbance.[28]

In the 1980s, police standing orders in Victoria, as elsewhere, still advised non-interference 'in the private business of others'.[29] Police directions were sustained by strong cultural and social organisational norms which legitimised low levels of intervention and approved or excused male violence in particular. Judges, no less than police or settlers, might excuse male violence, ranging from beatings to shooting and knifing, on the grounds of female spouses' failure to live up to their husband's demands. Hence Judge Pring in New South Wales in 1904 agreed with the jury's recommendation for mercy in the case of a returned Boer War veteran who had shot his wife in 'a moment of frenzy', after her repeated refusal to leave Sydney to come with him to New Zealand: the 'prisoner was driven by his wife's disgraceful conduct to commit the crime'.[30]

The all-male character of the different levels of the criminal justice system (judges, police, juries and lawyers) did not help matters, but there were important exceptions in perceptions of what constituted acceptable behaviour between spouses. And contemporary norms and realities sometimes cut across the sex divide. Hence on the Darling Downs in 1862 the local police magistrate and mayor of Toowoomba was presented with a petition of residents for mitigation of punishment on a man he had sentenced to six months hard labour in Brisbane gaol, for an aggravated assault on his wife. The petition was signed by the man's wife (the victim) and 31 other residents who did not dispute the justness of the sentence, but deplored the disgrace to the family from his 'being paraded through the streets as a common felon'. The magistrate could not support the petition, as the wife had presented before him:

> a most shocking spectacle – her face and body a mass of bruises; not the first time, since she complained to him when he first arrived in Toowoomba but refused to lay information.[31]

In this context, the policing of violence was principally a matter of actions by individuals. In the days before social security and state-sponsored family maintenance, the great responsibility for prosecuting these kind of assaults lay with the individual rather than the police. We might conjecture that dealing with a violent husband entailed *unforeseen* consequences. In all likelihood, however, the consequences were all too visible and well-known. A private summons on the husband for assault, a very common form of action in the nineteenth-century Magistrates Court, if it was pursued, could mean departure of the bread-winner, to prison or out of the home. Desertion of such a husband would require a further summons for maintenance, again a common business of the lower courts by the late nineteenth century. The desirability of successful action against the husband on either count had to be weighed against the possibility of an outraged husband inflicting further violence or misery on the family.

A less gloomy outcome might be that the summons was taken against the husband as a warning: the proportion of discontinued actions of this kind is noteworthy, suggesting women using the law strategically to manage the social relations of the home. The perceptions of a Victorian gaol governor, used to housing a large number of imprisoned deserting or offending husbands, was that some women were adept at negotiating the legal possibilities provided by their power of civil action against their husbands:

> Most of the men have been bound over to keep the peace for threatening their wives with violence.... Many stay several months and constantly are laying their cases before the Visiting Justice...It is amusing to hear how the women assume an authority in the matter—they will let their husbands out if they will undertake to do so and so & they will keep them *in* to the bitter end unless they give them the fullest satisfaction. There is no doubt most of the men are bad-tempered & drunken but some of the women who own them are enough to sour the disposition of the best of mortals.[32]

In such a world, police were also called informally to intervene in domestic disputes. If so, they might face the risk of another man's rage, in this often most dangerous form of policing. They also had to face the weight of rule-made and culture-made norms against their becoming too involved, let alone recognising the legitimacy of the woman's need for protection. Not surprisingly then, this was a domain where everything conspired to preserve a boundary between the public and the private.[33]

In consequence, the involvement of police was extremely limited, if we take the level of prosecutions as our index. More subtle forms of historical investigation, through the use of police diaries and other paperwork, might suggest a higher level of informal policing in this area, though the thinness of the police resource is unlikely to have left much time for domestic policing of this kind, even were police willing and able.[34]

Indicative of the dominant police perception that this area of their work was outside the domain of normal policing was its development as a priority duty for women police. Important evidence from the early history of women police indicates both the high incidence of domestic violence and conflict occasioning police notice and the degree to which this policing took place outside of the purview of the courts.

The example of the South Australian police is instructive. By the 1930s that State had an active women's police establishment of 13 officers, having been the second police department in Australia to appoint women police (in 1915, shortly after New South Wales). Their role initially was principally a child-saving one, with major attention being paid to diverting young girls from prostitution. By the 1930s, the diversity of tasks undertaken by these police had broadened to include a wide-range of 'social work' tasks, making inquiries into public relief cases and emergency housing needs as well as attending to the policing of neglected children. The annual report in 1935 suggests also that what it called 'domestic discord' had become a significant area of concern. Over the year, the women police had dealt with 559 cases under this head, cases which made no appearance in official police statistics: the police had given advice and assistance to couples, 'at all times endeavouring to effect reconciliations, if practicable'.[35]

South Australia was regarded as having the best commitment in this area of policing in the inter-war period.[36] Its policing arrangements, however, appear to have been conditioned by an unusually strong tradition sustaining a broader concept of policing, the department's operation of an ambulance service being another instance of a like kind. The emphasis in the policy of the South Australian women police on advice, assistance and reconciliation suggests the emerging influence of diversionary strategies in policing—Annie Cocks, the first principal of the women police in South Australia had been earlier a clerk with the state children's council and the first female probation officer for juvenile offenders in South Australia.[37] She was not alone in bringing such a background to the police force of an Australian State.

In New South Wales, an inspector in the state children's department, Maude Marion Rhodes, was appointed along with Lillian Armfield (who had worked as a mental nurse at Callan Park hospital in Sydney) to the police department in July 1915.[38] Comments by Rhodes to the press in the wake of their joint appointment invoked a different concept of policing to that which tended to prevail in the masculine world of the New South Wales police:

> The work which Miss Armfield and I are now undertaking will not so much require physical strength as tact, experience, straightforwardness in dealing with questions that are too often waived, and commonsense and a certain amount of brainpower for dealing with those questions.[39]

The impact, however, of these ideas and expertise on policing overall must be regarded as nugatory in these decades. By 1929, one State (Queensland) still did not employ any women police in this work, while all others had very limited numbers of women police. Even when Queensland finally appointed women in 1931, they were not sworn officers. And in New South Wales, where the colonial secretary had boasted in 1915 that the 'women police would be police in the full sense, and have all the powers possessed by the men of the force', women police remained only special constables, without superannuation rights until 1965.[40]

During the long (and only slowly changing) period in which the role of women in policing was seen as limited specifically to the 'domestic' arena (including the protection of women and children and the dealing with them as victims of crime), the commitment of all police departments in staff and resources to this area was parsimonious in the extreme. Ultimately, the only lever of change was the political one. It was politics, in the activity of feminist organisations,[41] which brought about the appointment of women police in New South Wales and South Australia, leading the way for the other States. The renewed feminist interest in domestic violence from the early 1970s resulted in a more intense focus on the role or indifference of police in addressing the problem. Reform legislation in some places gave police a new mandate to intervene pre-emptively through initiating protection orders and involving themselves in community-based education and prevention agencies.[42]

The changes indicate the transformation over a century of the family domain as a site of government concern and intervention. The law, and with it, police, tended in the nineteenth century to leave untouched the relations of spouses. Interventions in protection of the interests of children and of women's property interests heralded a new order. But they were accompanied at the turn of the century by postulates about the nature of family life and social order which recast the issue of domestic violence as a problem not so much of law and policing but of medical and psychological pathology and remedy.[43] The high age of the psychologisation of social conflict, from the 1900s to the 1960s, may well have resulted in a lower rate of reporting and prosecution of domestic violence as alternative solutions were sought by police, courts and a growing number of social agencies.[44] Thereafter, the rise of a new wave of feminism and a critique of the inadequacy of prevailing legal and policing indifference to the issue of domestic violence has brought legal remedies back on stage in a significant way.

The critiques of this new wave of feminism have signified more general changes in the operation of the prosecution process and available remedies since the nineteenth century. As discussed earlier, the main resort of women who sought to restrain or punish their husbands for violence or other domestic offences (eg desertion) in the nineteenth century was a civil action: in this way the law signified this domain as 'the private' and gave only limited mandate to police to become involved. Of course, in the enforcement of court orders the police role might be crucial, but the difficulty of tracking maintenance order breaches limited police enthusiasm for this work anyway, regardless of their perceptions of its importance.

Late twentieth century innovation has demanded of police a more constructive and proactive role in the policing of domestic violence. Principally this has been through the recent legal option of a domestic restraint order. While this may be sought by women themselves, the law also increasingly empowers police to take this action in cases where women have not.[45] In this way, the arena of domestic violence has become not just a matter for public law, but one in which police themselves are expected to play a significant enforcement role.

Yet the public obligation on men to account for or restrain their behaviour in the home has been constructed only slowly and hedged around with qualifications. Police themselves perceived their shortcomings in this area: surveys conducted for the Neesham inquiry into Victorian police in the 1980s suggested that domestic violence and conflict was an uppermost need in training for the police role.[46] From being a domain which police should keep out of, the family has become a focus of intensive policing concern.

In spite of this change over the last century or more in the range of government interventions possible in family life, the evidence of police resistance to the need for peace-keeping or crime-detecting actions in relation to domestic violence remains. In a review of the conditions affecting Aboriginal women's experience of violence, Audrey Bolger reported in 1991 that in spite of domestic violence legislation enabling police to take preventive action over domestic violence (by way of obtaining restraining orders against suspected violent offenders), police were still perceived by many women to be reluctant to get involved:

> The action of calming things down and then leaving was the one women complained about most. Their interpretation was that the police came and did nothing. The police argument was that unless the man was drunk or the woman was obviously injured there was little action they could take.[47]

The importance of providing a specific statutory power of intervention in the area of domestic violence has nevertheless been demonstrated by changing police practice in some jurisdictions. While police reluctance to use the restraint order option was at first evident in South Australia, Bolger reports that police were soon taking out the majority of applications for orders. In Queensland, this was evidently the case from the beginning of this legislative change.[48]

The growing role of police in the development of a public response to domestic violence is probably as good a contemporary example as any we could choose of the way in which the work of police is subject to historical change. The paradox of policing in the last two decades is captured in the expansion of police powers into a domain previously regarded as too sensitive and too private for public intervention. Such a development has occurred exactly at the moment when police functions and powers and the use of them have been subjected to extended criticism, in public life and in academic research.

The changing function of police seen in this perspective reflects the important symbolic as well as instrumental function of police in modern government. In the absence of other means of modifying or preventing harmful behaviour in the home or on the streets through self-policing, the strongest statement of government is one which passes to police the power to intervene at their discretion. Even in the age of privatisation or of community policing it remains inconceivable that these powers will not remain of central importance to the government of the population. In such a context, the stakes are that much higher for ensuring that this policing is carried out justly, given that its effectiveness is always imperfect.

CHAPTER 6

The Government of Aborigines

If any characteristic has distinguished the police in Australia from their original models in England and Ireland, it has been their continually changing role in the government of Aborigines. The police as an institution was not present at the first dispossessions in eastern Australia. But the formation of police forces from the 1830s on added to the colonial state an apparatus of great power and flexibility in completing the process. By the late 1980s, when the issue of deaths of Aborigines in police custody focussed unprecedented attention on the relations between the two, there was a long, violent and frequently changing history to trace.

It is tempting to give an account of this history as one in which the police oversee and facilitate dispossession, exert totalitarian control during the era of protection, and act as guardians of white peace and order during the modern period of Aboriginal citizenship. In fact, such an account would be more satisfactory than most attempts to capture a complex process in a neat historical lineage. Nevertheless, it is also necessary to remind ourselves that we are dealing with local and regional histories of often great contrast. Just as Aboriginal groups were quite differently situated in relation to settlement, so police, no less than other settlers, operated under different laws limiting or expanding their power over Aborigines.

Thus a conventional distinction might be to contrast New South Wales, Victoria and Tasmania, where dispossession was accomplished to a greater extent earlier, with the other States and the Northern Territory, where protection systems dominated policy and practice during the first half of the twentieth century. But such distinctions are in danger of ignoring the continued role of police in the colonisation of the older and long-settled States. Thus, for example, the vigour of removals policy in New South Wales after 1909 legislation left a history of conflict between police and Aborigines which is no less consequential than that in the States which had protection systems.

The task here, however, is less to review the incidence of violence in these different histories than to explore the forms of government of which police were such a key instrument in the different parts of Australia. For the government of Aborigines involved police in work which was quite distinguishable from their other duties. If police work conventionally meant street policing or detection of crime, the policing of Aborigines meant in addition to this, interventions in family life, surveillance of itinerant Aborigines, management of Aboriginal money, inspection of work arrangements, handing out of blankets and rations, and other duties.

None of these duties in itself was unique to the policing of Aborigines, at least as a mechanism of policing. But their combination in the one office directed towards the one population was what defined the particular nature of police-Aboriginal relations over many decades. The contemporary task for policing is to reverse the intensity of this relation. But achieving this objective is elusive, given the history of police attitudes and the functions that police have been expected to perform.

TAKING THE LAND

If the history of Aborigines in Australia is the history of dispossession, then the history of their policing defines one of the means of enforcing that process. The historical feat achieved by the law in Australia of so comprehensively legitimating this process gave the police a remarkably free hand in relation to Aborigines. We can understand the particularity of the role of police in this process by contrasting with it the somewhat different history of Maoris and settlers in New Zealand.

Settlement in New Zealand entailed an institutional recognition through the Treaty of Waitangi of original Maori dominion, requiring that land be acquired rather than simply seized by occupation. Moreover, the terms of settlement also implied to some degree a conjoint responsibility for keeping the peace and enforcing laws. Hence, the management of law and order at the outset of settlement in New Zealand was characterised by what appears from an Australian perspective to be a quite remarkable recognition of the legitimate role of Maori peace-keeping procedures. The erosion of this achievement is part of the subsequent history of colonisation, but the difference with Australia is striking.[1]

Equally notable is the presence in early New Zealand policing of the Maori constable. Urban police forces in the colony frequently included Maori members, whose role extended to the management of pakeha (settler) order where necessary. Again, such a situation was eroded over time by settler intolerance, but its very appearance signifies an important difference from the Australian colonies. The notion that Aboriginal people might serve in the office of constable in Australia, with an authority over white settlers, was scarcely contemplated. However, it was not entirely beyond the bounds of possibility — in the Camden area west of Sydney in the 1820s, the settler elite appointed a local Aboriginal named Bundal a constable. Attempts by James Macarthur to appoint him on a full wage were not successful, in spite of the help given by Bundal in helping police capture 'thieves and runaway convicts'.[2] In 1837 it was contemplated that Aboriginal police in Victoria have some degree of interaction with the settlers, for it was intended that Aboriginal recruits to the native police 'must be made to discriminate between the different classes of white people, showing respect to the upper and well conducted, and prevented from associating with those who may instruct them in vicious and disorderly habits'.[3]

Aboriginal social order was for the most part opaque to colonial settlers in Australia. Opportunism as well as ignorance of the forms of Aboriginal relation to the land generated the conditions for dispossession. For most decision-makers, Aboriginal law and custom could not conceivably be recognised as prevailing in the colonies,[4] and the subordination of Aborigines in the colonial world view was so complete as to preclude a significant role for them in the formal structures governing the British colonies. Indigenous constables in urban areas, possible for a time in New Zealand, were far from the realms of imagination in Australian settlement.

Nevertheless, a significant role for Aborigines was constructed in aid of the process of securing the land for European settlement. This was in the form of the native police, a controversial innovation in colonial policing. Historians drawing on the evidence of urban colonial political hostility to the symbols of authority have emphasised the bloody role of the native police in the dispossession. By contrast, some have more recently drawn attention to the inevitable ambiguities of their role and urged attention to the enlistment of troopers in terms of the mentality and social context of the Aborigines themselves. In the latter view, enlistment in the native police offered to Aborigines in Victoria material and social benefits which were intelligible in their own societies.[5]

Our concern here, however, is primarily with the role that the native police were expected to play in governing the Aborigines. That role was inevitably linked with the more general tasks of policing a colonial society, some of which also affected the Aboriginal populations.

The fluidity of the conception of 'police' in the 1830s is evident in the correspondence on the formation of the first native police in Victoria. Whatever the later uses of the native police, the earliest discussions of it stress its potential as part of the civilising process. To the more familiar tasks of incorporating colonised people into the governmental structures ruling them was added the objective of using the servitude of the native police constable as a means of changing mentality and behaviour. Indeed, in the process of establishing the native police corps, an entire 'Native Village' was to be established, with huts for the police and their families, and land reserved for a considerable distance around to keep the squatters away. Developing this theme, the prominent missionary, L. E. Threlkeld, in fact suggested to the New South Wales governor that the name of this body be changed from 'Police Corps' to 'Melioration Institution', linking its establishment to the need to satisfy the 'just claims of the Aborigines'.[6] Others, like the prison reformer Alexander Maconochie, urged the necessity of some system 'to protect the natives from insult and injury, or to keep these lawless whites in due order and subjection'.[7]

Conceived in these terms, the native police were something both more and less than the settler police at the time. Perhaps inevitably the multitude of objectives which this conception of police involved limited its potential achievement. This confusion of policy and administration, ending at one point in another missionary taking charge of the native police corps, led within little more than a year to its collapse.[8]

In contrast to the relatively benign function which it has recently been argued was the function of the native police in Victoria, the function of the same-named body in northern Australia was much more military in character. Operating on the principle of 'dispersal', the native police in New South Wales and later Queensland governed through 'force of arms' with a view to pacifying or eliminating black opposition to settlement. The rough justice of the bush did not always bow to the requirements of due process or other tenets of the common law in its pacification of the frontier. The standards of justice were frankly documented by a former officer of the native police in an interview with commissioner Cahill of Queensland in 1910. Ex-sub-inspector Walter Cheeke recalled risking his life to save a settler family at Windorah in western Queensland in the late 1870s. Having been tipped off that 'Long-Toed Paddy and his gang of wild blacks' were about to attack a settler family, Cheeke set out with a number of native troopers:

> I got on to the track of the blacks immediately. Force of arms had to be used. Three of the blacks were shot, two were flogged, and although I never saw two dead bodies, I believe one sank in deep water. I followed Long-Toed Paddy's tracks for 700

miles. He was in the flooded country. I ran him out at Oontoo Water Hole. He crossed into South Australia near where Birdsville is now. I ran his tracks to Ferrar's Creek when I sent word to the South Diamantina Police that Paddy was in the District, and I returned to my Barracks after being absent 5 months. Long-Toed Paddy was a notorious scoundrel. A Reward of £50 was offered by the Squatters for his capture. He killed a man on the Diamantina and was himself afterwards shot. He came to life again and was shot again by Sub-Inspector Eglinton, and burned to make sure that he would not come to life again. That was the last I heard of him.[9]

As this account suggests, the degree of control over the native police in Queensland was limited in the decades following separation from New South Wales. These were police serving an unashamedly repressive function, securing possession of the country for the settlers moving in to new land. When the South Australian government ordered the raising of a force of native police in the Northern Territory in the 1880s, it was against the wishes of the chief policeman and the Resident in the Territory, both of whom considered the Queensland experience one to be avoided. The guidelines (predictably ignored) drawn up for the Territory force pointedly repudiated a policy of 'dispersing the Natives' which 'simply means shooting them'.[10] The far-flung nature of settlement in central Australia, with no superior court in Alice Springs, meant nevertheless a sustained degree of violence in the 'pacification' of the Aborigines in that region.[11]

In Western Australia in the late nineteenth century, the regular and native police were equally an instrument of squatters' possession of the new cattle country in the Kimberley. There a major cause of conflict was the incidence of cattle killing by Aborigines. By the end of the century the colony already had a large number of black prisoners, with gaols at Roebourne and Derby full of them.[12]

Behind the frontier, in settler Australia, Aborigines were already occupying a dual role, as worker and as offender, in their interactions with white society. In many parts of Australia, Aboriginal people became a crucial source of labour supply in the late nineteenth and early twentieth century. This role brought them into contact with police in the mundane ways shared with other labouring people, sometimes in the context of the application of master and servant legislation, more frequently through public order offences.[13]

In a historic shift at the end of the nineteenth century, the establishment of a new mode of government of Aborigines, the system of protection, marked the end of the native police. Their rationale had been diminishing in many parts of the country. But the means of their success, brute force without the hindrance of administrative or legal accountability, had also met its limit in the rainforests of North Queensland. There the Aborigines continued to hinder the activities of timber-getters and agriculturists into the 1880s. Senior police in Queensland faced the option of increasing the use of force or attempting conciliation through bringing the blacks into a relation of dependency through providing basic resources like food and blankets. In choosing the latter policy, they initiated a process which resulted eventually in the enactment of protection legislation in Queensland in 1897. It was to be the model for similar acts in Western Australia in 1905 and in the Commonwealth-administered Northern Territory after 1911.[14]

The colonial nature of 'native policing' continued in the aftermath of the disbandment of the native police per se. In Queensland, numbers of Aboriginal troopers were kept on as trackers, with low pay and other entitlements such as maintenance of their 'gins'. The informality of some arrangements between police and Aboriginal employees was disclosed in Western Australia in 1905 when the Queensland chief protector of Aborigines, Dr W. E. Roth, was commissioned to inquire into 'the condition of the Natives' in that State. Under the head 'Native Police System', Roth reported that strictly speaking there were no native police, but rather trackers employed by the police. However, in spite of obligations to engage these trackers under contracts Roth had heard of only one case of such an agreement in the north and north-west. In spite of this, it appeared that trackers were left in charge of black prisoners and assisted in their arrest, a practice which had led to at least two cases of fatal shooting of prisoners by trackers.

The trackers were paid nothing for their services, according to Roth's informants. Money was paid to their supervising officers who were expected to sustain and clothe them. But the commissioner suspected that officers were profiting from the money by rationing on a low scale, or leaving the tracker to find his own food with a shot-gun. Not surprisingly, in view of these findings Roth recommended that the employment of trackers be put on a strict contractual basis, that they not be supplied with firearms, and that their duties be restricted to tracking and 'horse-boys' rather than being used for any police enforcement purposes.[15]

The passing of the native police did not go unnoticed. Queensland police commissioner Parry-Okeden vigorously defended the institution, though not its excesses, as late as 1897, following severe criticism of it by a special commissioner of inquiry, Archibald Meston, in 1896. Parry-Okeden's defence articulated the ambivalent objectives of policing policy. On the one hand the justification of the native police was the:

well-known fact that the only control possible to be obtained at the outset and maintained over wild or uncivilised blacks is by the exercise and exhibition of superior force by people whom they recognise as capable of competing with them in their own tactics ...

The only whites capable of doing so were bushmen. But if the native police, with its white officers experienced in bushcraft, were to be disbanded then from where were such men to come?

To find even a few such men it would be necessary to recruit from the stations in the far North — that is, from a place and from a class where and among whom at the present time are to be found masquerading under white and yellow skins, some of the blackest scoundrels alive — wretches who have wrought deeds of appalling wickedness and cruelty, and who think it equal good fun to shoot a nigger at sight or to ravish a gin. So long as such villains escape hanging and live in our country, the blacks must be — and shall be, if I have a free hand and my native police — protected.[16]

Protection of the victims of settler exploitation and violence was a noble objective. But 'protection' as a system of government, one in which police were to play a crucial role, carried with it the seeds of further destruction of the means of Aboriginal livelihood and self-respect.

PROTECTORS

The genesis and administration of the system of protection was crucial to the development of the modern-day identity and historical memory of Aborigines. Police were the *sine qua non* of this system, acting as agents of a system of state control which was founded on the principle that Aboriginal individuals and society were not the equals of white Australians but instead required specialised forms of government administration. The word protection summarises an era, from the mid-nineteenth century for one hundred years on, but in fact covering a variety of regimes.

The adjacent States of New South Wales and Queensland epitomise the different styles of intervention. In the former, the 1909 *Aborigines Act* legitimised a system of State controls and powers which were aimed primarily at breaking up centres of Aboriginal population. Additional powers obtained by the Aborigines Protection Board in 1915 enabled welfarist intervention by police into Aboriginal families, leading to large scale removals of Aboriginal children from their parents into white-controlled institutions or the care of white families. Not all Aborigines were subjected to the formal control of the Act, but living outside it was perilous and uncertain, with police and local council incursions into the settlements.[17]

In Queensland on the other hand, the 1897 *Protection Act*, model for later forms of administration in northern, central and western Australia, provided even more extensive controls over Aboriginal life, while aiming not at 'dispersal' of the Aboriginal population but rather at concentrating it. On the premise that there were socially significant distinctions between full-blood and mixed-blood Aborigines, the Act oversaw the removal of the former onto protected reserves, while providing for police scrutiny and control of the working conditions and wages of those in employment. By the operation of a system of exemptions from the provisions of the Act, the State in principle required of police a degree of surveillance of all Aboriginal people which created a lasting legacy of suspicion and hostility on both sides.[18]

Police-Aboriginal relations, however, were not defined solely by the formalities of the statutes which applied to Aborigines. For outside those who were specifically the target of this legislation, Aborigines were among the classes of the population most vulnerable to policing control. This was to become even more the case in the aftermath of the transition to citizenship from the late 1960s. But even before that, police were inclined to attend to Aborigines as part of their requirement to surveil and govern the lower classes. If Aborigines were in employment, their occupations were most likely to be labouring or domestic work. Their living conditions in towns or out of them were such as to make them objects of police surveillance in ways which they shared with many poor whites.[19]

Protection was in fact a criminalising system. Its effects, that is, were not limited to the powers of surveillance and control which the parliaments had delivered to police over Aborigines. Rather it made criminals out of people in ways that would not have been tolerated had they applied to white society. That is the conventional view at least. It needs to be modified to a certain degree by the fact that there *were* sections of the white population which were targeted in somewhat similar ways. Contagious diseases Acts had made criminals out of prostitutes whose work was tolerated in various legal and illegal ways. Vagrancy legislation from the 1820s in England and Australia delivered very substantial powers to police over some members of the poor and working classes. Child welfare legislation in its paternalism and interventionism is a symptom of the changing form of government of the population of which Aboriginal protection was the most highly toned Australian variant.

What distinguished Aboriginal status in policing terms was the potential control over all whom the protector (and hence police) deemed to be Aboriginal. This capacity is well illustrated in incidents in Northam, Western Australia, during the 1930s depression. Against a background of some decades of rural white hostility to the presence of Aboriginal town camps, the Northam council in 1932 sought the removal of Aborigines living in the district following a medical report on the occurrence of scabies. At the instance of political leaders, including the local member and Premier, Sir James Mitchell, the minister ordered the removal of all Aborigines in the district to the Moore River native settlement. Not only were all town camp members rounded up by police, but warrants for removal were also taken out against 90 Aborigines in the surrounding district, in spite of many of them being in local employment. A policing duty which earned the police great praise from the chief protector was incomprehensible in white Australia.[20]

Invasive as the system was, the extent of police contact arising out of minor charges in the petty sessions courts appears limited during the years of protection, as compared with more recent decades. Certainly the reorganised administration of Aborigines in places like Queensland and Western Australia may have initially diminished the volume of prosecutions for minor offences. In 1914–15, police had prosecuted 322 Aboriginal males and 66 females in Magistrate Courts in Western Australia; a decade later the numbers were down to 188 males and 12 females. Cattle killing remained a significant cause of police intervention, but public order offences such as drunkenness were far less noticed though still contributing a good proportion to the numbers of Aboriginal people incarcerated. With the decline of protection and a consequent greater presence of Aborigines in towns in the 1950s, the numbers of police prosecutions began to increase rapidly. So too did more intensive development of remoter regions of north Australia result in the same phenomenon.[21]

Notably, in view of the generation of a high probability of Aboriginal experience of police or prison custody, police power was exercised disproportionately as a power of arrest rather than summons. When legal researcher Elizabeth Eggleston observed this in practice in the mid-1960s, she argued that the greater likelihood of Aborigines being arrested on a police charge rather than summonsed was to be explained in terms of the nature of charges which they faced, since traffic Act offences, which were more common in the white community, were usually brought by summons, whereas public order offences were usually preferred by arrest. Her data did not enable cross-tabulation of arrest and Aboriginality by charge or by sex, however, disguising the extent to which, even within similar categories of offences, Aborigines were more likely to be arrested than summonsed.[22] In the mid-1950s, for example, while Aboriginal and white experience of arrest on a charge of drunkenness was similar, there were marked differences for another important public order charge—that of disorderly conduct.

Table 7 Arrest and summons, disorderly conduct charge, WA, 1954–5

	arrest (%)	summons (%)	total
male			
Aboriginal	134 (97)	4 (3)	138 (100)
Non-Aboriginal	631 (80.3)	155 (19.7)	786 (100)
female			
Aboriginal	61 (98.4)	1 (1.6)	62 (100)
Non-Aboriginal	32 (74.4)	11 (25.6)	43 (100)

Source: Annual Report of the Commissioner of Police, 1955, Western Australia *PP*, 1955.

The disparity in police treatment which these figures suggest has become the object of more sustained investigation in recent years in attempts to explain the high incarceration rates of Aboriginal people. The explanations pay attention to factors of the operation of the criminal justice process, to the social condition of Aboriginal people, including their greater exposure to police attention and to the cultural determination of police behaviour towards Aborigines, including racism. The evidence of disparate treatment from a period predating the rapid escalation of incarceration in the 1960s and later suggests that all of these factors have a long history.[23]

Although incarceration of Aborigines for minor offences was not yet at the levels of the 1970s and after, policing in the protection era was already making its contribution. While sustained statistical examination of the historical patterns of local policing against Aborigines is yet to be carried out in Australia,[24] the use of special powers of police against Aboriginal drinking was already evident. Haebich suggests that incarceration of Aborigines from southern Western Australia after the 1905 *Protection Act* was substantially incurred for alcohol offences. The web of controls drew in ever more Aborigines in the aftermath of protection in that State, as changes to the law in 1911 included even Aborigines living in 'European' fashion in the prohibition of alcohol. Exemption from the Act was possible, but was in itself dependent on police inquiry and recommendation and might be revoked on police opinion.[25]

The other side of protection was the putative surveillance of whites, preventing them engaging Aborigines without work contracts, having sexual contact with the women, or supplying liquor to them. While there is evidence of some police actions consistent with the intention of these laws, it is meagre. Where police did act, they might be frustrated by legal, judicial or magisterial indifference or partiality. Both crown law advice and Magistrate's Court judgments effectively mandated occasional white male access to Aboriginal women in Western Australia.[26] Settler magistrates might find it difficult to convict compatriots against whom police had proceeded for sexual or supply of liquor offences. The powers of protection which were intended to provide some measure of remunerative justice to Aboriginal employees were rarely exercised in their favour. Perhaps the powers of wardship never were: in the most comprehensive review of Australian legal cases affecting Aboriginal interests, John Mc Corquodale was unable to discover a single instance in which an Aboriginal administrator ever prosecuted 'a tortious action as legal guardian for and on behalf of his wards.'[27]

In ways which are evident in other histories of policing, the contribution of policing to inequality is also evident in the very process of prosecution and intervention under the protection Acts. Police control of the money of Aborigines through the trust accounts established under the Queensland Act rendered them dependents. The full story of the control of Aboriginal trusts has not yet been told, but historical evidence suggests abuse of a systemic as well as individual kind. In Queensland in the 1920s, the police had to be stopped from using money from the trust accounts as reimbursement of expenses incurred in tracking absconders from settlements.[28] In Western Australia, their initial control of rations after the 1905 Act had to be curtailed following suspicion that some police were profit-taking: reorganisation of the system produced such substantial economies that suspicions were confirmed.[29] In an evident continuation of this phenomenon, police in Western Australia were still in the 1990s receiving a 'meal allowance' for each prisoner in custody: the Royal Commission into Aboriginal Deaths in Custody concluded that the system was open to abuse and might well have contributed to a high number of arrests of Aborigines in that State.[30]

At the heart of the government of Aborigines through police protectors was the breadth of responsibility and authority in the police role. In a period in which the capacity of state intervention in the government of populations increased so enormously, the personnel of the state had not yet been sufficiently specialised to address the changed conditions: police were the agents for all conceivable purposes in the government of Aborigines. The two-fold character of the role was well recognised by royal commissioner Moseley in Western Australia in 1935 in criticising the inequities in the trial of Aboriginal offenders. The prosecution relied many times on the 'admission' of accused Aboriginal offenders (for example in the frequent cattle killing cases), an admission obtained by a police officer who was not only the arresting officer responsible for bringing the case to court, but also in remote areas likely to be a local protector as well. Inevitably, Moseley considered, the constable faced a conflict of duty:

> It must necessarily occur that the constable will be confronted with two conflicting sets of instructions, one from his superior police officer, and the other from the Divisional Protector.[31]

From the point of view of Aboriginal experience this may not have made a substantial difference — the statutory definition of their position rendered them unequal whatever the agency of control. But separation of the role of protector and prosecutor might well have established at least the possibility of an agent responsible for acting truly in the interests of Aborigines, as had been done for example for Melanesian migrant labourers in Queensland in the 1880s.[32]

From the point of view of police, the mix of welfare and more regular policing roles was not one for which they were well prepared or to which they adapted successfully. The ambiguities of the policing role were heightened by the delegation to them of certain statutory powers which in fact made them all-powerful over a significant portion of the Aboriginal population. Being in effect administrators rather than law officers their actions were only rarely subject to accountability by independent agencies: few of their actions over Aborigines came before the courts and there was of necessity only limited scrutiny of their practices by the chief protectors.

The potential of legal scrutiny was nevertheless enough to make them nervous. In 1932, Queensland police were instructed not to make notes on the orders issued for removal of Aborigines, as these orders might be required for production in court.[33] When their practices did become subject to scrutiny, as after police participation in punitive expeditions or other maltreatment, the consequences by the 1920s were much negative publicity but insufficient attention to measures of redress. Hence, even a report critical of police practice in many respects, like that of Moseley, could still find reason to justify chaining of detained Aborigines in 1935.[34] Hence too the response was in the 1930s for policy to move towards assimilation rather than address the consequences of difference in cultural and social status in ways which would not reproduce detrimental police behaviour.

KEEPING THE PEACE OR AGGRAVATING DISORDER?

If anything, the protracted demise of the protection system in its various forms aggravated relations between Aborigines and police. The outcomes of policing became more visible, but in the longer term also more vulnerable to challenge. The challenge, however, was very long in coming and conflict-ridden in the very process of being addressed. As in preceding cases of public exposure of police behaviour in relation to the policed, police practices towards Aborigines became controversial not through the mundane inequalities of their everyday practice, but in their violent and tragic outcomes.

The acceleration of Aboriginal detentions after the 1950s provoked political controversy on a national and international scale by the 1980s. The intense focus on Aboriginal incarceration which resulted from the Royal Commission into Aboriginal Deaths in Custody highlighted the close links between the criminal justice experience of Aborigines and their historical experience of Australian society since settlement two centuries before. Reporting on the death in custody of one Aborigine in New South Wales, the commissioner identified this relation:

> there was a rare fiercely violent struggle with police, after which he said 'This country belongs to us blacks. You whites stole it off us', and went on to talk about the rights of Aborigines.[35]

Subject to the detailed scrutiny of social science, the incidence of Aboriginal deaths in custody in the mid-1980s was shown later to be no greater than that for others detained in police cells or prison. But the inquiries of the commission, appointed in 1987 and reporting in 1991, identified what Aborigines already knew — that police interventions in their lives were far in excess of those of other Australians. Aboriginal people, as opposed to Aboriginal prisoners, were far more likely to die in custody because they were far more likely to be in police custody anyway. In the course of its inquiries, the commission conducted a national survey of detentions in custody in August 1988. The survey confirmed the extent of the inequalities in policing in Australia. The resistance of long-established patterns of policing to change, even in the face of substantial criticism and review of practices, was evident in the failure over the following four years of attempts to reduce the disproportionate incarceration of Aborigines.

As so often, however, national figures distort local particularities. The national aggregation of results from the survey disguise substantial regional variations. These were not only jurisdictional in significance, though Western Australia and South Australia were notably excessive in their policing rates. The differences were also regional within jurisdictions. In Queensland, which has substantial Aboriginal populations in both urban and rural regions, the survey indicated much higher arrest incidence and length of police detention in

Table 8 National Police Custody Surveys, 1988 and 1992

	1988	*1992*
State	*% Aboriginal*	*% Aboriginal*
New South Wales	14.3	16.2
Victoria	4.1	3.8
Queensland	28.8	23.5
Western Australia	54.2	57.3
South Australia	21.8	19.5
Tasmania	7.5	5.4
Northern Territory	76.3	80.0
Australia	28.6	28.8

Source: *Deaths in Custody Australia*, No. 2, 1993, Australian Institute of Criminology, Canberra.

Cairns than in metropolitan Brisbane. Brisbane is the location of over 10% of the State's Aboriginal population. Cairns (in fact the far north including the Cape York peninsula) contained about 25% and included the majority of the State's former Aboriginal reserves, which became trust lands after 1984 legislation.[36]

In New South Wales, the incidence of detention of Aborigines by police appeared less excessive than in the northern and western States. But country areas of New South Wales, especially towns with substantial Aboriginal populations, were shown to have extremely high rates of detention. This had already been well established in earlier studies by government research agencies which had described and analysed the intensity of policing in the so-called 'Aboriginal towns' of western New South Wales.[37]

By the late 1980s, the story of police relations with Aborigines was almost uniformly gloomy. Excessive detention rates were dominated by occasions of minor offending, drunkenness above all. Even in those States which had abolished it as an offence, drunkenness continued to be the occasion for numerous police contacts with Aborigines, often leading to time in a police cell (in 1992, 33% of police detentions of Aborigines in Australia continued to result from non-offending intoxication). Police, however, were also significantly involved in Aboriginal detentions for a range of violent inter-personal offences. Symptomatic of the state of affairs in some Aboriginal communities was the criticism by Aboriginal women that police were insufficiently attentive to protecting women and children from the violence of drunken Aboriginal men and youths.[38]

As our previous discussion has suggested, the nature of police interactions with Aborigines had not always been so well documented. Both in the nineteenth-century period of dispossession and frontier policing and in the twentieth century-period of protection there had been very significant levels of police intervention in Aboriginal lives without coming to statistical or other publicly-recorded notice. The militaristic mandate of much nineteenth-century policing of Aborigines had avoided legal accountability. Many forms of policing during the protection era had been within the administrative sphere, again avoiding public scrutiny through the courts.

Central to the genesis of the intense policing of Aborigines during the post-protection decades was their changing status in Australian society. Citizenship recognition in the wake of the constitution referendum in 1967 was the centre-point of this transition in formal legal and political terms. Specific disabilities remained, especially in Queensland until repeal of the last vestiges of protection in 1984.[39]

But the complex of changes was more varied than entailed in the constitution amendment. Changing employment relations saw on the one hand affirmation of Aboriginal rights to equal pay while at the same time opportunities for employment were reduced through increasing mechanisation and other transformations of the rural industries which had been nurtured in many areas on cheap Aboriginal labour.[40]

For Aborigines in some of those areas, such as western and northern New South Wales, the changes were accompanied by increased policing. During the era of protection, Aborigines in many areas of New South Wales had been continually moved on by police responding to the desire of local municipal government to exclude Aboriginal enclaves on the outskirts of towns.[41] The slow erosion of these powers meant an increasing permanent presence in some towns of Aboriginal people who had previously been excluded. Police attention to Aborigines seemed by the 1980s to be especially severe in those towns with substantial Aboriginal populations, sometimes prompted by law and order campaigns which were organised by prominent white citizens and in some instances sustained by police involvement and support.[42]

Quite different pressures were experienced by Aborigines and police in other contexts during this period of rapid change. An influx of white settlers combined with the mobility of Aboriginal populations in more remote districts in Western Australia lay at the origin of conflict between police and Aborigines in notorious incidents at Skull Creek in January 1975. In the early 1960s, Laverton, a couple of hundred miles to the east of Kalgoorlie, had been a tiny centre of population of just 40 whites with a local Aboriginal population of some 400. These ratios were reversed over the following decade as mining development in the area led to a major influx of white population which was some 1,200 by 1973. The Aboriginal numbers had remained static.

In December 1974 Aborigines from surrounding country gathered at Laverton for ceremonial meetings connected with a rain-making ritual. Regular congregation of Aborigines around the hotel at Laverton during December and early January led to a number of incidents involving arrest. News of a further influx of Aborigines from Warburton, over 300 miles east, in early January led police to revise their tactics. Deciding to block the entry of these people to Laverton the police organised a convoy with 22 officers. Three vehicles, including a truck, carrying about 40 men, 15 women and 21 children were stopped. There were clashes between the police and some of the men who got out of the truck:

> A few people, perhaps only two, were involved in this first violence, but immediately thereafter the police officers set about arresting all able-bodied men on the truck and the old men, women and children were told to go away.

A royal commission appointed some months later to review the incident and its background concluded that this mass arrest:

> was done pursuant to a direction or understanding made either before the police arrived at the truck or immediately after the first violence occurred and the result was that possibly all and certainly the great majority of the twenty-five men then arrested were arrested without cause.[43]

Not surprisingly these unjustified arrests provoked further physical confrontation which police claimed was inspired by a desire to attack them. The royal commissioners did not agree, observing that:

> [w]e accept ... that there was a good deal of shouting by the Aborigines. We are not satisfied they were encouraging attacks on the police. On the contrary, it is likely that they were protesting at the behaviour of the police.

Compounding the aggravation of an already substantial breach of law in making unjustified arrests, the police then proceeded to concoct stories which would justify the circumstances of their intervention. The commission concluded for example that:

> a common story was worked out as to the circumstances in which the police would say the offences were committed. As a result summaries of fact were prepared, the great majority of which alleged or implied that when the police arrived Aborigines were fighting among themselves or commenced to do so shortly thereafter, which was admittedly false but which if true would have justified police intervention.[44]

In the course of inquiry, the commission was unable to say why a further extraordinary development occurred in which one set of police briefs, alleging that the Aborigines had been first observed fighting among themselves, was replaced later by a second set, prepared for the commissioner of police, in which the 'first violence seen was of Aborigines fighting police'.[45]

Remarkably, such evidence of police perversion of the course of justice did not lead the commission to recommend charges against the police involved. Instead, various recommendations were made concerning the 'underlying causes' of these sorts of incidents. The Laverton incidents indicated a pattern of police response which amplified and provoked violence rather than prevented it. It was not the last of incidents in which large numbers of police have been directed to respond to a perceived threat of disorder and ended up aggravating the situation. It was understandable only against a background in which police, like most of the white community from which they came, perceived Aborigines as a source of disorder requiring firm treatment and occasional retaliation. Such a perception justified some bending of the requirements of the law to provide a reason for arrest and charge.

It was a failure of police administration and of government policy which allowed these events to continue in many parts of Australia through the following decade. Hence it was that commissioner Muirhead, in his 1988 interim report of the Royal Commission into Aboriginal Deaths in Custody, was brought to recommend careful screening of recruits to ensure that people with racist views did not become police or prison officers.[46] Yet the events at Laverton, like others before and after them, suggested that the need for reform went beyond personnel to the policy and operations of police in their interactions with Aboriginal communities.[47] Equally, it was necessary to pay attention to the state of public order and drunkenness legislation, offences against which constituted a very high proportion of causes of arrest by police of Aboriginal people. Some States had already proceeded to decriminalisation of public drunkenness, though not always with success in relation to Aboriginal people.

Citizenship changes which removed restrictions on Aboriginal access to the range of commodities enjoyed by many other Australians included the crucial area of alcohol. While controls on Aboriginal access to alcohol had been indicative of second-class status, the widespread abuse of alcohol which became endemic in parts of the Aboriginal population led to frequent contact with the police. It did so in at least two important ways.

First, the broad definition of public order offences, including drunkenness, disorderly behaviour, obscene language and vagrancy (no visible means of support) had historically given police wide-ranging discretion to police public spaces in ways which were oriented primarily to the defence of white sensibilities. The removal of broad restraints on the control of Aboriginal residence and movement exposed Aborigines to the attention of police as they more permanently occupied public spaces in rural towns and inner cities. The outcome was an accelerated rate of detention for minor offences and, in some States, of imprisonment for these.[48]

Second, alcohol abuse, widespread in demoralised communities, led to increasing levels of inter-personal violence. A consequence was increasing police interventions in response to serious offending.[49] For the course of police–Aboriginal relations, this development was crucial. Already entrenched police attitudes to the intractability of Aboriginal behaviour were confirmed. The fact that many police in Aboriginal communities in rural Australia were very young and transient, doing their country posting before a more desirable city or coastal assignment, limited the capacity of police to develop responses which were less aggravating to an already inflamed situation.[50]

Given the history of Aboriginal–police relations outlined earlier, it is not surprising that police policies as well as practices were found to be so deficient in managing their relations with Aborigines in the post-protection period. There were exceptions to this rule, as halting moves were made towards a 'community policing' policy in some Aboriginal communities in the 1980s. But on the whole, police departments, conservative in management and policy formation, had done little to address the problem of Aboriginal difference, except in ways which were detrimental.

Some recognition of a need to deal differently with Aboriginal detainees was embodied in police rules dealing with arrest and interrogation.[51] Otherwise there was an evident indifference to the social impact that intensive policing was having. Education and training of police in the culture and history of Aboriginal people was almost negligible. The incidence of harmful conduct and racist abuse of Aboriginal people was not limited to police. But the official condonation of such attitudes and behaviour through failures of discipline or administrative reform contributed to its perpetuation.

The possibility of police reform in relations with Aborigines was one of the most pressing needs identified by the royal commission. In some parts of Australia there had been significant if piecemeal changes in police practices. Some individual police with particular responsibility for policing Aboriginal communities were noted for their initiatives in establishing liaison with those communities. Other changes were based in the demands of Aboriginal communities themselves. In the Northern Territory, the responsibility of communities for policing their own areas underlay the initiative of Aboriginal women at Tennant Creek in organising night-time patrols.[52]

Yet, even during and after the hearings and reports of the royal commission, police attitudes and practices in other places proved intractable. In New South Wales, the shooting of David Gundy, the police raid on Redfern, and the continuing demands by western New South Wales local government for new regulatory powers against Aboriginal drinking, all reflected the deeply rooted sources of resistance to reform of policing and legal regulation affecting Aboriginal people.[53] As the phenomenon of local government demand for new police powers for removal of Aborigines has demonstrated in at least three States (New South Wales, Queensland, Victoria),[54] police are operating in a context which is highly politicised, providing support for resistance to changes in police practices which would reduce the kinds and incidence of police intervention in the lives of Aborigines.

The outlook for successful implementation of the positive reforms recommended by the royal commission remains gloomy. Indeed, as we have seen, such is the slow pace of change in spite of sustained scrutiny of the policing of Aborigines that by 1992 the proportion of Aborigines in police custody had in fact increased over the previous four years. The continuing high international visibility of Australia's treatment of its indigenous peoples, however, is likely to sustain the political demand for reform, as agreed by the Federal and State governments in the wake of the royal commission.[55]

The history of policing of Aborigines in Australia has epitomised the contradictory position of police in the structure of government. The putative neutrality of police in the task of governing has always been qualified by the socially specific focus of their work. In the case of Aborigines, the interaction of legal regulation directed at the control of the poor, the homeless and the disruptive, with the socially marginalised status of indigenous people in Australia worked to the detriment of good policing. Where policing might have worked more consciously towards peace-keeping, in fact police interventions were often the stimulus to confrontation.

Police were not neutral agents in these situations but agents of government presiding over dispossession and attempting to reconstruct or eliminate by assimilation the whole Aboriginal population. This was the most ambitious governing project in which police in Australia were involved—and the most fatal to its targets. The opportunity of constructing new relations between police and Aborigines presents itself in the wake of the royal commission. But once again police will not be the neutral nor the sole agencies in the government of Aborigines. Reducing police interventions, and reducing the need for those which do occur, will call for new forms of government, ones which might for the first time address the possibility of self-government as a means among other things of self-policing.

Governing the Police—Hidden Histories

Often the history of policing appears characterised by nothing more than periodic crises of corruption or malpractice, followed by halting moves toward reform. Only during these crises do police practices tend to become the subject of wider public scrutiny. At those moments it has historically been the figure of corruption which has dominated the public stage in debates about policing. More infrequently (as in England after the urban riots of the early 1980s, leading to the inquiry by Lord Scarman, and in Australia in the developing concern over deaths of blacks in custody which led to the establishment of the royal commission in 1987) the matter of police procedures in relation to particular sections of the population has also figured.

The value of such historical moments for understanding some of the forces organising policing in any particular jurisdiction is of course immense. But they can also beguile. A common pattern is the investigation of particular incidents or of a particular section of a police force with a view to rectifying perceived abuses. The public view of police revealed is usually unflattering, even highly damaging. But the moment passes quickly, the forces for reform become divided, disillusioned or lose power—the obstacles to sustained reform are immense, as the Fitzgerald Report warned in 1989. For a brief moment, some details of the inner workings of a police department may stand revealed. But before long that door is closed again. The organisation of policing remains visible only through official reports or the occasional legal case touching police practices.

Hence, the matters dealt with in this section of the book are largely hidden from history. Histories of policing have paid little attention to the problem of the maintenance of good policing, especially compared to the inevitable and understandable concern with the bad. That is not to say that there has been little concern with whether police or their practices and priorities were good or bad. But this has been little dealt with as a 'problem', a question to be addressed and answered. Acclamatory histories of the police presume that police in general act for the public good, critical histories presume that police act for the benefit of some class, or for their own calculated benefit. To address this question then is to touch on a difficult and unappreciated area.

Whereas we were concerned in section 2 with some of the functions and effects of police in the government of the population, we will be concerned in this section with police as themselves the object of government. Here we take a contemporary concern with an old problem, the government of the self as the centre of the modern problem of government, and extend it to the police. For the hidden histories I discuss below show us that the problem of police discipline was of primary concern to early police administrators. Moreover, the techniques (of discipline, of training) which were applied to the government of the police are of considerable complexity if we dig below their surface meanings. And although it is difficult to judge their success, it is arguable that where they were taken seriously they were effective in limiting police use of their extensive powers (their monopoly of legitimate violence above all).[1]

These techniques, however, were subject to considerable transformation over time. A further hidden history is contained in the slow erosion of commissioner authority by the achievement of police unionisation, as dealt with in chapter 2. The emergence of rights of appeal on promotion, the application to police work of principles of industrial rights, were undoubtedly *achievements*. But it cannot be disputed that, together with the other conditions of police work which help create 'police cultures', they have contributed to a very significant alteration in the lines of effective authority in twentieth-century policing.

We start then with a review of some of the forms of police training in Australia, addressing the question of why the system of 'craft or on the job' training remained prevalent for so long and why the contemporary period is marked by a move towards professionalised and external training.

Second, we explore the systems of order and discipline which developed in the police forces in Australia, with the benefit of a historical review of police staff files in Queensland. The problem of internal governance of the police is central to the maintenance of not only effective but just policing, ends which have been frequently undermined by police misconduct. It is closely related to, but certainly not identical with, the demands for public accountability in complaints procedures, in ways which will be discussed.

The remaining chapter will address what happens when police misconduct becomes public. Corruption inquiries have been one of the major sources of image creation of policing in Australia. They have also historically been one of the few avenues for sustained public inquiry into the police — until the 1980s there were few other inquiries into police management or effectiveness and even fewer which addressed problems of police behaviour, attitudes or conduct towards those with whom they come in contact. The 'scandal' approach to law reform, as it has been dubbed recently,[2] tends to be the historical record in Australia — this contrasts with England where there were important general public inquiries into police powers in the 1920s and 1960s.

Hence, the histories of government of the police which follow present little comfort to those who favour a progressive view of history. While contemporary debates about policing offer more by way of sophistication and information than was available in the public arena before the 1970s, the mechanisms for ensuring that policing is just, fair and effective remain as imperfect as they have long been. There have, however, been significant changes in the nature of these mechanisms and what follows identifies some of these and offers explanations of the transformations.

CHAPTER 7

Police Training:
Apprenticeship or Education?

Turning raw recruits into efficient, serving police officers has been a preoccupation of police administrators since the foundations of the new police. Indeed, while the critics of the new police in England feared their use as instruments of a repressive government, those who advocated a reorganised police emphasised the advantages to good government that would come from well-trained and disciplined police whose presence would help keep good order in the cities. In the colonies these arguments were reproduced as conflicting forces in colonial society sought to define the conditions of colonial life. The problem of producing efficient and disciplined police has remained ever since a controversial issue.

For most of the history of police, the mode of training has been on the job. Apprenticeship as a police officer was short. The emphasis was on experience, with subordination in a rigid hierarchy the means of producing compliant constables. Training was closely related to questions of recruitment. Standards of entry could not be high for neither remuneration nor the anticipated duties were expected to require it. Periodically a new commissioner would attempt to encourage a greater attention to quality of officers through redefining the promotion criteria. Only very recently, however, has there been a concerted move towards advanced training, extending in some jurisdictions to a long-term objective of recruiting only tertiary educated graduates.

Understanding the conditions under which police training changed requires attention to some of the wider relations of policing. Styles of training were closely related to perceptions of what capacities police should possess. Changes in these perceptions, sometimes coinciding with crises in policing, including corruption scandals or crime panics, have stimulated new directions in training as well as in organisation of the police forces themselves. We can explore some of these directions by examining in order, the militaristic persuasion in nineteenth-century policing, the relations of examination and specialised training to the career structure in early twentieth-century policing, and the ideas and forces producing the most recent emphasis on university training.

MILITARY MODELS

The creation of the colonial police necessitated decisions about dress, accommodation, work routine and private life which signified the importance of the military model in colonial policing. When the police in South Australia were first put into special uniform, the model was that of the 6th Dragoon Guards.[3] The example is significant since South Australia had a more localised police than the eastern colonies. Other military influences included of course the very personnel of the police, both in the ranks and among officers. In Victoria, the work of civilianising the police style which had been a characteristic of the police there since the 1850s was explicitly challenged from 1870, with the introduction of a recruitment scheme which required police to have served with the colony's artillery corps.[4] The importance of the military as a preparation for police work continued in the twentieth century, having a substantial impact in the inter-war period, when a large number of Australian police forces were led by experienced war-service soldiers.[5]

While many colonial police resided in one or two-man stations, sometimes of transportable make, the congregation of substantial numbers in urban areas justified their collective accommodation in a police barracks or 'depot'. The regulated routine of police beats and patrols left little time for what today we would call private life. This was a life of extraordinary rigidity by twentieth-century standards. Such was the all-encompassing reach of service in the police that in Queensland in the early twentieth century, married police were still being cautioned to observe hours of curfew when not on duty, and were forbidden to wear non-police clothing in public without permission.[6]

To produce police capable of serving in such an occupation required training and discipline of quite specific kinds. It might also suggest that recruits, at least those who survived for prolonged service, were distinctive in their personal attributes. Much work might be done on police personnel files to explore the backgrounds of recruits with a view to examining such a proposition.[7] All the same, a reading of personnel files from the nineteenth century suggests the ordinariness of police backgrounds. These were people who were looking for a job, any sort of job, but to be accepted in the police they had to meet some minimum standards of literacy and physical standards of height and health. Once accepted in the police, their fate was determined by a mix of circumstances and opportunities which saw initially a rapid turnover of police.

This was the result in part of the nature of the colonial economy, with its opportunities for reward in non-public service occupations fluctuating with the fortunes of the wool and gold markets. Economic boom-times made it difficult to hold police in a relatively low-paid occupation.[8] The high turnover and the lack of discipline were notorious and the subject of much comment and criticism. In Victoria, the government established a special prison at the Richmond police depot in 1854 to cater for the regular parade of errant constables, charged with drunkenness and other more serious offences.[9] Much administrative energy would subsequently be spent in devising disciplinary remedies to such problems.

By the 1860s and 1870s many recruits came to the colonial police with the desired background: military or police service in the British Isles or other colonies featured prominently. Thus in Queensland, New South Wales and Victoria, recruiting in the mid-1860s drew in the majority from those with police background, in Ireland especially, but also from other colonies as well as Britain.[10] For others of different background, however, police service was one of the many means of obtaining a secure footing in the new country. Accompanied by references from parish clergy, country gentlemen, or former employers, Irish migrants to Brisbane in the 1870s and 1880s looked to the police as only one of the possibilities of secure income. But few other male permanent occupations had such an insatiable thirst for new recruits: police work was one of the main forms of government employment, after railways.

An insight into the orientation of such migrants as they contemplated police service is offered in the diary of a recruit in Brisbane in the early eighties. As the boat neared port, this young Irishman, perhaps advised by a fellow passenger with colonial experience, noted down the various work possibilities in the city:

> Apply for employment at the undermentioned places. Surveyor generals office. commissioner of water works. commissioner of public works. commissioner of police. At Brisbane all these resides Make seperate applications Doant make it known at one place that you applied at another.[11]

The high proportion of Irish in the colonial police in some colonies has frequently been remarked on. Some imply that the low skill and literacy levels of the early police may explain the high proportion of Irish.[12] But a different emphasis in explanation might be offered. Irishmen who arrived in the colonies after the 1860s were usually as literate as their British counterparts.[13] Report writing was the *sine qua non* of the maintenance of police organisation and Irish migrants increasingly possessed the minimum skills needed, those provided by an elementary education available in Ireland from the 1830s. We should not underestimate today the significance of the achievement of mass literacy in the nineteenth century and its implications for the organisation of policing, an occupation which depended on the written word.

Regardless of the specific composition of the police forces, a more general explanation of the high migrant intake of the colonial forces is the simple fact that such a high proportion of the adult population was immigrant. The pool of recruits was gradually 'Australianised' as the native born population increased. By the first decades of the twentieth century, nearly 70 per cent of the New South Wales force was colonial born and the tendency strengthened from then. After the First World War the Australian police forces were overwhelmingly Australian-born: by 1926, 90 per cent of the New South Wales force was born in the Australian States or New Zealand, while in Victoria 93 per cent of the striking Victorian police of 1923 were native born.[14] Increasingly, the immigrant country was policed by non-immigrant Australians.

Only with the genesis of concern over police relations with non-Anglo-Celtic Australians in the 1970s and 1980s was there a move towards addressing the monochrome character of Australian police, overwhelmingly male and Anglo-Celtic. Most recently, the conflict between police and Aborigines turned attention at the end of the 1980s to the very low rates of employment of Aborigines in Australian police forces.[15] Equally there was by this decade concern over the poor representation of ethnic minorities in the various police forces.[16] Over time, a variety of historical forces had produced a tendency to great uniformity in the personnel of Australian police, notwithstanding the evident atavistic survival in Queensland of some tensions between Catholic and Protestant officers, a tension also alleged to be evident in New South Wales until mid-century.[17] By mid-twentieth century, the development of particularistic entry requirements meshed with the social inequalities of Australian society to produce police forces which were overwhelmingly male, secondary-educated to mid-level only, and Anglo-Celtic in origin. Increasing the proportions of women, opening up the forces to tertiary graduates, and encouraging the recruitment of Aborigines and of those of ethnic background required positive initiatives on the part of policy-makers.

Such initiatives had to contend with a century and more of quite different presumptions in police recruitment and training. While the earliest recruitment was of the most elementary and even informal character,[18] by the late nineteenth century, entry to the police was controlled by routine scrutiny of the physical and other capacities of the intending constable.

The form of application made out by the Queensland recruits may serve as an instance. It required details of parental origin, education, previous employment, and references. An elementary test was conducted of the applicant's arithmetical competence, while the ability to write reports was assessed through a dictation test, read from one of the pages of the police manual. Moral standing was required: the application form required answers to the questions, 'have you any illicit entanglements with females' and 'are you the parent of any illegitimate child'. Such questions warned police of their need to avoid compromising obligations, likely among other things to cause scandal in small communities.[19]

Physical capacity was important, especially in a period when many police had to serve in remote areas of harsh climate. Mortality from disease and broken health was a greater risk than the fatalities resulting directly from policing duties. But more significantly what was seen as essential was the height and weight to lend physical force when needed. The presumption that policing was in essence a physical task persisted. In 1947, New South Wales police officers responsible for training recruits emphasised the priority accorded to physical capacity:

> Physique is a matter of particular care in these years of training, it being recognised that, in a policeman, a good big man is better than a good little man.[20]

Such thinking, reflecting a perception that policing was essentially a physical force task infused police departments. Reporting the formation of anti-larrikin squads in South Australia in 1959, the police commissioner advised that each was composed of four men, of average height 6 foot 3 inches and 'well proportioned'. The height and weight of recruits has continued to be a matter of controversy into the 1990s, as some police continue to insist that physique is critical to the capacity for the job.[21]

Recruits who met the elementary criteria in the colonial period might, as in Victoria before the 1870s, be placed on a list from which they would be called for service as the opportunity arose.[22] In general, the initial period of service entailed a rudimentary training at the police depot in the capital city. In Queensland, even this might be foregone for recruits enlisted in the northern reaches of the colony—there it was difficult enough to place constables at any time, let alone recruit them, and at one time the police commissioner was content to bypass normal entry standards in order to ensure that policing needs in the north were satisfied.[23]

Training in the depot had two basic objectives. In the first place, recruits had to be judged capable of conforming to the elementary requirements of the police department — observing rules, obeying superiors, showing some minimum standard of personal propriety. Evidence of drinking or laziness in the first few days of service at the depot in Brisbane quickly resulted in discharge. After a period which was never longer than three months in the nineteenth century the new constable would be posted to a large station, under the supervision of the officer-in-charge. Here the main elements of police work were imparted through an apprentice relationship to more senior police.

The second objective was to establish a practical understanding of police work, with some attention to the task of law-enforcement and regulatory administration. Colonial police manuals emphasised the knowledge of public order offences and criminal matters as the centrepiece of the policing task. Only quite late, in New South Wales evidently as late as 1898, did formal lectures in police methods and duties consolidate the routine lessons of the manual.[24] Service under existing officers provided the culture in which the elements of discretion involved in policing offences could be developed. Hence the critical response of commanding officers to those police who proved incapable of exercising appropriate judgment, arresting respectable people for minor offences, or failing to investigate matters called to police notice.[25] As commissioner Parry-Okeden in Queensland advised a Cooktown inspector in 1895, the actions of a constable in issuing 42 summons for illegal employment of Kanakas was 'unnecessary and injudicious without previous cautioning and reporting': such a constable would be promptly advised of the need for discretion in future.[26]

Public inquiries around the turn of the century found little to commend in the low-key approach to police training which the colonial forces had developed. But there were few, if any, voices for a substantial alternative. Hence, while the militaristic tones of much police organisation during the nineteenth century appears obvious to our eyes, the 1883 royal commission into the Victorian police considered that recruits lacked discipline in their training because of the absence of military-style drill. This was the lynch-pin of disciplined police and its absence in Victorian training, where the 'police authorities ... appear to have acted on the principle that a constable is born, not made', was considered one of the causes of police weakness in the face of the Kelly gang:

> The police are no doubt intended as a civil force ... but experience has demonstrated the danger of so demilitarising the police as to render them comparatively valueless for other than patrol or beat duty.[27]

Drill prepared constables for coordinated response in crowd control and was regarded as character forming. While the Victorian commissioners of inquiry in 1883 painted a picture of a force which had sought to divest itself of militaristic trappings, they saw military models as desirable for a disciplined police. Other police authorities of the colonial period and shortly after sympathised with such a direction. Hence commissioner Cahill in Queensland (1905–1916), with a background in both the Irish constabulary and then in the part-time Queensland militia, retained a strong emphasis on drill for police recruits in their training at the depot in Brisbane. And two decades after the Longmore commission, the Victorian police inquiry of 1906 stressed the importance of 'systematic drill' for probationers and reminded police that their work necessarily meant they must be regarded 'as semi military or *quasi* military bodies', subject to the strictest discipline.[28]

From such a perspective we can understand the characteristic recruiting or graduation parade photos which adorn police histories and museums. A photographic essay appended to the 1915 annual report of the Western Australian police summarised the means and aims of training characteristic of the police anywhere in Australia between the 1880s and the middle of the twentieth century. The 'finished article' in 'The making of a policeman' is a uniformed and capped constable standing in a line of similar sized men. Along the way the recruit has been instructed in the criminal code, Police Act, Aborigines Act and other legislation, and municipal regulation. For the rest, the photos depict the physical orientation of training in body building, swordsmanship, musketry and revolver instruction, wrestling and self-defence. This is supplemented by instruction in some elementary needs of policing, such as first aid, and criminal investigation, including the taking of footprints as well as the use and classification of fingerprints.[29] This was the mould in which the average twentieth century constable was to be cast for the next half century.

THE POLICE CAREER

The first half of the twentieth century witnessed only slow change from the patterns of the colonial period. Few police authorities, however, could fail to recognise the appearance in North America and England of an increasing attention to training, both at recruit stage and later.[30] This move was part of a larger concern with enhanced administration of the police inflected differently in various jurisdictions. In the United States, for example, much of the impetus to professionalise originated in a desire to distance the police from urban political machines, regarded as the source of police corruption and inefficiency.[31]

The issues in Australia were not ones of professionalisation as a means of contesting urban political control, since such direction was not part of the organisation of policing in the colonies. Rather, they seem to have been more intimately linked to questions of police leadership as a problem of management. At the beginning of colonial policing, it had been characteristic to look to both social caste and military background to provide a source of leadership. Neither was a guarantee of success in policing, but there were no practical alternatives in colonial conditions. By late in the century, however, a repetitive theme was the need to provide another criterion besides length of service to fill the ranks of senior police.

In this context, the system of examination had developed, though not always with happy results. Two decades after the 1883 Victorian royal commission had recommended promotion by examination, 'to be conducted in the same manner as those in connection with the University',[32] another inquiry concluded that efficiency had not been enhanced by the comprehensive introduction of examination. 'Cramming' and the 'imbibition of book lore' were characteristic of such a system, and the 1906 commission concluded that many meritorious officers had been passed over through their lack of time for exam preparation. 'Effective preservers of law and order can only be trained in the school of everyday practice', observed the report. Failure in the written examination should not debar a potential candidate for promotion who should have the opportunity for oral examination by the proposed board for promotions.[33]

As this consideration implies, the tasks of study and bookwork had a strictly limited currency in turn-of-the-century policing. They were linked less to ethical concerns about the formation of the police officer than to the need of the organisation to maintain its efficiency and effectiveness by promoting the meritorious. It was to become a recurrent theme in every phase of reform in twentieth-century policing. A spirit of self-improvement was encouraged by police commissioners concerned to make their own forces more efficient. Hence Cahill in Queensland, himself well-educated and recruited from outside the ranks of the force, made it known that progress through the ranks was dependent on police educating themselves and maintaining their physical competence.[34] 'There is a very mistaken idea prevalent that a policeman has nothing to do but to walk about', commented the Western Australia commissioner in 1925, ' but a great deal of general knowledge combined with common sense is required of every member of the force.'[35]

Before the 1920s, however, there was little attention to implementing the rhetorical calls for improved training.[36] Undoubtedly, the tendencies towards specialisation of police functions added some impetus to change in police training. It was just such a direction which an outsider, lieutenant-colonel Sir George Steward, brought briefly to the Victorian police force in 1920, with a special course for prospective detectives. Again it was a commissioner recruited from outside the force, C. J. Carroll, who undertook to address in Queensland what he saw as new requirements of policing in the 1930s. One indication was the establishment of Italian language classes at Roma Street, intended to improve the capacity of Queensland police in their duties with the Italian migrant population in the north. Another was the 'Police Educational Series' of lectures on various aspects of policing: these were circulated from 1935 to be read to police at their stations by the officer in charge. The effect of such initiatives must be questioned. In 1937, the necessity to read these lectures to the assembled officers was repealed.[37]

Even where there appeared innovation in police training in these years, the tendency was muted. Above all, the question of training was intimately linked to issues of police promotion. In Western Australia, for example, a system of examination for promotion was introduced in 1914, but it scarcely went beyond the elementary objectives which were sought in judging the suitability of recruits: the subjects consisted of 'Statutes', Reporting, Arithmetic and Dictation. Standards were nevertheless applied—five of the 22 applicants for the NCO positions failed the dictation test in 1915. A decade later, 'progress exams' were introduced in recognition of the well-known shortcoming of exams, 'the idea that once an examination is passed by a man, it is not necessary to study any further'.[38]

A more sustained and important development was nevertheless evident in South Australia in the 1930s. There the police department established a police training college (initially called school), with its motto 'Salus Populi est Suprema Lex' ('the people's safety is the highest law'). Its task was the moulding of career police from the earliest stages of their recruitment. The long-serving South Australian commissioner and ex-brigadier, Raymond Leane, expressed a view of policing as a vocation in his comments on training in the mid-thirties. It was best to start training at an 'impressive age' in order to produce constables who were energetic, trustworthy, with 'sound judgment, and...worthy of upholding the principles of British freedom and justice'. Leane's vision of the young constable was shifting the burden of police work from the routine tasks of patrol or the excitement of crime detection to a conception of the constable as 'protector or guide'. In such a role police needed 'not only courtesy, integrity and capacity, but a cool judgment and a sense of proportion':

> The police officer may at any time be called upon to exercise a level-headed discretion in matters of difficulty, and to act promptly and decisively with but little time

for reflection. Anything which relieves the position from temptation to crime; anything which helps to take young people away from evil surroundings and implant in them instincts of honesty and virtue is true Police work; and Junior Constables are taught that they should throw themselves heart and soul into such work as readily as the ordinary work of detecting crime.[39]

Whether the South Australian system met the high-minded objectives for police training outlined by Leane in 1935 may be questioned. The winds of change were slight and the notion of the well-educated cop implanting instincts of honesty and virtue in the otherwise potentially criminal youth of South Australia appears more rhetorical than practical. In its suggestion of such a broadly defined police vocation, however, Leane's observations marked an increasingly self-reflective occupation.

By the mid-1940s recruits to the South Australian training school came from two sources. Junior constables, of average age 18 years at recruitment, spent six months learning the fundamentals of policing. Technical requirements such as shorthand and typing, which were taught by staff from metropolitan business colleges, were supplemented by instruction in basic police duties, especially legal powers and obligations. A strong emphasis on physical instruction, for disciplinary reasons as well as physical development, was characteristic of the introductory training.

Shortages of police at the end of World War Two led to the extension of the recruiting and training programme at the College to ex-servicemen. These were enlisted as special constables while they undertook training. For both groups, the introductory period at police college was supplemented by service in a variety of different divisions of the police department.[40]

In New South Wales about the same time, the forms of training were little different though not conducted at a 'Police College'. A police cadet system was introduced by commissioner MacKay in 1933. Again it involved an initial period of formal instruction in elementary policing duties, with an emphasis on physical training, endorsed by two police commentators on the system on the grounds, as noted earlier, that 'a good big man is better than a good little man'. Legal instruction in this routine was just that — the shortage of relevant texts meant that instructors dictated legal principles and statutory powers to the young cadets who were subsequently tested on them. After their initial training, the cadets were posted in six-month blocks to divisional head stations, criminal investigation branch, traffic branch, police headquarters or the police depot. In New South Wales, the completion of the cadet period was marked by the award of an 'Annual Silver Baton' to the outstanding recruit, an award which carried with it twelve months seniority in the force.[41]

The preoccupation with physical training and the clerical tasks of shorthand and typing indicate the continuity of this system with its nineteenth century predecessors. Yet the traces of a later interest in the benefits of more advanced training are evident in the interest with which an ancillary outcome of the cadet system is commented on in 1947 — several former cadets had gone on to university studies, with a number taking out law degrees at Sydney University.[42]

Moreover, the frequency with which psychological and sociological theories and postulates are addressed in the early years of the *Australian Police Journal* shows that a number of police were pursuing their education, even if not formally, in areas other than the law. The influence of a developing mode of reflection on the contexts of police work is evident in the appearance in the journal in 1949 of one of the first Australian statistical inquiries into the incidence of crime. Significantly perhaps it came out of South Australia, and one of the co-authors was Detective Constable Ray Whitrod, later to head the Commonwealth investigation service, playing an important role in establishing the Australian Police College in Manly and, most famously, heading the Queensland police for six years, where one of his major ambitions was the enhancement of police education.[43]

TRAINING OR EDUCATION?

Police colleges were the police solution to what was seen as a police problem, how to train police in the practical requirements of their work, including police 'duties', but extending at the higher levels to matters of management and administration. The establishment in England of a police college in Warwickshire extended the possibilities but still preserved the task as one for police to manage themselves (that college itself began to play some role in Australian policing through the visits of some police to it during the 1950s).[44]

In 1960, the changing environment for police education and careers was signalled by Ray Whitrod, beginning a period as Commonwealth police commissioner, in a perceptive and historically-minded essay on police administration. Whitrod addressed the need for a different approach to the administration of police departments in Australia which he considered lacked a depth of leadership which might be fostered through the establishment of an officer class or, as he preferred to put it, an 'administrative grade'. Referring to a British home office review of 1946 into 'Higher Training for the Police Service', Whitrod drew attention to the weakness of a police service, or any public administration, which was administered by officers whose primary qualifications were life-long experience in the police force, developing what the home office study had epitomised as 'a certain stiffness in habits of thought'.[45] While there had been some innovation in terms of preparation for administration in officers' courses, as in Victoria in the late 1950s, the efforts were regarded by Whitrod as savouring 'of an attempt to lift oneself up by the boot-straps'.[46] Clearly he favoured a sustained innovation in police education which would prepare officers from among the best recruits, and at an early age. The need was especially evident, considered Whitrod, in view of the changing demographics and education level of recruits to the police service. While the Australian police forces had obtained a high standard of recruits during the economic depression of the 1930s, owing to the reduced opportunities elsewhere, post-war affluence had possibly diminished the pool of intelligent recruits:

> Indeed there could be a widening gap between the average standard of intelligence and education in the community and that possessed by police recruits.[47]

Much of the essay was based on personal observation, since Australian police departments did not collect data on the attributes of their police, except in individual files: Victoria for example had begun to record the 'intelligence quotient of its recruits', but the data could not compare past and present. It was scarcely an endearing portrait of the administrative capacities of the Australian police and its observations on the resistance of rank and file police to the creation of an 'officer class' were prescient of Whitrod's later difficulties in Queensland.

Nevertheless, Whitrod's essay epitomised many of the themes which were to characterise the debate over police education and training in the following three decades. Producing change in the system was also dependent, however, on external pressures. The transformation of the conditions of policing in recent decades has many faces. But policing has not been alone in its move towards an enhancement of its managerial and professional organisation. Along with many other occupations there has been a tendency to move towards more intensive and sometimes broader pedagogy and training. A comparison with the occupation of nursing helps to highlight what is distinctive about the developments in police training which have culminated in an increasing expectation that police attain tertiary educational qualifications during the last decade of the century.

Like police-work, the history of the occupation of nursing was characterised by on-the-job training. The work of nursing, however, takes place in an institution which is dominated by another occupational status, that of medicine.

Moreover, a certain ethic of service and discipline, allied with the gender-skewed orientation of the nursing role, produced an occupation of quite distinctive standing. In the 1970s and 1980s there was a major move to reorganise the conditions of entry to nursing, a move in which tertiary education, outside the boundaries of the hospital, came to be pre-eminent. The reasons for this change are complex, but they include pressures from within nursing ranks for improved status and income. As well, there was a demand for a formal recognition of nursing as a particularly skilled occupation, not subordinate to medicine (and other para-medical knowledges, such as psychology, physiotherapy etc), but different from it.[48]

While the move to 'professionalise' nursing, through removing initial education from the control of the doctor-dominated hospital, can be seen in some ways as arising strongly from the demands of nurses themselves, the parallel move in Australia towards police tertiary education came from quite a different impetus. It would be overstating the case to ignore the opposition to tertiary status of some elements of the nursing workforce, including nursing educators. But the contexts of the move towards new forms of training were significantly different from those affecting police.

An important difference was the institutional autonomy of police. Where nursing operates in an institutional subordination to medicine, police work is substantially autonomous. While there are elements of subordination within the police ranks (through the employment hierarchy and the rule structures), the external constraints are limited in their impact — neither judiciary nor political figures can substantially affect police in their everyday work. While the knowledge required of police in some of their work is highly specialised, it is for the most part routinely organised and acquired. And while police had and have complaints about their salary and conditions, they have long had unions active on their behalf which have been defensive of existing standards of pay and conditions rather than over-anxious about something as elusive as professional status.[49]

It is true that there had been recognition within police forces for some time of the diversity of skills and dispositions which policing demanded. In its early years the *Australian Police Journal* had registered this approach. 'The police no longer exist for the sole purpose of thief-taking', noted an article in the journal in 1951. 'Police work is a great social work'.[50] The stated demand for enhanced professional training at tertiary level has come from outside the police forces. Perhaps the most public moves in this direction came in the course and aftermath of the Fitzgerald inquiry in Queensland from 1987, but its concerns had already been prefigured in some ways by the less controversial but very substantial reviews of police organisation in New South Wales in 1981 and in Victoria in 1986.[51]

Analysing the 'police culture' which had developed in Queensland, the Fitzgerald Report observed that, as a group, police officers received:

> inadequate instruction in public ethics and proper relationships within the Police Force and with the government and the community, with training substantially carried out by older police at least some of whom are officers imbued with the police culture.[52]

The system described earlier in this chapter had always presumed that police training should be a police matter, carried out within the organisation for the purpose especially of maintaining a system of promotions. From the elementary police manuals of the nineteenth century through to the establishment of the police colleges in their various forms from the 1930s, the making of police officers had been police business, in which there was little if any input from outside.[53]

It was this history which was challenged by Lusher in New South Wales and Fitzgerald in Queensland. Fitzgerald noted the claims of several submissions that the Academy (for induction training) and the College (for in-service development) lacked independence, and that the 'examination branch at headquarters exercises a great degree of control over the curricula, marking tests, and determining which officers pass or fail'.[54] Not only did the Academy appear to lack independence, but the isolation of trainees in such an institution contributed to the narrowness of police culture, separating police trainees from the public at the earliest stage of their careers:

> Since a significant amount of police work involves community service, the wisdom of training police in isolation from the rest of the community, and confining the study of the social sciences to a small proportion of the course, must be questioned.[55]

These criticisms reflected a process of re-evaluation which was taking place within Australian policing over the previous decade. In New South Wales, John Avery, a senior police officer later to become commissioner, had signalled the change in his research thesis, subsequently published as *Police: Force or Service?*.[56] He drew on research showing the substantial community rather than crime work done by police in their everyday duty. Reviewing the orientation of police education programmes in the mid-1980s, Dale Sullivan from the external studies programme of the Victorian police drew attention to the disjunction between police work and police training:

Although [only] 10–20 per cent of the police role involves crime-fighting activities, by far the greatest emphasis in pre-service and in-service training for officers is placed on the law enforcement nature of policing.[57]

The inadequacies of police training in the area of social and inter-cultural relations were the object of severe criticism in the interim and final reports of the Royal Commission into Aboriginal Deaths in Custody (1987–1991). Although there had been elementary moves in some States to acquaint police with the specific nature of their responsibilities in relation to Aborigines, the commission regarded these as inadequate. This was particularly the case in that the inquiries revealed repeated evidence of racism towards Aborigines and Torres Strait Islanders. The occasional lecture by a visiting Aboriginal person to a group of trainees or serving police was scarcely adequate to redressing the long-established ignorance and antagonism which police recruits and officers shared with many non-Aboriginal people in Australia.

There is some evidence, not limited to the writing of senior police such as Avery in New South Wales, that police themselves were increasingly critical of the limits on their training. In Victoria, a major review of police management and administration in the mid-1980s included a substantial survey of police attitudes to their work. Ranking areas where they saw themselves as ill-prepared for their everyday tasks in the community, many of those surveyed pointed to crime prevention, youth matters and domestic violence in particular as a problem for which police required better training.[58] It was a need endorsed strongly by Fitzgerald:

> Police need an education which equips them with a sense of balance in both enforcing the law and serving the community. As well, they need preparation to cope with the traumas associated with police work. The military model of training, applied to young school leavers, cannot achieve these objectives.[59]

Was tertiary degree study appropriate to redressing the poor formation of police officers in their relations with those they policed? Increasingly the tendency was to answer 'yes.' Lusher had recommended changes in police education which would ensure police trainees had contact with non-police as students and teachers. Fitzgerald concluded that 'Education programmes in Colleges of Advanced Education or other tertiary institutions which provide basic knowledge of criminal justice processes and foundations of social science are needed.'[60] That was substantially the model which developed in Queensland from 1991, with major new programmes at two Brisbane universities.

Already in the 1980s there had been moves elsewhere in such a direction. By 1984 there were a number of diploma study programmes at tertiary colleges in most States.[61] In addition, following their predecessors since the 1940s, a number of police were regularly undertaking university degree programmes — a 1982 study suggested that South Australia, the Northern Territory and Victoria were the most likely to have serving officers possessing degrees or graduate diplomas. At that time, two police forces, those in Tasmania and Western Australia, provided no salary increment for obtaining these qualifications.[62]

The transition from training to education in Australian policing has been a long time developing and is far from resolved. The presumption, as in the 1906 Victorian royal commission, of inevitable conflict between the 'imbibition of book lore' and the practical tasks of policing, remains a powerful theme in debate over contemporary policing. Continuing tension between the short-term recruiting needs of police departments and the longer-term expectations of a more highly qualified police service bedevils the recent commitment to police education. Ingrained suspicion of book learning is evident in comments of police, senior and rank and file, about the necessity of practical training.[63]

To recall the nursing comparison again it can be seen that policing is not alone in this regard. In each case an alternative argument might be mounted that both 'book-lore' and 'practice' might need to change to address the putative gap between general education with its emphasis on personal formation and the everyday demands of police or nursing work. Certainly the presumption in the case of policing has been that university education will positively change practice, in producing a police officer capable of better exercising judgment in police matters. But to understand adequately the change that is embodied in the shift from the 'military model' of training to the idea of police education, it is important to recognise some other changes which are affecting the personnel structure of the police forces.

The task of training and education in the making of police officers is now one which applies to a different composition of recruits. Height requirements, gender restrictions, and other components of recruiting policy which historically characterised policing in Australia have changed since the 1970s. In addition to removing discriminatory provisions, police departments have increasingly been required to adopt affirmative action policies in recruitment to redress the disparities in ethnic as well as gender composition of police. Recent recommendations of the Royal Commission into Aboriginal Deaths in Custody, for example, enhanced the potential for addressing the need to recruit Aborigines and Torres Strait Islanders as well as to transform the culture of police training and education in order to produce more deep-rooted change in the policing of these people.

Hence the presumption of colonial policing, that it was an office to be held by men, of Anglo-Celtic origin and of a certain height and physique, has given way to a more diverse conception of the desirable police force in Australia. Whether the achievement of this greater diversity in personnel and the acquisition of higher education means better or worse policing will remain a moot point, an element in the constant political debate between the nostalgic protagonists of the virtues of the past and the advocates of a different future.

CHAPTER 8

Rules and Discipline

Police work on the streets may be characterised by a high level of discretion, but police departments are inconceivable without rules. From the beginning of the new police, rules made in law, by regulation, or by directive of a commissioner or other senior officer have served to organise the work of policing. The (ideal) conformity of police to rules does not characterise policing alone, since other occupations (nursing, public service) place a high degree of emphasis on rules and procedures. But appreciating the historical and cultural nature of the specific rules of policing helps to understand the limits, constraints and possibilities of the police exercise of power.

There are, however, different kinds of rules. Three can be distinguished in understanding police behaviour and the culture that produces it. First, to the extent that police actions are accountable in court, there are rules that judges or magistrates apply in determining whether or not police have acted legally. Yet, secondly, many police activities not falling within the view of the court are in any case regulated by departmental rules. Finally, there is the body of informal rules which apply in any workplace, but which have been perhaps particularly powerful in police work. The sociological term, 'cop culture', intended to capture the living reality of these rules, but particularly the role of informal rules, has been recently influential in official inquiries and reform programmes.

If there are rules, there are also sanctions. Again, we need to consider the reality of both formal and informal sanctions. Since their inception, the capacity of police organisations to exert authority over the behaviour of police has been a controversial matter in policing. Discipline has been exercised in a variety of ways which deserve historical scrutiny. The history of informal sanctions is much less accessible, for obvious reasons — only the memoirs or oral histories of police or the occasional surfacing of these informalities of police behaviour in official inquiries or police files can assist in this most hidden of police histories. Australian historians of the policing of Aborigines are familiar with the telling silences which denote the use of unregulated violence, including murder, in the nineteenth century dispersals of Aborigines. 'Tale-tellers', or in modern parlance 'whistle-blowers', people to be avoided in many work places, not just those of police, are few and far between in these histories.[1]

Within the space available here two issues deserve analysis. One is the history of rule-making itself, a history which must explain the changing form and content of rules as well as limits and obstacles to their observance. The second is the history of police discipline. What forms of regulation of police conduct existed within police departments and how were they administered? How did they change over time and were any related to changing relations of policing more generally? The relation of these questions both to the chapter which follows (on corruption) and to the earlier discussion of police commissioner authority and autonomy needs to be remembered in the analysis which follows.

RULES AND RULE BOOKS

The putative independence of the constable was early qualified by the emergence of formal rules and regulations governing the organisation of police. To a limited degree these were legislated in the various police (or police regulation) Acts. The genesis of these in Australasian forces was significantly influenced by the Victorian legislation of 1853. The organising statute was supplemented in 1856 by the issuing in Victoria of a *Manual of Police Regulations*, which guided subsequent rules and publications elsewhere in the colonies.[2] Even before this, however, the idea of a police manual had been given its colonial airing in South Australia, where the police commissioner published a *Police Manual* in 1845, its dictum being 'the absence of crime will be considered the best proof of the complete efficiency of the Police.'[3]

Police statutes and gazetted rules and regulations were of little use unless police were somehow made aware of them. Moreover, they were poor guides in many respects, applying only to the broadest conception of what police work involved. The true dimensions of bureaucratic policing become most evident in the gradual development of other forms of regulation. The rule books, published and circulated in various forms, provided a means of orienting police to their work. But supplementary means of governing police behaviour emerged in the form of circular memoranda and general orders. In the simple structure of nineteenth-century policing, organised on a district basis, with inspectors the only intermediaries between commissioner and stations, there was also provision for district orders. The content of these administrative devices suggests the ambition of centralised control. At the same time, there is evidence of the difficulties of maintaining observance of the rules. The informalities of local practice are only occasionally hinted at, but often tellingly so as commissioners' cautionary directions on the necessity of observation of the rules show.[4]

Modern research on the effectiveness of police rules suggests the need for mechanisms of monitoring and education of police in their observance.[5] These objectives were historically sought for example through station meetings. Evidence from Queensland suggests the practice of a collective reading of the general orders as new ones were made and circulated. Monitoring of observance was possible where procedures involved feedback of documents to the central office and inspectors were expected to oversee the receipt and filing of new rules and circulars, as magistrate inspectors had before them.[6]

What about the rules themselves? What forces moulded their content? The apparently mundane world of police rules and the bureaucratic circular is yet capable of demonstrating some important dimensions of the modes of governing the police. The statement of rules embodies some highly symbolic observations on the preferred modes of policing. The symbolic and political character of police rules is the product of decisions taken in their formation. The rules embody statements of the law, or preferred ways of proceeding in interactions with the policed, as well as procedures in police administration. These statements thereby involve choices between different ways of acting as police.

The content of a colonial police manual can tell us something about the expectations and norms of policing in the field. It has been observed in other places that modern manuals have increasingly become technical documents to an extent which conceals the policy choices in policing decisions.[7] Yet nineteenth-century manuals were produced quite pointedly as a guide to young police constables. In the absence of extended training they were, in effect, policy guides to policing.

Colonial manuals aimed to instruct in basic police duties and powers as well as outline some policy considerations in policing. The 1876 Queensland *Manual of Police Regulations*, for example, was arranged alphabetically under subject headings (arrest, assault, beats, beggars, and so on) and was aimed not only at reprinting the rules and regulations and acquainting constables with statutory police charges, but also at forming the capacity of officers to use their discretion in making policing interventions. Hence, while beggars (especially those 'deformed, blind or suffering from offensive or contagious diseases') were to be arrested and charged under the *Vagrancy Act*, police were advised of the extent of discretion to be used in intervening in assault cases, especially between 'a man and his wife'. In policing indecent offences, police concealment (for purposes of entrapping offenders) was not to be used and generally charges of indecent exposure were not to be lightly made, especially where 'it is supposed that there is no improper intention'. Extensive instructions were laid out guiding police responsibility for the care of prisoners, and more generally for any matters bearing on arrest and interrogation.[8]

The range of matters covered and the rhetoric of approach suggests the practical orientation of the manual. However, as a guide to practice it faced the hazard of obsolescence over decades of use in a changing society. Hence, in a number of colonies the need for updated manuals was regarded at the turn of the century as an important administrative impediment to better policing.

In Victoria, the constant amendment of the police regulations of 1877, by means of publication in the *Government Gazette*, produced a situation of uncertainty regarding the rules, which the Victorian commissioner, Thomas O'Callaghan, sought to put right by producing a new 'Police Code' in 1906.[9] Contemporary with the Victorian commission, the 1906 royal commission in Tasmania, charged with a general inquiry into the administration of the Tasmanian police, recommended a new manual, to replace that of 1871, long out of date. Without a 'modern Manual', observed the commissioners, it was:

> obviously unreasonable to expect that subordinates, and particularly those who are removed from immediate control, will acquire that knowledge of the functions of the Department and of their own duties and responsibilities which is essential to efficiency.[10]

In Queensland, the 1899 royal commission had heard evidence that constables could be disciplined for offences against rules which they had never seen. The commission recommended in favour of a new and more widely distributed rule-book.[11] The arguments in favour of a comprehensive and comprehendible rule-book seemed particularly compelling in bureaucracies of such extended coverage as those of Australian police forces, where a large part of the police force was well beyond the reach of everyday supervision by superiors.

Not all police manuals are likely to have been the subject of bureaucratic wrangling between police and other agencies. But the absence of overt conflict may mean merely the dominance of one particular view of the responsibilities and duties of police. The modification of police rules would in the twentieth century be usually governed by the administrative priorities of the police department, mediated only by the need to consider the occasional injunction

of a judicial decision. The political meanings of this process were very clear in
the only documented account of the writing of a rule book in the Australian
police forces.

In the first years of the twentieth century, Queensland's principal magistrate, Robert Ranking, together with the attorney-general, J. W. Blair, decided
to adapt a reputable English police manual for Queensland purposes. Their
choice was Howard Vincent's manual, an established authority on urban policing of the English model, written by a former head of Scotland Yard and peri-
patetic Imperial law reformer. It was an influential publication, having been
cited for example by the Victorian Longmore commission in 1883 in cautioning against the use of informers in criminal investigation.[12]

Vincent's Manual was characterised by an especially cautious introduction
on police powers, an address to constables which advised them of the need to
observe the liberties of the policed and the requirements of the law, especially in
regard to arrest and interrogation. Together with the attorney-general, Ranking, who had been and continued to be critical in court of police practices,
drafted a revised edition for Queensland and hoped to have it printed for circulation in the force by 1905.

In that year, however, W. G. Cahill was appointed commissioner of police,
having previously been under-secretary of justice, following an earlier Irish
career in the constabulary. Cahill was aggressively jealous of his department's
autonomy. The proposed manual drafted by the chief magistrate and the
attorney-general was offensive to Cahill's sense of authority and police autonomy. In voicing his objections to the government, however, Cahill articulated a
series of propositions about the nature of police work which give us a sense of
how police rules prioritise particular ways of behaving.

The commissioner's criticisms of Ranking and Blair's *Police Code* were spelt
out in a 1907 memorandum.[13] In some cases (Cahill instanced twenty matters
of substance which he claimed would mislead Queensland police practice), the
commissioner was able to establish simply that procedures, regulations or
statutes had changed since the enactment of the criminal code (1899). The age
under which a child could be deemed 'neglected' had been raised from 15 to
17; police rather than police magistrates were now responsible for ordering
post mortems; armlets (to distinguish police on duty) were no longer worn by
police in Queensland. On these matters Cahill's opposition to Ranking's *Code*
was primarily grounded on his opposition to any outsider's attempt to define
police practices — specifying minor inaccuracies was the means to a larger end.
On matters of criminal law and investigation, however, the commissioner and
the magistrate were more sharply distinguished.

In the most substantial issue raised by Cahill, that of 'cautioning a prisoner', Ranking and Blair had simply followed Vincent's *Code:*

> before a prisoner in custody is asked any questions however necessary...he should be distinctly cautioned that his answer may be given in evidence against him. The law is very strict on this head, and does not permit persons charged with offences to be interrogated by police as to their guilt.

The point was reinforced in the *Code* by reference to the introductory address of Lord Brampton which was much concerned with advice to constables on the limits of interrogation. Cahill took exception to this statement of 'the law'. The advice was simply 'wrong'. He made no reference to police practice, to general orders or to his instructions (which had recently drawn attention to the 1876 manual's warning about confessional evidence), but cited in support of his opinion two Queensland judgments affecting the admissibility of evidence.[14] Cahill had judicial mandate on his side: the judges in the mid-1890s had affirmed that confessional evidence obtained by questioning while in custody could be admitted so long as it had not been induced under threat or promise. His extensive citations from the relevant cases suggest his determination to sustain police powers at their broadest limit, while retaining his own prerogative on internal directions to the force.

In reply, Ranking suggested that 'Doctors Differ' and fell back on Howard Vincent and Lord Brampton to sustain the advice given in his manual. But the magistrate did not leave it there, considering as he did that this was one area of police practice which required closer scrutiny. Strong justification for a strict interpretation of the 'caution' in an educative manual was advanced: 'as a fact, the right to question accused prisoners after there had been found an intention to arrest them subsequently, is constantly abused by the police, and it is as well therefore that the line should be drawn clearly'. Coming as it did from a magistrate who was not averse to condoning the exemplary use of police powers to stop and question suspects,[15] this criticism was pointed. It is consistent with what Ranking saw as the larger interest involved in producing a manual intended to educate and make more accountable a police force which was increasingly independent of external controls or criticism.

Cahill's concern with the possible impact of Ranking's advice on police procedure in criminal matters was also evident in his criticism of the directions regarding charges and depositions taken at a watch-house. According to Ranking and Blair, these should be taken in the presence and hearing of the prisoner, and 'no statement relative to the charge should be made except in the hearing and presence of the prisoner'. As a norm this seemed unexceptional, but Cahill disputed its publication at all. 'Such an order', he considered, 'could not possibly be carried out. The confusion would be simply appalling and the number of police required to attempt to carry out such duty could not be afforded'. The gulf between Cahill's and Ranking's expectations of a code of procedure was demonstrated in the latter's response to the commissioner's criticism of this prescription. The wording on the mode of taking a charge was transcribed from Vincent's Code. 'As the practice is found workable in England', Ranking added 'and is stated by commissioner Cahill to be impracticable in Queensland, the inference is that method and discipline are less effective here than in England'. This surely begged the question whether such a prescription for police practice was carried out in everyday policing in England.

At the same time, another inference of Cahill's dissent from the Vincent guide to police was that these procedures represented an unwarranted burden on police resources for the sake of the person being charged. In other matters of criminal law and police procedure, Cahill attempted to bring the force of judicial mandate in Queensland and Australia against Ranking's *Code*. A cautionary note on the use of circumstantial evidence was strongly attacked by Cahill who was able to cite Sir Samuel Griffith's judgment in the famous Kenniff case that in some cases circumstantial might be preferred to direct evidence.[16]

On another matter, however, Cahill's reliance on case law rebounded on him. The arrest without warrant of a person charged with vagrancy ('no lawful visible means of support') had been limited by a Victorian court, leading Cahill to issue a circular memorandum to Queensland police warning them against such arrests. He therefore disputed Ranking and Blair's statement of the law on the subject. By the time of Ranking's reply to this criticism, the Victorian case had been overruled in the High Court and the *Code's* statement of the law was formally correct.[17]

The process of negotiation or confrontation over the drafting of an adequate manual illustrates the range of factors involved in defining the police rules. Judicial decisions were clearly taken seriously and helped define policy, whatever the practice. In areas left untouched or ambiguous by case law or statute, administrative convenience and efficiency were important considerations. Hence Cahill's concern that advice about police responsibilities in the matter of gathering evidence against a prisoner should not err on the side of caution. The only restrictions which should be felt were those prescribed by the statutes, by rules and regulations, or by the courts in case law. Rules should be framed in ways which recognised some important local conditions of policing, not least those caused by greater sparsity of population, great distances, and limited numbers of police at any one station.

Beyond its demonstration that rules and the wording of them have a history, the significance of the episode epitomises a particular style in Australian policing—its bureaucratic and centralist mode. Importantly, this example suggests that this phenomenon of police defensiveness can arise in circumstances which are not just symptomatic of a certain police culture. Cahill's position was not formed through long service in the police force, for he was appointed from outside it, like most reformers.

Rather, resistance of Cahill as commissioner to the role of other non-police authorities in the definition of rules and procedures was conditioned by the structural position of police forces, agencies responsible for the forceful control of individual and collective behaviour but with limited accountability for their actions and little inclined to direction from outside. The time for magisterial direction of police duties in Australia had been, if only briefly, in the mid-nineteenth century. Ranking and Blair had challenged 'the order of things as they ought to exist' as Cahill so forcefully put the matter on another occasion.[18]

Rule-making and rule-books changed in the course of the twentieth century. While police work remains highly discretionary, there has been some movement towards a comprehensive statement of the boundaries within which police actions should lie. Rule-books are drafted by specialist units, taking account of the effect of legal decisions as well as legislative changes. Their efficacy and relevance are matters for further research and evaluation in Australia. But there have been signs in recent years of failures in police departments to ensure both that rules are up to date and that their observance is adequately monitored. Administrative malaise, conflict, and lack of priorities, evident in the tortuously long process of revising the Queensland rules, as discussed above, is a problem that may affect the operation of policing now as much as then.

The inquiries of the Royal Commission into Aboriginal Deaths in Custody, for example, uncovered a number of areas where rule-making and observance had failed to protect those in custody from harm. In one of the most critical areas of police powers, the commission found it difficult to discover any process of monitoring the observance of the common police injunction that arrest is a power of last resort. In South Australia, despite departmental policy being clear on this, there was no evidence of statistical monitoring of the use of arrest. The Western Australia police commissioner had to repeat in 1989 his 1985 Instruction on the use of arrest:

> Arrests are not to be made purely as a means of inflicting a penalty on offenders, or because it is an easier method of process. Depriving people of their liberty is an action to be given careful consideration, as it can have serious repercussions on the police image if it is done without due discretion.

The wording of the Instruction suggests the police department-oriented mode of much rule-making, concerned with the image and interests of police, with the citizen-oriented issue of unnecessary arrest becoming secondary.[19]

Other inquiries which brought police operations and administration into the public eye suggested police rule-making was deficient in its lack of observance of matters such as legislative change. In Queensland, the Fitzgerald inquiry found the legal and training branch of the police department deficient in its capacity to state the law on various policing matters.[20] But this was only part of a larger malaise in police administration which results from a police determination to possess the field of policing and resist outside attempts to direct it. Reviewing the attitudes and operational practices of New South Wales police, Dixon has concluded more generally that 'criminal investigation and policing generally... are at a stage where law is often regarded as a flexible resource and is sometimes ignored, but is rarely taken as a constitutive and directive part of policing.'[21]

POLICE RULES AND POLICE DISCIPLINE

Rules are deficient without means of obtaining compliance. In the case of police work, a variety of modes of discipline have been used, as well as forms of supervision and inspection mentioned earlier. In the wake of the numerous police inquiries in Australia in the last two decades, it is difficult not to be impressed by what looks like a repeated failure to observe the rules, even when they may be more oriented to preserving the police image than to guaranteeing whatever may be regarded from the citizen point of view as good policing.

Our second concern in this chapter then is to address briefly the issue of discipline within the police forces. What have been the main modes of disciplining police when training and supervision fail, and how have they been administered? The subject cannot be easily separated from two other concerns — the issue of corruption (discussed in the next chapter) and that of public complaints. Nevertheless, the matter deserves preliminary treatment here because it is part of the history of internal administration, tied so closely to our preliminary concern with how police were formed as social actors with particular capacities and dispositions.

Compliance with police rules and administrative requirements has, since the nineteenth century, been an object of divided responsibility. At law, police have continued to be potential objects of criminal or civil action for abuse of their powers or harm done to others in the course of their work. This legal regulation of police misbehaviour was reflected in the administrative structure of some of the colonial police forces at various stages: police were subject to the inspection of magistrates and might be charged in the magistrates court for offences against the Police Act or regulations.[22]

Nevertheless, the prosecution of police for minor or major offences, whether against police regulations or the criminal law, became a matter of last (and not hopeful) resort. Police discipline was increasingly a matter for the authority of the commissioner, and he had a range of means at his disposal. These included fines (deducted from wages), demotion, and dismissal. Short of these types of penalties were admonitory advice and cautions. These were frequently used and of considerable interest as indicating the administrative sophistication of colonial police. All these modes of discipline have continued through the twentieth century, but appear to have changed in incidence over time.

Police personnel files indicate that the full range of disciplinary means was constantly employed in police administration during the later nineteenth and early twentieth century. A large number of police were affected at one stage of their careers by actions of their superiors over some aspect of their conduct. In the early decades this concerned particularly matters of personal decorum. Much research in Australia and elsewhere has shown that the most common cause of action against nineteenth-century police was on account of drunkenness.

Punishment for drunkenness ranged from caution or reprimand through fines to dismissal, the latter occurring mainly in aggravated circumstances where other grounds for dissatisfaction may have existed. In South Australia, the offence was initially considered sufficient to warrant immediate dismissal, though this was considered too harsh by an 1867 select committee which recommended it not be mandatory to dismiss an officer on a charge of drunkenness.[23] Hence, the context of the offence became crucial. That this is the case may be deduced from the fact that a number of police had persistent offences of drunkenness without punishment ever extending beyond a fine. Where drunkenness was seen as having impeded duty it was regarded as more serious, and where it took place in a hotel where police were forbidden to socialise, the offence could lead to the most serious consequences.[24]

Police drunkenness reflects the widespread incidence of the phenomenon in the society at large but it has been endemic to police culture. Palmer's research on the Irish constabulary suggests that drunkenness accounted for over 50 per cent of dismissals in the 1830s, this in a force which had a much lower turnover rate than the London police. Studies of the police in New Zealand and the Australian colonies confirm the picture. Among those dismissed in Queensland from 1880–1930, a similar proportion had drunkenness defaults in their records.[25] Other historians of police have frequently confirmed the endemic problem of drunkenness in police work, while a contemporary sociologist of police corruption has recently suggested that his status as a non-drinker seriously interfered with his capacity for researching the practices of the Amsterdam police.[26]

The problems for police administration posed by drinking were made more serious by the public scandal it might incur as well as its debilitating consequences for the effectiveness of police work. Early cautions for drinking were a warning of troubles ahead. Michael O'Brien's brief service in Brisbane and then Maryborough in 1882–3 was marked by four offences in less than two years—drunk on duty, fined 20/-; absent from beat, fined 10/-; absent and drunk, fined 10/-; and a final charge of being drunk twice which led to his dismissal.[27] The short career of Patrick Carr (1914–18), ex-Irish constabulary, included a fine of three pounds after he was found to be absent from his beat in a hotel 'in suspicious proximity to a bottle of liquor'.[28] The instances of minor and serious offending against rules and against the law are numerous enough in the Queensland files to show why strict inspection was necessary, if it could be achieved.

As an occasion of discipline, concern for the image of the police was perhaps matched only by determination to ensure strict subordination of junior to superior in the police hierarchy. Consequently, after drunkenness the common causes of disciplinary action were insubordination, disobedience of orders or absence from beat duty. When eleven police defied commissioner Peterswald's order to wear uniform to a police public concert in the Adelaide Town Hall in 1886, they were all reduced in rank.[29] Insubordination was a category allowing a superior to address a broad range of defects in personal disposition; for example 'Identifies himself too strongly in religious matters' was an inspector's judgment on the behaviour of an insubordinate constable in Queensland in 1896.[30]

The burden of police discipline tended to be oriented to the maintenance of the organisation, through attention to routine duty rather than directly related to the quality and effectiveness of policing itself. In spite of the relative frequency of official corruption inquiries in Australian policing history, corruption charges appear relatively infrequently in police disciplinary proceedings, at least on the evidence of the Queensland personnel files. This might be explained of course by a low incidence of such practices in police forces over time in Australia. Or it might be simply that these charges are of necessity difficult to prove and therefore likely to be below the threshold of official notice much of the time. Without systematic examination of a large volume of police personnel files over a substantial period of time, we cannot know what is the more acceptable explanation in the Australian case.

What were the means of investigation and discipline which brought these offences to book? The matter was variously the subject of legislation or of regulation from the beginning of centralisation in the middle of the nineteenth century. The unifying theme was the singular authority of the commissioner, but this was qualified both by the nature of offences and by the occasional responsibility of other officers for their subordinates. Some variation was evident also in the role of magistrates in the process of discipline, a role which was to diminish over time in line with the police preference for internal management of their own affairs. There is something of a countervailing move in this century in terms of some restrictions on the freedom of the commissioner to discipline his underlings.

The Victorian disciplinary procedures may be taken as an example of the changes which occurred in most Australian forces over time. From 1853 the chief commissioner was empowered to discharge or dismiss constables and the power was freely used in the early years of the colonial force. The 1873 *Police Regulation Act* set out the procedures under which inquiries into misconduct or insubordination were to take place. Essentially these distinguished between provisions applicable to sergeants or superior officers and those applying to constables. Penal powers resided in the hands of the commissioner or his delegate (a superintendent or other officer appointed by the Governor in Council) in relation to constables or others who could be fined or imprisoned for misconduct offences, the charges having been heard on oath. For all intents and purposes, the chief commissioner and his inquiry officers were acting as justices in these cases. While appeal to the higher courts was not provided, there was alternative provision for the hearing by a three-person board of the charges, with the board itself having disciplinary powers.

The only substantial change to this arrangement prior to the Second World War was the elimination in 1938 of imprisonment as a penal option. In 1946, however, Victorian police association lobbying of a new Labor government succeeded in curbing significantly the power of the chief commissioner in disciplinary matters. Dismissal became an option only able to be recommended by a a police discipline board, comprising a magistrate (nominee of the government) and a superintendent (nominee of the chief commissioner). At one level this simply formalised the earlier provision for a board to act as an alternative to the commissioner in disciplinary cases, where an officer charged so desired it. But the restriction on the powers of the commissioner to recommend dismissal was an important change in proceeding.[31]

The creation in the nineteenth century of what was effectively an appeal board with such powers as that which existed in Victoria was an unusually innovative step in the management of police discipline. Most of the other colonies/States were to wait until after the First World War at the earliest to establish such a mechanism — New South Wales in 1923 and South Australia in 1928. Few jurisdictions in fact spelled out in such legislative detail as the Victorian legislation the means by which discipline would be maintained through the charging and punishment of police offenders against regulations and rules. Most left such statements to the rules and regulations gazetted under the relevant police Act.

Hence in Queensland, for example, proceeding on disciplinary charges was regulated by rule 96 of the 1869 rules. Amendments in the 1890s devolved power to officers to hear evidence and decide forms of punishment. In 1906, however, commissioner Cahill, evidently eager to pull back to the centre powers which had issued to the periphery, ordered officers to obtain direction from him before charging police with misconduct. Four years later he went further, withdrawing from officers the power to make a decision in a disciplinary hearing, requiring instead that they forward the results of inquiry to him for final determination.[32]

As discussed in chapter 2, much of the attention of police unions in the twentieth century has been focussed on disciplinary provisions, especially those relating to the seemingly autocratic powers vested in the commissioner and the alleged weakness of appeal provisions. However, how did the various commissioners use their powers, extensive as they were? A reading of police staff files leaves little doubt as to the potential power of the commissioner to determine the fate of subordinates. The effectiveness of such disciplinary powers was undoubtedly in the end dependent on the flow of information between local stations and the central office, dependent that is on the capacity and characteristics of inspectors and superintendents. At the same time the substantial powers of the commissioners, should they want to use them, were frequently evident.

The measure of the commissioner's authority lies in the early frequency of what were to become harsh or unusual punishments in police administration. The constantly changing nature of official reports make it difficult to judge the trend, but Queensland data from official reports show an average of one officer dismissed per year between 1942 and 1957—a significant change from the 19 per year between 1882 and 1893. Certainly the style of a particular commissioner made a significant difference at any time. Cahill in Queensland dismissed an average of 20 officers in his first three years in office, a notable increase from the 8 per year under Parry-Okeden before him.[33]

It is difficult to compare these results with other States for which the information is even more inadequate in official police department reports. In Victoria, the commissioner's power to dismiss was lost altogether in 1946, in the wake of complaints about the allegedly arbitrary character of its use.[34] The difference between nineteenth and twentieth-century practice, however, is evident in the declining use of discipline prior to this date. In New South Wales, in a department which had dismissed regularly more than 20 officers a year before 1900, the number declined to well under ten in the early decades of the twentieth century.[35]

More recent history provides some confirmation of the historical norm which developed that made dismissal a comparative rarity. Most notably, the career of commissioner Ray Whitrod in the Queensland police was marked by the re-assertion of the commissioner's authority in discipline matters, including dismissal. The reaction of many police and their union was predictably hostile.[36] Attempts in other States to deal with police misconduct through the punishment system have been similarly countered, notoriously in Victoria after the Beach inquiry, where police resistance made impossible the pressing of charges and disciplinary proceedings relating to corruption.[37]

While dismissal was common in the early period of policing, demotion also had its place. It is not uncommon to find police even of senior rank who had earlier suffered demotion for some offence.[38] A notable instance is the Victorian chief commissioner, Thomas O'Callaghan (1902–13), who survived an early demotion while in the detective force, as well as other breaches and scathing criticism from the Longmore royal commission, to become head of the force.[39] Senior constable Grimes, responsible for training police recruits at the Petrie Terrace police depot in Brisbane and a valuable witness on police training before a royal commission in 1889, had himself been discharged for seven months on a charge of drunkenness in 1882.[40] An implication of these and other cases is that demotion served its purpose as a positive disciplinary tool.

Besides these substantial penalties, the disciplinary modes available to the commissioner, and in certain circumstances other appointed officers such as superintendents and inspectors, included monetary fines, cautions and admonishments. The modern resort of counselling has its origins in the means of administering a caution, a process which involved a superior overseeing the reading of the written instruction by the offending police officer, who was then required to sign the caution. It was a process which reflected not simply the bureaucratic imperative of ensuring that directives reached those to whom they applied, but carried with it perhaps an element of shaming as well as encouragement of personal reflection.

Whether these methods proved capable of remedying the mundane or more serious police infractions was doubtless conditional on the context of its application. With evident justification, the 1899 royal commission in Queensland criticised the overbearing conduct of some inspectors in the colony's force. Michael O'Sullivan recalled with jaundice just such a superior in his early years as a country policeman:

> After three months training I got orders to proceed to Roma on transfer... Next day I proceeded to Roma, a big remount centre, which was considered, at the time, the penal establishment of the Police Department. Inspector Armstrong was in charge of the district, and Senior-Sergeant O'Shea was in charge of Roma Police Barracks. O'Shea was undoubtedly a most tyrannical little creature, who seemed to delight in getting his own men into trouble. He reported me nine times in two months and failed eight times to substantiate his charges, and would have failed on the ninth if I had kept my head and not used the words "damned liar". I was fined ten shillings by the commissioner.[41]

Police officers learnt early that breaches of discipline could be summarily and often harshly punished.

It was nevertheless a system which could take note of virtue built up over a number of years of service in an occupation which provided numerous temptations or accidents of fate to trap the unwary or careless as well as the simply venal. For while defaults were noted, so too were favourable mentions and one could cancel the other out. Commissioner Cahill in Queensland noted of one somewhat chequered career that the constable had four unfavourable and four favourable mentions, on his default sheet, hence amounting to a record 'without blemish'.[42]

Flexibility in administrative control (which unionisation of police and other workers has limited significantly, at least till recent years) was arguably a powerful and positive disciplinary tool. Whether it was exercised to the public good, rather than to the narrower interests of organisational performance, or even at the arbitrary whim of superiors, is a much more difficult matter to judge.

The harsh disciplinary standards of the early years of the new police may have been influenced by the desire of police administrators to establish the legitimacy of the new arrangements among the allegedly resistant working class and to allay the fears of a suspicious middle class. But whatever the stimulus, the more important effect was the routinisation of disciplinary mechanisms as a stratagem of organisational conformity. As conformity to hierarchy became a less prominent concern, with the consolidation of police work as a career, the use of harsh disciplinary methods declined. Peer pressure and institutional culture produced their own disciplinary standards appropriate to what were seen as the interests of police as workers in a unique occupation, set apart from other groups.[43]

Some recognition of this new culture is evident within the ranks of police themselves over time. The first issue of the national *Australian Police Journal* in 1946 produced a commentary by a New South Wales chief superintendent on the role of discipline in policing. For Superintendent Wickham there had been a 'retrogressive tendency' in police work over the last twenty years. Police were the 'shock absorbers, as it were, between all sections of society. Therefore, it is absolutely necessary that discipline should be more pronounced in us than in any other people'. For Wickham the old concept of discipline in the 'strict military or police sense of the term' was less relevant than 'self or individual discipline, as a basic principle in the mental analysis of crime and criminals'. What was needed in police work, especially in an organisation such as the CIB, was self-discipline as a basis for team-work and comradeship.[44] Such an appeal may be taken as an emblem of the modern style of discipline, replacing reliance on the swift and severe punishments which could be meted out in the colonial forces.

PUBLIC COMPLAINTS AND POLICE DISCIPLINE

The management of police forces was for much of the time a matter for police administrators, having an eye on the efficiency and morale of the force itself. As this chapter has suggested, the norm against which individual police behaviour was to be measured was one set by police departments themselves. Disobedience, insubordination, drunk on duty, absent without leave—all these were offences whose rationale was primarily internal. Of course, this behaviour might be a symptom of other infractions affecting citizens and others. But the essence of the police disciplinary system was its internal orientation. Just as police training for most of the historical period we are reviewing was conducted by police for police, so too was the discipline system.

It would be inaccurate, however, to presume that thereby police were quite unaccountable for their behaviour when challenged by citizens. And it would underestimate the readiness of citizens to complain of police behaviour or take action against police for assault or other harm or neglect. The highly politicised conflict of the last twenty years over police complaints procedures suggests not so much the emergence of a new readiness of the citizenry to complain as it does the creation of new institutions to deal with them. Reading police personnel files of the nineteenth century leaves little doubt concerning the frequency of public complaint and the seriousness with which at that time it might be treated by police authorities.

In the nineteenth century, the mechanisms of public complaint were of two kinds — complaints to the commissioner, and civil actions against police for assault or other offences. On the evidence of the Queensland files in the late nineteenth and early twentieth century, commissioners regarded complaints seriously — internal investigation could be rigorous and punishment harsh, leading in many cases to dismissal as the earlier discussion has suggested. It may be that the situation varied between States. The New South Wales police, led by police from the ranks throughout this century, appears on evidence of other research to have been particularly hostile to citizen complaint. In this it was supported by key justice figures like the crown solicitor who, in 1918, warned that 'the apaches of Sydney would soon be out of control altogether if the Police were not supported in the performance of their dangerous duties'. Seggie concludes that 'complaints from the public concerning police behaviour were rarely followed through to involve any disciplinary action'.[45]

Retributive satisfaction for public complainants, however, was alternately the province of the courts. As today, the chances of successful civil action against police by citizens was probably slender, but it was far from unknown in the nineteenth century. However, these two forms of citizen complaint, administrative and legal, did not altogether exhaust the possibilities for aggrieved citizens in the twentieth century. A third arose from generalised political pressure, sometimes exercised through the media, at other times through politicians. Some commissioner investigations of police conduct began or were reluctantly prompted in this way. In a number of rare but occasionally important cases, such instances prompted formal parliamentary inquiries or even royal commissions. These were typical of an increasingly politicised environment for policing in the 1950s — the inquiries into the convictions of McDermott in New South Wales (1951–2) and Stuart in South Australia (1959), as well as that into assaults on a number of detainees at the Hobart criminal investigation branch in 1954–5.[46] The process by which incidents such as these became matters of public inquiry are well illustrated by the Studley-Ruxton case in Sydney in 1954.

In that instance, David Studley-Ruxton alleged he had been assaulted by police at Darlinghurst Police Station in central Sydney. Ruxton had been on a binge for a number of days, during which he was pursued by police looking for a stolen car. The circumstances were mundane enough. But while in custody, Studley-Ruxton sustained a number of injuries, which a subsequent inquiry by a judge concluded could not be explained, though some of them were suspected by him to have been caused by one or two of the interrogating police. The appointment of a royal commission in this case followed the vigorous advocacy of Ruxton's case by a Sydney solicitor, who managed to attract the interest of one of the city's major newspapers, the *Daily Telegraph*. The solicitor's interest appeared to arise from the fact that a number of his clients had recently complained of police assaults, with two of them unsuccessfully charging their prosecuting police — but Justice Dovey also suggested that the solicitor hoped to gain some publicity for his new criminal law practice. The newspaper's involvement was undoubtedly political, whatever the merits of the case and of the journalists' motivation for pursuing it. The publicity given to Ruxton's allegations occurred in a climate of controversy between the Labor government and the opposition over the administration of the police force. In this atmosphere, the newspaper's interest was perhaps less than disinterested — the *Daily Telegraph* not only paid for a Queen's Counsel and Junior Counsel to represent Ruxton at the inquiry, but also paid his accommodation and living expenses for its duration.[47]

As inconclusive as the Ruxton case was, its occasion highlighted some of the conditions which were needed by any complainant dissatisfied by the administrative or legal channels of appeal against police misconduct. Publicity of the kind accorded the Ruxton charges against police was grist to the mill of parliamentary oppositions and of some newspaper organisations. The politics of the media-police relations were as real in the 1950s as they were before and since. As the President of the Australian Journalists Association told a police dinner in 1957, journalists involved in a 'newspaper campaign story when the newspaper is aiming, often for some political motive, to expose some alleged weakness in police administration' might be asked by employers to write stories to justify an attack on police or government.[48] Godfrey's examples included vice stories and police assaults, two of the stock in trade of urban tabloid journalism. This evidence about the questionable interest of the media does not belie the legitimacy of claims of police assault or other misconduct. Rather it points to the complex of conditions which underlie a successful attempt to gain public exposure of such allegations. That is to say nothing of the notorious difficulty of proving to judges or magistrates or royal commissioners the truth of allegations against the police in cases involving no other witnesses—a difficulty faced in this case by Ruxton.

Transitions in complaint procedures are for the most part a phenomenon of the late twentieth century in Australia. Since about 1970 there has been a multiplication of institutions in different jurisdictions oriented to opening a new avenue of recourse for citizen complaints. These have not so much replaced the older administrative and legal remedies as supplemented them. But their political impact has marked a new stage in the contexts of policing.

The limits of judicial regulation have been recognised by the emergence in recent years of a variety of tribunals or investigative bodies which are intended to deal with public complaints. Their frequently stormy histories suggest that the supplementation of legal by administrative regulation is not a panacea. In Victoria the establishment of a Police Complaints Authority, which saw its responsibilities as extending beyond a simply reactive response to complaints, led to substantial police and union resistance ending in its eventual demise. In Queensland, political attempts to foil corruption allegations led to the establishment of a Police Complaints Tribunal: its administration was compromised by its close relation to the police department and by a number of incompetent investigations. It did not survive the scrutiny of the Fitzgerald inquiry.

More generally, the tendency in Australia has been towards administrative review by an ombudsman's office, following the model recommended by an influential report of the Australian Law Reform Commission in 1975.[49] Such administrative review has not ended the possibility of legal actions against police by aggrieved citizens, nor internal administrative action by police departments themselves. But the emergence of these bodies is nevertheless a substantial ingredient to add to the mix of forces with a substantial interest in the directions and accountability of policing in Australia. The need for external review has long been the implication of the repeated inquiries into corruption and maladministration of police in Australia, the subject of our next chapter.

CHAPTER 9

Corruption and Reform

Writing to the Colonial Secretary from his post at Port Phillip in August 1838, police magistrate William Lonsdale reported that he had:

> this day suspended Chief Constable Henry Batman from his office, for receiving a bribe of one pound from another constable to alter his tour of duty and telling me a falsehood in stating that it was such a constable's tour of duty when it was not. He confessed the offence when I brought proof before him. I have for some time suspected that he has received bribes from the inhabitants to neglect his duty, and am now quite satisfied my suspicion was correct.[1]

Corruption is one of the most intractable of historical problems to investigate in policing. Its prominence as a subject of public inquiry in recent years in Australia has highlighted the obstacles to understanding its incidence and genesis.

We should first distinguish the varieties of corruption before assessing their incidence historically. The most popular image of corruption is of police on the take, receiving money in return for taking or not taking certain actions. In reality, the varieties are many—individual police receive favours in the course of incidental actions, for example, bribes for not issuing a ticket; groups of police receiving favours in return for protection of particular interests (often illegal industries such as prostitution and gambling); groups of police conspiring to obtain benefits through participating in criminal activities, for example, in theft rackets.

These activities involve the police in direct remuneration to supplement their income. But income-generating activities are not the only forms of corruption. Indeed, in its discussion of 'Police Misconduct', the Fitzgerald report instanced first a different type of behaviour, that of distorting the forms of law through practices such as 'verballing', the manufacture of evidence to produce a conviction.[2]

While such practices may in some cases be related to the maintenance of the former types of corruption for direct personal benefit, their prevalence must also be explained in terms of the particular nature of police work and its institutional context. For Fitzgerald, police misconduct was a symptom of the power of police culture. The notorious difficulties facing investigators of police corruption complaints have been seen as symptomatic of the closed shop character of policing. Our comments on long-term changes in the organisation of policing in Australia have shown how at the level of both police administration and police unionism there have long been tendencies which contributed to the construction of a wall about police work which have contributed to the invisibility of corruption and maladministration.

In this chapter we will examine some of the historical forms of police corruption in Australia, made known principally through public inquiries. For this purpose, corruption will be understood to involve activities of police involving benefit to themselves through decisions or actions which pervert the purposes of the law. Such a definition, however, will emerge as itself problematic since 'the law' itself (if by that we mean the common and statute law as interpreted by the courts) has been one of the conditions fostering corruption. Understanding corruption historically requires therefore an analysis which takes account of the interaction of the law, police practices and the organisation of police activities. Before bringing these areas together, we need first to consider some historical problems in studying corruption in Australian policing.

TALES OF CORRUPTION

The evidence for police corruption has been scattered and never examined systematically in Australia. Assessing its reliability is inevitably a hazardous business — allegations of corruption can be made as readily against the innocent as the guilty. The necessity for corrupt dealings to be kept secret is the major barrier to historical as to legal scrutiny of its incidence. Yet the patchwork of evidence is compelling in favour of the view that corruption has been present in Australian forces since the colonial period, though more rampant in some forces or sections of them than others and at varying levels of intensity over time.

Most historical evidence of corruption must come from the many official inquiries which have addressed the issue. Some comes from the popular press, some of which thrived on stories of corruption in police and government — John Norton's *Truth* has been a fruitful source of historical speculation on the incidence of corruption for this reason.[3] A rarely used source, however, is the personnel files of the various police departments. Access restrictions in some States (for example, New South Wales and South Australia as compared to the more open archives in Queensland) make this a lesser resource than it might be. Yet the same files which can tell us about the modes of discipline and punishment in the police force also provide some evidence of the mundane instances of corrupt practices.

Partners in the Cairns police district, Kreutzmann and Perkins, were implicated by their district inspector in 1911 following their failure in an opium possession case.[4] Perkins, the senior officer, had been cabled to search a Chinese arriving at Aloomba by train — in spite of the warning, they failed to discover the opium which was later detected. The inspector suspected that both were involved in taking bribes from Chinese in the north, protecting sly-grog and opium dealing, but proceedings could not be pursued because none of the Chinese involved would give evidence. Perkins was disciplined by admonishment and transferred without promotion to a small station near Mackay, the inspector advising his new superior that he requires 'strict supervision'. His promotion was delayed another five years.

The case against Perkins was not on the basis of failed cases and poor police work alone. The inspector reported confidentially to Brisbane that Perkins' family had been living in 'great style'. Kreutzmann was similarly doubtful. He had been in the district only three years but appeared to have a considerable amount of money. He had taken holiday leave in the south of the State at a reported cost of £50 (at a time when a constable's annual pay was no more than £150). He was still believed to have £140 in the savings bank and had applied to get married. Inspector Malone considered he could not have saved this sum from his salary.

Further scrutiny of Kreutzmann's file suggests an erratic career marked by repeated questions about possible corrupt involvement. Some police files are remarkable for their lack of incident. Kreutzmann's was not one. The defaults began early in his career with a breach of leave from barracks and a charge of neglect of duty. During his time in Cairns district he arrested a licensee in a room of his own hotel in circumstances which are obscure but which it was believed would bring the police into contempt if prosecuted. In the course of a strike in 1911 he had entered a union meeting and got involved in a potentially serious altercation with unionists. During the war he was on plain clothes duty in Brisbane, but numerous incidents and allegations surfaced by 1919, leading to him being returned to uniform and transferred to Blackall in the west of the State. He had been allegedly associated with a brothel keeper and a sly-grog seller, and received commission from cab drivers for chasing up fares owing. Interviews with a prisoner and other 'reliable' police information suggested that Kreutzmann and another police officer received payment for protecting a two-up school in Brisbane city.

Kreutzmann's career, the incidents *and* the recording of them, touches most of the elements which make up the complex of corruption and the difficulties of dealing with it. The 'strict supervision', advised for Perkins, might have been all that would save Kreutzmann from his misdeeds and indiscretions, but what if the supervisor was suspect, what if he was in on 'the joke' too? Strict supervision was the mode of governing the police which made nonsense of the notion of the constable's independence and absolute discretion. But if it was the only means of stopping petty or large malfeasance, then it was also utopian — not every police officer in every situation could be watched.

At almost any point of the allegations made against Kreutzmann, the problems of evidence loomed large. Were these problems serious obstacles or convenient ones for supervisors who might be unwilling to publicise corruption and conflict within the police force? And which of the allegations might have been manufactured to serve some other end? When Kreutzmann charged a man with obscene language in 1915, the subsequent case was said to have resulted in two defence witnesses perjuring themselves in order to 'harm' Kreutzmann. But if the motive was harm, what was the reason? By this stage, Kreutzmann's career was so patchy that confidence in any action against the perjurers was weak: Kreutzmann's inspector wanted to proceed against them, but commissioner Cahill would not assent.

Behind Kreutzmann's suspect behaviour lay a network of laws and regulations and police practices which made his behaviour possible and his survival in the police force predictable. The laws affecting prostitution were highly ambiguous, guaranteeing its survival under conditions which police were primarily responsible for determining. Gambling on two-up was illegal, but other forms of gambling were legitimate — popular culture endorsed both, and police were expected to police both in the interests of good order and to protect the State revenues.

In their work, police were expected to maintain, as the rules put it, 'a friendly intercourse with all the respectable inhabitants, and a *useful knowledge* of all the bad characters'.[5] Every member of the Force, advised Cahill's manual, in terms which had been familiar in police texts since the 1830s, 'should make himself well acquainted with the persons and haunts of the criminal class (habitual criminals, thieves etc) in his district'. Optimistically, these manuals suggested that police should not hold 'aloof' from such characters 'but act kindly, endeavour to induce them to abandon crime and live honestly.'[6] This prescription for pastoral care and counselling was hardly taken seriously, given the nature of relations between police and the 'criminal class'. But these sets of rules, embodied too in later systems of training (for examples, in the guidance given in training New South Wales police in the use of informers),[7] form part of the conditions which legitimise police contact with law-breakers in ways which are not restricted to the detection and prosecution of offences.

Were Kreutzmann and Perkins alone in their enterprise, if such it was? Scarcely. The incidence of bribes sent to police by Chinese gamblers was such that a circular memorandum in 1904 directed that these bribes be paid into the police reward fund.[8] Five years later, commissioner Cahill sought advice from the Attorney-General on the mode of prosecuting bribery of a police officer. It was a Queensland criminal code offence (section 87) covered by the fact that police officers were public servants, opined the Attorney-General: all police were informed, again by way of circular memo.[9] Proving an attempted bribery offence was inherently difficult. Hence, in northern Queensland in 1911, one Sun Lee was convicted for illegal sale of liquor to an Islander. But a second charge of attempting to bribe the arresting constable failed in the district court at Cairns.[10]

If bribes were being offered, how many were being taken, rather than paid into the reward fund or made the subject of prosecution? We cannot know, but the commissioner and his inspectors knew or suspected that the problem was serious enough to warrant such general warning as well as attending to individual cases. Henry Baulch's short career of three years in the Queensland police ended with his dismissal in January 1904 after being convicted at Chillagoe for taking 'hush money' to stop a prosecution for gambling. The original charge had been 'extortion', suggesting that Baulch was perhaps rather more than a passive recipient of a bribe.[11]

Estimating the extent of this level of police corruption has always been difficult. Occasional public inquiries in other States confirmed the significance if not the actual incidence of corrupt dealings in the twentieth century. A striking example was offered in the course of the Victorian royal commission into off-the-course betting in 1958. Inspector Healey, chief of the gaming squad, testified that illegal bookmaking had survived there because 60 per cent of the gaming enforcement police were corrupt. The systematic nature of this corruption was notable. In reviewing police files on gaming cases, Healey had discovered that no people were ever arrested, that prosecutions were of people with fictitious names and addresses, and that prosecution briefs in gaming cases were prepared in advance of any police action, leaving the police to fill in only the desired names of defendants and other variable details. This was the practice in a police force which McCoy argues was cleaner than that of New South Wales, owing to its systematic cleansing by repeated royal commissions from the 1880s on.[12]

The organised character of police corruption on this scale was not unique. Similar evidence exists for New South Wales policing of starting-price betting from the 1930s on. At mid-century the testimonials for senior licensing squad police, attended by large numbers of bookmakers and hoteliers, attracted the critical scrutiny of a New South Wales royal commission into the sly-grog trade in 1950. In Western Australia, the evidence in the 1930s and after suggests an organised system of public deception as police sought to maintain the pretence of legal prohibition of street betting. In spite of widespread public complaints about the extent of corruption enabling the maintenance of this farcical situation, neither of the State's major inquiries into starting-price betting (in 1948 and 1959) subjected police behaviour to scrutiny.[13]

It is, however, perilously difficult to estimate the likelihood of the existence and survival of historical evidence about corruption in such circumstances. Public inquiries themselves may be diverted or subverted from discovering evidence. The conditions for establishing an inquiry which is capable of breaching the usual wall of silence around police departments are rarely present. When they do exist, the results can reveal the extraordinarily organised nature of police corruption in the regulation of industries such as prostitution and gambling. Evidence before the Fitzgerald commission demonstrated the perversion of the criminal justice process by police protecting organised prostitution and starting-price betting, as well as other forms of gambling. In that case, police developed over a number of years a practice of charging prostitutes under the vagrancy Act on a pre-arranged basis. The fines would be small and the frequency of charging not such as to inhibit continuing work in the sex industry. Police were able to show that they were continually active in the policing of the industry—but the prosecution figures were to all intents and purposes a fiction:

> members of the Licensing Branch toured Brisbane's night life, socialising and drinking in the brothels, nightclubs and gaming establishments which were supposedly so difficult to enter, noting and participating in the various activities which they observed, charging prostitutes and sometimes receptionists (usually with their co-operation) on a rotational basis, occasionally prosecuting prostitutes from escort agencies or their drivers and underlings engaged in unlicensed sales of liquor...More energetic treatment was reserved for those prostitutes and other offenders who were out of favour with individuals or groups within the Licensing

Branch, and those who were not paying protection and whose protection was unwelcome to those who were.[14]

In these cases police work had moved from the routine regulation of illicit trades to an active role in their modes of organisation. The long-term seriousness of this for the legitimacy of policing could not be underestimated. Fitzgerald's response was equal to the occasion, demanding nothing less than a wholesale reconstruction of the police force. But the report of this commission went beyond the usual limits of such inquiries, to ask whether other adjustments in the political, legal and administrative cultures of the State also needed fundamental reform.

Such an outcome points to the need to understand the relationship between police corruption and its context. That context includes not only the forms of law but also the changing social and economic relations of Australia and its constituent regions.

CONDITIONS FOR CORRUPTION

Bad laws help sustain corruption, though they may not directly foster it. The persistence of some legislative frameworks deriving from the extraordinary growth of statute law in the nineteenth century and after has played a powerful role. Classically, those areas most associated with the incidence of corruption by way of police protection — prostitution, gambling and liquor trading — had been made the subject of substantial government intervention in the late nineteenth century. More recently, the twentieth-century regulation and prohibition of drug consumption has produced a context facilitating the corruption of police. The popular press as well as popular and academic histories tend to characterise these interventions as an instance of Australian 'wowserism'. In truth, the nature of these legal interventions owe as much to the diversity of governmental concerns in the nineteenth and early twentieth centuries as to cultural determinism. Wowserism as a cultural phenomenon was articulated through the debates around the nature of these legal remedies for what were widely seen as social questions.

These social questions occasioned great conflict reflected in legislative outcomes. The specific form of the law affecting prostitution needs to be understood as a conjunction of a number of different factors, including the nineteenth-century move towards the regulation of health, the critique of prostitution by social reformers, especially feminist and temperance groups, the interests and motives of police and, last but not least, the influence of masculine prerogatives. Moreover these factors were inflected differently in various jurisdictions. In a society as apparently homogenous as Australia, regional/State differences were capable of producing quite different forms of legal regulation of prostitution. In Queensland, one of only two colonies which introduced contagious diseases legislation, the patterns of police oversight of prostitutes were early set by the discretion afforded by health regulation. In New South Wales and Victoria, much more affected by the political conflict around social purity, the legal situation was dominated by the public order question. Vagrancy law and its offshoots proved powerful tools in the police regulation of the industry and opened the way to extensive involvement in protection.[15]

As police often lamented, the act of prostitution was not in itself an offence in English law. That is, the individual sale of sexual services by any person, female or male, was a matter of indifference to the law. The law's boundary-setting of the domain of privacy precluded legal scrutiny of the circumstances of such a trade. Yet the population of those who provided these services became an important target of policing throughout the nineteenth century. By the beginning of this century the organisation of prostitution was not imaginable without the guiding or constraining hand of police. The long-term consequences of this relationship were deleterious to the public reputation and efficiency of the police force. In Queensland, the Fitzgerald inquiry uncovered arrangements amounting to the licensing of particular prostitution operations, arrangements which have a long, if difficult to chart, history.

We have noted earlier some of the factors which contributed to the preoccupation of police with the maintenance of public order. The legal framework which mandated police peace-keeping and patrolling activities also delivered to them substantial powers of surveillance and arrest of a wide range of street people in the early nineteenth century. Central to the police power on the streets was the re-organisation of vagrancy law in England subsequently extended to the Australian colonies. The legislation was unusual in policing statutes in being directed not at acts or behaviours but at statuses of people under police observation. Hence, while the act of prostitution was not an offence, the fact of being an idle and disorderly prostitute, one who walked the streets or frequented other public places, was a justification for arrest. These powers were predicated on a demand for urban order, clearing the streets of the idle and disruptive.

Nineteenth-century statutory reform however, developed more extensive and ambitious modes of control. The prime example affecting prostitution in mid-century was the English Contagious Diseases Acts (1864, 1866 and

1869). Forged in the anxiety of the Crimean War, the Act had the putative objective of maintaining imperial strength through guaranteeing armed forces access to prostitutes free of venereal disease. The Act enabled police to stop and question women in proclaimed areas suspected of being prostitutes. The burgeoning scope of government interventions in the public health domain gave the legislation its rationale.[16]

In Australia, the British navy's presence encouraged the enactment of similar legislation in Queensland and Tasmania. In other colonies, and eventually in these, opposition to the legislation limited its impact. But even after Queensland effectively nullified the Act in 1911, similar police powers continued to provide police with the duty of surveying the work of prostitutes. Health legislation enabled police to direct prostitutes to the venereal diseases clinic, while other public order legislation gave them power to harass prostitutes. In New South Wales, amendments to the Police Offences Act in 1908 provided substantial power to police to determine the future shape of the prostitution industry. In Western Australia, the choice of police was control and regulation of the industry rather than its eradication. From one point of view, that is explaining how prostitution persisted in the face of such constant surveillance, it matters little whether this police involvement connoted corruption or not. Rather, such legislation and its policing, it has been persuasively argued, set the industrial conditions under which the work of prostitution would be carried out in Australia.[17]

Another condition affecting the regulation of prostitution was the more pervasive cultural attitude to sexual relations. In this society there was not a consensus about sexuality, but rather a deeply divided one. In what has been characterised as the 'double standard', men were considered to have rightful access to the sexual services of prostitutes in order, as William Acton said, to protect the virtue of the women of the middle classes. Propositions of the innate sexual drives of males requiring an outlet for their satisfaction drew on medical authority to legitimate the social role of prostitution. This was endorsement at an ideological level of a cultural attitude and practice of much longer standing. Hence, the repeated retort of (always male) politicians that prostitution was the world's oldest profession or that young men could not be prevented from sowing their wild oats.[18]

These attitudes did not stand alone in the field of debate over sexuality and the appropriate role of government and police. Drawing on the puritanism of the Judeo-Christian tradition in its attitude to sexuality outside marriage, the social purity movement of nineteenth-century evangelicals and others saw prostitution as the 'social evil'—prostitutes had to be saved and their male customers reformed to a stricter code of moral conduct, centred on the family. From a different perspective, first wave feminists went beyond social purity to attack prostitution as a practice which degraded women and, for some at least, epitomised the danger of 'the animal in man'.[19] The political strength of this alliance, which touched other social issues as well, especially the liquor problem, was insufficient to alter the direction of policing policy. Rather it provided a politically cogent reason for reinforcing conventional regulatory controls with a high level of discretion effectively residing in police.

This mix of concerns and predispositions on the question of prostitution was shared to a good extent by police. But centrally involved as they were in the very process of surveillance, they had interests of their own. These interests have now been shown conclusively through the Fitzgerald inquiry to extend to an intimate involvement in the very organisation of prostitution, through arranged prosecutions and sexual services in return for protection. The masculinity of the police, a factor which is important in understanding the forms of organisation of policing, is in this case central to the definition of police interests. Hence the retort of South Australian police commissioner Maddely in 1904 that a local social purity leader represented a 'section who would do away altogether with brothels and prostitutes': such a view endorsed the maintenance of prostitution as part of the social order.[20] Thus a pertinent issue here is the role of police departments as agencies which are responsible not just for enforcing the law, but which came to play an active role in describing its contours.

As we have argued earlier, the police had already in Australia been political actors by virtue of their initiatives in policy matters in areas such as Aboriginal policy and management of labour disputes. In defining what the proper role of government should be in response to prostitution, police at the turn of the century also contributed very significantly to ensuring its continuity as work which should be closely observed and dependent on police regulation. The move towards summary jurisdiction for a range of offences connected with prostitution (including soliciting, brothel keeping and pimping) was enthusiastically embraced by police in New South Wales who thenceforth had extensive powers to regulate the operators.[21] Regulation did not *necessarily* entail corruption, but the forms of regulation which the law laid out made it possible.

Gambling and liquor legislation has also varied between the States. Here the ground of state interest was different. There was in fact not one but two principal sources of state interest in each area — revenue collection on the one hand, and social regulation of the conditions of consumption or use on the other. Unlike prostitution, where the forms of state legitimation were always somewhat circuitous and the financial returns to the state negligible if not negative, by the early twentieth century governments were intimately involved in the generation of state revenues through gambling and liquor taxes. The legalisation of the totalisator at racing clubs was accompanied by a state tax and decisions made thereafter about the forms and legitimacy of betting on racing on or off the course would always be accompanied by considerations of the impact of any measure on the state revenue. The founding of Tatt's lotto and its phenomenal commercial success led eventually to the initiation of state-run lotteries, Queensland's Golden Casket being a notable forerunner in the 1920s. In the Queensland case, what had begun as a war-time fund-raiser was institutionalised after the war as a means of funding public hospital and health programmes. As revenue drained into neighbouring States which had lotteries, other States were moved to adopt the winning formula. Calculations of the social policy benefits which the new source of revenue made possible were significant in the decisions legitimising gambling in the inter-war period.[22]

The taxes raised by liquor were an equally important rationale for government legitimation of an industry which provided a good part of police work through the adverse effects of consumption of its output. Equally, the potential profits for those who could evade the government revenue or controls on the hours and points of sale made the 'sly grog' trade a highly attractive venture. A substantial police effort developed over many decades to limit this evasion of the taxing state.[23] Police involvement in these duties had to be hedged with various cautions—the employment of informers was essential to police success but potentially corrupting in itself. It was unpopular work in any case, potentially contaminating police reputation. When the Queensland Cabinet decided in 1910 that sly-grog work should be brought under the control of the police, the commissioner was careful to instruct his officers that it should be kept entirely separate from ordinary police work.[24] In Otago, New Zealand, the work had been regarded as so unpopular in the 1860s that it was shifted from the responsibility of the police to that of the inspector of distilleries.[25]

Enhancement of the revenue, however, had to proceed in some tension with the countervailing pressures of powerful political opposition to gambling and liquor. The impact of these forces was varied although nowhere in Australia was there a State-wide prohibition on gambling or liquor. But the social reform campaigns led (in the case of liquor) at least to restrictions on opening hours and days of sale, and even to dry areas through local option in others. In gambling, despite the interest in Western Australia and South Australia in the possibility of off-course legal betting, the political costs of legalisation could not be broached by governments in the larger States.[26]

In any of these areas, police were often left with the responsibility for regulating practices which were in a limbo of legality. In Western Australia, a 1937 inquiry into charges of political corruption against the Premier, J. C. Willcock, absolved him but uncovered a legal muddle in gambling regulation which has been typical of recurrent problems in policing so-called 'victimless' offences.

Under the criminal code, gambling in its various forms was forbidden in Western Australia. Yet Labor colonial secretary, J. M. Drew, instructed the commissioner of police in 1915:

> With reference to art unions, and other games of chance, these, although illegal, as you are aware, are being held in aid of charitable, patriotic and other worthy objects, with the approval and support of the public and even some of the most respectable persons in the community. If we enforce the strict letter of the law, we should suppress all these devices for raising money. To do that would mean the closing up of many channels of benevolence and departing from the rule followed by all previous Governments. I think, however, this movement should be regulated, and I feel you will be doing all that is required if you take no action except in cases in which the object, or part of the object, is individual gain or profit, and in which the funds are not controlled by responsible persons who may be reasonably relied upon to see that the money raised goes to the benefit of the object. In applying this test common-sense must be used in each case.[27]

The royal commissioner concluded that Drew had left a wide discretion to the police commissioner to allow illegal games as long as there was 'no individual gain, if he were of the opinion that the funds were controlled by responsible persons'. Increasing gambling during and after the war, in the context of this government policy led to the commissioner requesting in 1920 a further clarification of the need to regulate 'spinning jennies' and other gaming instruments. Cabinet subsequently approved the suppression of the latter, but by default left lotteries and sweeps alone. Four years later, a commissioner sought a further statement of government policy after being faced with the decision of whether to prosecute some gamblers when others had been left alone:

> I submit the whole question of gambling should be considered by Parliament, for if the majority of people desire to gamble it would be much better to regulate same by act of Parliament than to carry on as we are going, for there can be no doubt *that successive Governments have permitted the gaming laws to become a dead letter.*[28]

The government subsequently reverted to the policy established in 1915, again allowing spinning jennies, but without amending the criminal code prohibition on gambling. Under such conditions it is not difficult to see how readily suspicions of favourable treatment and corruption, both among police and politicians, could be aroused. It was all too possible for police on the ground exercising the maximum discretion available to them to become effectively judge and jury of decisions about permissible illegal activity, with or without financial or other benefit to themselves.

The confluence of such forces and interests constituted the politico-legal conditions which nurtured corruption. The ambiguity of the law and of government policy in effect created a large area of discretionary enforcement for police. Personal dispositions, formed in their own class and sex backgrounds, perhaps made many police little sympathetic to the objectives of laws which sought to prohibit some forms of vice while leaving others untouched. What made gambling on the racecourse a sporting activity but on the street vicious? If the organisation of prostitution was illegal, why was the act not an offence?

Law was only one of the means of sustaining corruption. The law regulated certain types of economy or industry—the scale and type varying in locale and over time. Hence, the most detailed historical examination of organised crime in Australia has argued that changes in the urban political economies of Sydney and Melbourne can tell us much about the phenomenon of corruption. The greater vulnerability of Sydney as an *entrepôt* compared to the longer-term stability of Melbourne as a centre of manufacturing may have influenced the degree of corruption in the former. But the creation too of new markets for illegal products of high demand, such as occurred in the post-Vietnam era in the expansion of the drug trade, points to the necessity of understanding the formation of corruption in a particular socio-economic as well as legal context.[29]

Beside law and the economic organisation of illegalised industries, we need to take account finally of the phenomenon of police collective behaviour. The idea that there is a 'cop culture' which sustains corrupt practices was given its most extensive Australian airing in the Fitzgerald inquiry in Queensland. However, it is scarcely a recent phenomenon. Our earlier examination of some of the historical features of police organisation suggest the foundations for an idea of the unique nature of police work.

This extended from the idea that police were not simply public servants, that they could not be subject to the normal political controls of other public servants, to the impact of police unions in contributing to a defensive and collectivist organisational posture. Further, in the very work practices which characterise policing—the partnership system in patrol work, the team identity of some units, the impact of the uniform in creating a distinctive identity — the police lived in an environment which limited external scrutiny of their actions.

Within the police environment it has been argued that there is a particularly powerful set of informal rules which operate beside or outside of the formal departmental rules. Breaching the informal rules, for example, through informing on other officers, is notoriously regarded as a reason for ostracism. Policing is not the only environment in which such rules or cultures operate, as workers in other collective enterprises, like universities or hospitals, know.

Nonetheless the contribution of this work culture to the historical development of corruption in police forces is notable. In particular, we may note the way in which such a work culture, with its sanctions against 'tale-tellers', made possible the systemic corruption by which illegalised industries were able to continue by way of arranged protection payments to high-ranking police. It was such systemic corruption which made police corruption a political *cause célèbre* at periodic intervals in the century from the 1880s.

INQUIRY AND REFORM

The moment at which rumours of police corruption grew into a clamour demanding exposure and redress has been a recurring motif in Australian political history for a hundred years or more. But what have the resulting public inquiries told us about police, policing and the genesis of corruption? What remedies have they sought or recommended? What impact have these periodic exposures of this aspect of policing had on the subsequent organisation of policing? Our concern here is less with the political impact of such inquiries than with what they can tell us about the modes of governing the police.

The impact of corruption scandals on the organisation of policing in Australia has for the most part been minimal. Police departments have been resilient in the face of public notoriety. The substantial changes in policing over time are much more the product of shifting social demands and political requirements. That is not to say that reorganisation of internal police affairs has not been a consequence of particular inquiries. But seeking redress for wrongs committed has been difficult. Recent experience in some States has illustrated just how deeply resistant police can be to demands for the application of the rule of law to their own behaviour.

A number of options have historically been considered and pursued in addressing the problems of police corruption and misconduct. They include changes to the laws under which police operate; specific treatment of the particular instances of corruption through the prosecution of offences allegedly committed by police; the internal reorganisation of police units and functions; and a more wholesale addressing of the organisation of police administration affecting issues as diverse as relations with government, recruitment and training, police discipline and law reform.

The prospects of any of these particular paths succeeding in its objectives is limited by the specific historical circumstances in which the corruption scandal has emerged. A calculation of what success means is in any case riddled with problems. Does the subsequent silence on issues of corruption indicate that the original problem has disappeared, or that it has merely become invisible, only to re-emerge in the future when the new arrangements, dependent as they are on a fragile melding of different interests, start to crumble? The historical analysis of this difficult issue remains to be undertaken in Australia. What we do have is evidence of the rediscovery in every generation of the phenomenon of police corruption.

Thus, the most thorough inquiry into nineteenth-century policing in Australia, that of the Longmore commission in Victoria, appears to have had limited consequence in terms of addressing those factors which had sustained corruption and inefficiency. Just two decades later, serious allegations regarding corruption in the same police force led to another substantial but even less consequential royal commission. Inter-war suspicions of corruption and misconduct on the part of police from the chief commissioner down again provoked official inquiries, addressing both specific charges and general organisation and practice. In the post-war period, allegations regarding corruption involving gambling in the 1950s and then abortion in the 1960s and 1970s again called into question the standards of control of police behaviour in Victoria. The serious opposition encountered by authorities seeking to discipline or prosecute police over alleged offences, in the wake of the Beach inquiry, has already been referred to.

This story might be repeated for other States, though the incidence of public inquiries into allegations of police misconduct or corruption has also varied from State to State. The difficulties faced by investigative authorities in New South Wales in the inter-war period were perhaps symptomatic of the more general problem posed by such allegations. For the second half of the 1930s Mr Justice Markell was occupied in a succession of inquiries into alleged police corruption and associated issues in connection with starting price betting in that State. Ultimately the inquiries proved fruitless in terms of addressing the long-term questions raised by the regulation of gambling and the institutional means of that regulation. Other inter-war inquiries in Queensland and South Australia similarly sought to address gambling and its regulatory problems, including corruption, but solutions adopted failed to suppress illegal gambling.[30]

The reasons for failure to address some of the sources of police conduct have varied. In cases where police themselves have recommended a significant change in laws to facilitate prosecution or else obviate it through redefining the categories of illegality, their opinion has sometimes counted for little. Commissioner Carroll in Queensland was in a minority in 1936 in recommending recognition of off-course bookmaking,[31] the government adopting the majority recommendations of a royal commission for stricter though selective prohibition. During the hearings of the Markell inquiries in New South Wales, commissioner MacKay indicated to his officers that he was less than happy with the unpalatable business of policing unpopular starting-price laws. Ambiguity at the level of police leadership can hardly have encouraged strict observance of the law's requirements by the constable on the street.

The perpetuation of bad laws by governments which found the prospect of changing them too difficult or too perilous has probably played as large a part in the sustenance of police corruption as any other factor. But official inquiries which have paid close attention to the organisation of policing itself have more recently sought to address the relationship between government policy, legal regulation and the organisation of policing as ways of combating the seemingly perennial issue of corruption and misconduct. Hence, as discussed in earlier chapters, it may be that the reorganisation of policing in Australia prompted in the last decade by major inquiries in New South Wales, Victoria, Queensland and Western Australia as well as at national level in respect of ASIO, will produce longer-term effects. In the meantime, the evidence of intransigence in the face of demands for change also suggests caution against optimism in such endeavours.

Conclusion:
Change or Continuity?

As I write, ten police from a Victorian armed robbery squad have been charged with murder over the shooting of two men in notorious incidents of 1989. At the same time, it is reported that a group of Hobart police have cheered as two of their colleagues have entered court to face charges over an alleged assault by a group of police on a handicapped man in a city street in broad daylight.[1] In Western Australia earlier in 1993 police authority attempts to dismiss an officer over an assault on a juvenile in custody have been overturned on appeal.[2] The recurrence of ugly and dangerous incidents involving police and citizens in a variety of circumstances has stirred again the endless debate over the functions and costs of modern policing.

This book has outlined some features of the history of policing in Australia which help to understand present conflicts which seem to represent a crisis in policing. For some decades it has been known that public respect and esteem for police has been low in Australia. The last two decades have also seen an unprecedented critical scrutiny of police practices and priorities. In some States, policing has been characterised over a long period of time by endless crises over leadership, conflict-ridden relations with government, and contentious relations with particular populations.

We need to be cautious, however, in considering the present as better or worse than the past on some imaginary scale of consent and dissent over policing. The same caveats which are entered in any discussion of a general phenomenon established on the basis of particular cases need to be entered here. The historian's message is in part that the past is easily forgotten and must be continually reconstructed if we are to forego the illusion that the present is very much worse or better than the past.

For this reason, the task of this book has been to show how policing may be seen as a historically-formed practice of government in a modern society. Recognising the close relationship between the police and government implies a number of important things about policing. The relation I discuss is not limited to the uses which particular governments make of police for the narrow end of asserting control over troublesome individuals, groups or populations. That use is part of the very rationale for the existence of police in the modern state. Its regulation by other constraints (legal, electoral, public opinion) is an important test of standards of justice and equality which apply in a particular society.

Recognising the historical dimension to policing entails both possibilities and constraints in future directions. There is much talk today about 'community policing'. It will be evident from the historical structure of Australian policing that community policing must necessarily be a somewhat different animal to the one which might grow in some other jurisdictions. Central control makes possible the extension of certain standards of practice and procedure in policing across a divergent number of circumstances in which police find themselves — procedure in relation to arrest and detention should in general be the same in Bourke as in Sydney. The responsiveness of police to community needs, however, requires recognition of very different social contexts between urban and rural centres. Sensitivity and judgment recognising local difference should be within the capacity of well-trained police and a well-managed centralised force. But beyond the delivery of local services by police on the street, police departments have to take account of needs and demands which arise from the State-wide nature of their jurisdictions. In policing, as in many other government functions in Australia, attempts to provide equitable service (equity on dimensions of urban/rural; rich/poor; Aboriginal/non-Aboriginal; male/female; young/old) face the difficulty of adjusting resources to fit the realities of dispersed and mobile populations which constantly change the meaning of 'community'. Whatever the strategy of policing pursued, the structural realities are those of the centralised bureaucratic control of personnel and resources. Policing has never been a 'community' resource in Australia, and is unlikely to be given the realities of governmental jurisdiction in this country.

If these comments point to constraint, other historical realities point to the possibilities for improved policing. Divided jurisdictions can be forces for highly differentiated policing practice. National coordination makes possible a more uniform address to contemporary problems. For most of the century, the State police commissioners have attempted to address the disadvantage of divided jurisdiction through exchanging information and personnel. The requirement that they address issues of potentially international notice, such as the police treatment of Aborigines, as a result of the Royal Commission into Aboriginal Deaths in Custody, will require the individual States to address new norms which are being established through national agreement. An important outcome of the last three decades of increasing criminological attention to policing in Australia is a growing consciousness of State differences, with an increasing expectation that differences which are disadvantageous to particular populations will be addressed through reform of policing practice.

The potential to deliver improvements in policing is, however, limited by the reality of the profound institutional conservatism of police forces. This conservatism is not limited to police, but when it results in the continuation of harmful policing its costs can be especially severe to individuals and groups who are the subject of unwarranted procedures. Police departments in Australia, by virtue of their jurisdictions, tend to be large and complex organisations. Changing them has been difficult. Police unions, with almost comprehensive coverage of their personnel, tend to be powerful and noisy advocates of sometimes very selective approaches to policing. Both department and union can be a fruitful source of media controversy for narrow political ends. Addressing change in Australian policing requires recognition of these realities.

The dominant focus of this book and of police research generally on the public police forces should not distract attention from the necessity of exploring alternative ways of policing. As the discussion of private policing in chapter 3 made clear, private policing has been a historical reality, though receiving limited attention in Australia as overseas. The temptation to see its current significance only in terms of a political agenda of 'privatisation' of public functions should be avoided. As with public policing, the questions for the future of private policing concern processes of monitoring and accountability of police actions and decisions. If there has been any achievement of the development of the rule of law as a means of governing in the modern, liberal state it has been the requirement (however weak this might prove to be in actual practice) that police and other state agents be answerable for their actions, that these not be simply a matter of whim. The problem with private policing is less the issue of profit or the devolution of governmental responsibilities, but the extent to which powers and duties of private police conform to fundamental values of justice and equality. The histories of policing in Australia show that in the process of seeking to guarantee order, both private and public police have been capable of performing poorly judged against those values. Making them central values in policing practice will continue to be the task of the future.

Endnotes

Introduction

1 D. Chappell and P. Wilson(eds), *Australian Policing: Contemporary Issues*, Butterworths, Sydney, 1989; P. Moir and H. Eijkman (eds) *Policing Australia: Old Issues New Perspectives*, Macmillan, Melbourne, 1992. The latter collection includes a couple of essays (Moore on Police Productivity and Hazelhurst on Aborigines and Police) which are historically sensitive.

2 J. Sutton, 'Women in the Job', in *Policing Australia*, Moir and Eijkman (eds), pp. 67–8.

3 See below chapter 5 on history of women police; also J. Allen, 'Policing since 1880: some questions of sex', in M. Finnane (ed.), *Policing in Australia Historical Perspectives*, NSW University Press, Kensington, 1987, pp. 212–213 and R. Haldane, *The People's Force: A History of the Victoria Police*, Melbourne University Press, Carlton, 1986, p. 162.

4 *Sydney Morning Herald*, 29 Dec. 1992, p. 3.

5 See *Police Regulation (Amendment) Act* 1934 and New South Wales *Parliamentary Debates*, 27 Sep. 1933, p. 705 for Lang's characteristically blunt comments on the government's motives; on Queensland and Western Australia see below chapter 2; on ASIO and Menzies see F. Cain, 'ASIO and the Australian Labour Movement — An Historical Perspective', *Labour History*, 58, 1990, p. 10.

1   A 'New Police' in Australia

1 R. Whitrod, 'Thoughts on the introduction of a police administrative grade', *Public Administration Australia*, 19, 1960, p. 122.

2 D. Bayley, *Patterns of Policing: A Comparative International Analysis*, Rutgers University Press, New Brunswick, NJ, paperback, 1990, pp. 17–18.

3   For a recent overview of the comparative organisation of police forces in the English-speaking countries see D. H. Bayley, 'Comparative Organization of the Police in English-speaking Countries', in *Modern Policing*, M. Tonry and N. Morris (eds), Chicago and London: The University of Chicago Press, 1992.

4   For critical reviews of the history of policing see especially R. Reiner, *The Politics of the Police*, Wheatsheaf Books, Sussex, 1985; C. Emsley, *The English Police: A Political and Social History*, Harvester Wheatsheaf, Hemel Hempstead, 1991; and, for Australia, M. Sturma, 'Policing the Criminal Frontier in Mid-nineteenth century Australia, Britain and America' in *Policing in Australia: Historical Perspectives*, M. Finnane (ed.), NSW University Press, Kensington, 1987; M. Finnane and S. Garton, 'The work of policing: social relations and the criminal justice system in Queensland, Part 1', *Labour History*, 62, 1992, pp. 52–70 and D. Moore, 'Origins of the Police Mandate: The Australian Case Reconsidered', *Police Studies*, 14, 1991, pp. 107–120

5   G. M. O'Brien, *The Australian Police Forces*, Oxford University Press, Melbourne, 1960, p. 2.

6   R. Haldane, *The People's Force: A History of the Victoria Police*, Melbourne University Press, Carlton, 1986.

7   V. Doherty, 'Western Australia', in *Police Source Book 2*, B. Swanton, et al (eds), Australian Institute of Criminology, Canberra, 1985, p. 428.

8   See H. McQueen, *A New Britannia*, Penguin, Ringwood, 1970; R. W. Connell and T. H. Irving, *Class Structure in Australian History: Documents, Narrative and Argument*, Longman Cheshire, Melbourne, 1980; A. Moore, 'Policing enemies of the state: the New South Wales police and the New Guard, 1931–32', in *Policing in Australia*, M. Finnane (ed.).

9   On the police in early New South Wales, see D. Neal, *The Rule of Law in a Penal Colony*, Cambridge University Press, Melbourne, 1991, ch. 6; H. King, 'Some aspects of police administration in New South Wales 1825–1851', *Journal of the Royal Australian Historical Society*, 42, 5, 1956, pp. 205–230.

10 S. H. Palmer, *Police and Protest in England and Ireland 1780–1850*, Cambridge University Press, Cambridge, 1988; D. Philips, ' "A New Engine of Power and Authority": The Institutionalization of Law-Enforcement in England, 1780–1830' in *Crime and the Law: The Social History of Crime in Western Europe Since 1500*, V. A. C. Gatrell, B. Lenman, and G. Parker (eds), Europa Publications, London, 1980; and for a sceptical view of the 'influential' Irish model, see R. Hawkins, 'The 'Irish model' and the empire: a case for reassessment', in *Policing the empire: Government, authority and control, 1830–1940*, D. M. Anderson and D. Killingray (eds), Manchester University Press, Manchester, 1991.

11 See Emsley, *English Police*, pp. 15–40; Philips, 'A New Engine' in *Crime and the Law*, Gatrell et al (eds).

12 See e.g. P. Pasquino, 'Theatricum Politicum: the Genealogy of Capital – Police and the State of Prosperity', in *The Foucault Effect: Studies in Governmentality*, G. Burchell, C. Gordon and P. Miller (eds), The University of Chicago Press, Chicago, 1991.

13 See O. MacDonagh, *Early Victorian Government*, Weidenfeld and Nicholson, London, 1977, p. 167ff; Philips, 'A new engine...' in *Crime and the Law*, Gatrell et al (eds).

14 For the implications of the broader notion of police see e.g. Emsley, *English Police*, introduction; L. Johnston, *The rebirth of private policing*, Routledge, London, 1992, pp. 4–6; E. Monkonnen, 'History of urban police', in *Modern Policing*, M. Tonry and N. Morris (eds), The University of Chicago Press, Chicago and London, 1992.

15 W. L. Burn, cited in O. MacDonagh, *Ireland: the Union and its Aftermath*, George Allen and Unwin, London, 1977, p. 34; see also MacDonagh, *Early Victorian Government*, ch. 10.

16 Cf Palmer, *Police and protest*; Hawkins, 'The "Irish model"' in *Policing the empire*, Anderson and Killingray (eds); R. Storch, 'The Plague of the Blue Locusts: Police Reform and Popular Resistance in Northern England, 1840–1857', *International Review of Social History*, 20, 1975, pp. 61–90; R. Storch 'The Policeman as Domestic Missionary: Urban Discipline and Popular Culture in Northern England, 1850–1880', *Journal of Social History*, 9, 1976, pp. 481–509; W. G. Carson, 'Policing the Periphery, 1798–1900', *Australian and New Zealand Journal of Criminology*, 17, 4, 1984, pp. 207–232.

17 Report of the Board of Inquiry, 26 July, 1856, *NSW Legislative Assembly Votes and Proceedings*, 1856–7, vol. 1, pp. 1149–50.

18 Ibid., p. 1149.

19 R. Clyne, *Colonial Blue: A History of the South Australian Police Force 1836–1916*, Wakefield Press, Netley, 1987, pp. 7–8.

20 G. Reid, *A Picnic with the Natives: Aboriginal–European Relations in the Northern Territory to 1910*, Melbourne University Press, Melbourne, 1990, ch. 6.

21 O'Brien, *Australian Police Forces*, pp. 42–3, for Western Australia; R. Wettenhall, 'Government and the Police', *Current Affairs Bulletin*, 53, 10, 1977, p. 22.

22 H. Golder, *High and Responsible Office: A History of the NSW Magistracy*, Oxford University Press, Melbourne, 1991.

23 D. Palmer, 'The making of the Victorian colonial police: from colonisation to the new police', MA (Criminological Studies) thesis, La Trobe University, 1990, p. 74 (16 Vic no. 24, s.xii).

24 Rules for the general government and discipline of members of the police force of Queensland, 1869, Queensland Legislative Council, *Papers*, 1869; W. R. Johnston, *The Long Blue Line: A History of the Queensland Police*, Boolarong Press, Brisbane, 1992, pp. 12–15.

25 Palmer, 'Making of the Victorian colonial police', pp. 96–100.

26 Clyne, *Colonial Blue*, p. 148.

27 The provision was eventually repealed by the *Police Act Amendment Act* (South Australia) 1938, s.3, South Australia Report of the Commissioner of Police, 1935, p. 33 *Proceedings of the Parliament of South Australia, 1935*, vol. 2, for amounts recuperated from corporations in the 1930s.

28 Wettenhall, 'Government and the Police', p. 22; H. Reynolds, 'That Hated Stain: the aftermath of transportation in Tasmania', *Historical Studies*, 53, 1969, pp. 19–31.

29 State of the Public Service, Report of the Commission, p. 7, Tasmania *Parliamentary Papers* (hereafter *PP*) 1857 and Wettenhall, 'Government and the Police', p. 22.

30 R. Wettenhall, *A guide to Tasmanian government administration*, Platypus Publications, Hobart, 1968, pp. 251–2; O'Brien, *Australian Police Forces*, pp. 32–37; Select Committee on Centralisation of Police, 1886, Tasmania *PP*.

31 Royal Commission on the Organisation and Administration of the Police Force, p. 2, Tasmania *PP*, 1906.

32 King, 'Some aspects of police administration', p. 214; in Victoria on the eve of consolidation in 1853, there were seven autonomous forces: Haldane, *People's Force*, pp. 27–8.

33 King, 'Some aspects', p. 216.

34 Ibid.

35 Board of Inquiry, 1856, p. 1151 (see above, note 16).

36 See NSW Public Service List, NSW *PP*, 1905.

37 See J. Allen, *Sex and Secrets: Crimes involving Australian Women*, Oxford University Press, Melbourne, 1990.

38 Haldane, *People's Force*, pp. 234–5.

39 Board of Inquiry into Police Conditions, p. 5, Tasmania *PP*, vol. 141, 1949.

40 See, e.g. M. Sturma, *Vice in a vicious society*, UQP, St Lucia, 1983; Neal, *Rule of Law*; R. Walker, 'Bushranging in Fact and Legend', *Historical Studies*, 11, 1964, pp. 206–221; Golder, *High and Responsible Office*; A. Davidson, *The Invisible State*, Cambridge University Press, Melbourne, 1990, pp. 110–118; P. J. Byrne, *Criminal law and colonial subject*, Cambridge University Press, 1993.

41 G. Friesen, *The Canadian Prairies*, University of Toronto Press, Toronto, 1984, p. 163.

42 See, on Canada, Friesen, *Canadian Prairies*; on New Zealand, R. Hill, *Policing the Colonial Frontier: The Theory and Practice of Coercive Social and Racial Control in New Zealand, 1767–1867*, Govt Printer, Wellington, 1984; on South Australia, Clyne, *Colonial Blue*; on colonial policing generally, see M. Brogden, 'An Act to Colonise the Internal Lands of the Island: Empire and the Origins of the Professional Police',

International Journal of the Sociology of Law, 15, 1987, pp. 179–208 and Anderson and Killingray (eds), *Policing the empire*.

43 Sturma, 'Policing the criminal frontier'.

44 See, e.g., debate between D. Neal, 'Free society, penal colony, slave society, prison?', *Historical Studies*, 89, 1987, p. 497, and J. Hirst, 'Or none of the above', *Historical Studies*, 89, 1987, p. 519.

45 See, e.g., R. Ward, *The Australian Legend*, Oxford University Press, Melbourne, 1957, and following him, McQueen, *New Britannia*, and A. McCoy, *Drug traffic, narcotics and organised crime in Australia*, Harper and Row, Sydney, 1980; on consent to policing in the later nineteenth-century Australia see S. Wilson, 'Police work: the role of the police in the Kalgoorlie community, 1897–1898', *Journal of Australian Studies*, 11, 1982, pp. 9–20, and R. Walker, 'Violence in industrial conflicts in New South Wales in the late nineteenth century', *Historical Studies*, 86, 1986, pp. 54–70.

46 Neal, *Rule of Law*, ch. 6.

47 Clyne, *Colonial Blue*, pp. 22–27; Hill, *Policing the colonial frontier*, Part 2, pp. 544–594.

48 NSW, 1903; Queensland, 1905; Tasmania, 1909.

49 Reynolds, '"That hated stain"'; L. Ryan, *The Aboriginal Tasmanians*, University of Queensland Press, St. Lucia, 1981.

50 Cf N. Loos, *Invasion and Resistance: Aboriginal–European relations on the North Queensland frontier 1861–1897*, ANU Press, Canberra, 1982, and Johnston, *Long Blue Line*, for Queensland; and A. Gill, 'Aborigines, Settlers and Police in the Kimberleys, 1887–1905', *Studies in Western Australian History*, 1, 1977.

51 M. H. Fels, *Good Men and True: The Aboriginal Police of the Port Phillip District, 1837–1853*, Melbourne University Press, Melbourne, 1988.

52 See Palmer, 'Making of the Victorian colonial police', pp. 109–111, on the significance of the Act's extension to Melbourne; also Haldane, *People's Force*, p. 15.

53 Cf Palmer, *Police and protest*; Storch, 'The plague of the blue locusts' and 'The Policeman as Domestic Missionary'; Sturma, 'Policing the Criminal Frontier'.

54 Cf J. Hirst, *Adelaide and the Country, 1870–1917*, Melbourne University Press, Carlton, 1973, on the later significance of Adelaide's dominance of the State.

55 Clyne, *Colonial Blue*, pp. 102–3.

56 Hill, *Policing the colonial frontier*, Part 2, ch. 7, for the influence of Victorian police in Otago.

57 C. Connolly, 'Explaining the "Lambing Flat" Riots of 1861', in *Who are our enemies? racism and the working class in Australia*, A. Curthoys and A. Markus (eds), Hale and Iremonger, Sydney, 1978.

58 J. Hirst, *The strange birth of colonial democracy*, Allen and Unwin,

Sydney, 1988, pp. 218–241; J. McQuilton, 'Police in rural Victoria', in *Policing in Australia*, Finnane (ed.); Johnston, *Long Blue Line*, p. 151.

2 Commissioners and Ministers

1 In this book, the term commissioner is used to refer generically to the position of head officer of the police in any particular colony or State. It was the preferred title in all States except NSW (until 1934 the chief officer was the Inspector-General) and Victoria, where the title was Chief Commissioner.

2 E. Whitton, *The Hillbilly Dictator*, Australian Broadcasting Commission, Sydney, 1989; P. Coaldrake, *Working the system*, University of Queensland Press, Sydney, 1989; S. Cockburn, *The Salisbury Affair*, Sun Books, Melbourne, 1979; A. Moore, *The Secret Army and the Premier*, NSW University Press, Kensington, 1989.

3 P. Sallmann, 'Perspectives on the Police and Criminal Justice Debate', in *The Australian Criminal Justice System*, D. Chappell and P. Wilson (eds), Butterworths, Sydney, 1986, p. 201.

4 Whitton, *Hillbilly Dictator*, p. 183.

5 See e.g. S. Egger and M. Findlay, 'The politics of police discretion', in *Understanding Crime and Criminal Justice*, M. Findlay and R. Hogg (eds), Law Book Company, Sydney, 1988; I. Freckelton, 'Sensation and Symbiosis', in *Police in our society*, I. Freckelton and H. Selby (eds), Butterworths, Sydney, 1988.

6 J. Allen, 'Policing since 1880: some questions of sex', in *Policing in Australia: Historical Perspectives*, Finnane (ed.).

7 M. Finnane, 'The politics of police powers', in *Policing in Australia*, Finnane (ed.).

8 Ibid.

9 M. Finnane, 'Police Rules and the Organisation of Policing in Queensland, 1905–16', *Australian and New Zealand Journal of Criminology*, 22, 1989, pp. 95–108.

10 Haldane, *People's Force*, p. 146.

11 R. Davidson, 'Dealing with the "social evil"', in *So Much Hard Work*, K. Daniels (ed.), Fontana, Sydney, 1984, pp. 171–2.

12 S. Walker, *Popular Justice: A History of American Criminal Justice*, Oxford University Press, New York, 1980, pp. 133–5; E. Bittner, *Aspects of police work*, Northeastern University Press, Boston, 1990; M. Brogden, *The Police: Autonomy and Consent*, Academic Press, London, 1982, pp. 60–71; Reiner, *Politics of the Police*.

13 See C. Emsley, *English Police*, pp. 80–88, 151–161.

14 See J. Summers, 'The Salisbury Affair', in D. Jaensch (ed.), *The Flinders History of South Australia-Political History*, Wakefield Press, Netley, 1986; R. Plehwe and R. Wettenhall, 'Reflections on the Salisbury Affair: Police–Government Relations in Australia', *Australian Quarterly*, 51, 1979, pp. 75–89.

15 Summers, 'The Salisbury Affair', p. 346.

16 Royal Commission on the September Moratorium Demonstration, *Report*, p. 82, *South Australia PP*, 1971–2, vol. 3.

17 Summers, 'The Salisbury Affair', p. 343.

18 See C. Procter, 'The Police', in *The Bjelke-Petersen Premiership*, A. Patience (ed.), Allen and Unwin, Sydney, 1985.

19 W. R. Johnston, *Long Blue Line*, p. 280.

20 R. Whitrod, 'The accountability of police forces—who rules the police?', *Australian and New Zealand Journal of Criminology*, 9, 1976, p. 16.

21 Ibid, p. 17.

22 R. Hogg and B. Hawker, 'The politics of police independence', *Legal Service Bulletin*, 8, 1983, pp. 160–5, 221–6

23 Ibid; see also Commission to Inquire into New South Wales Police Administration (Commissioner: E. Lusher, J.), *Report*, Government Printer, Sydney, 1981 (hereafter *Lusher Report*).

24 Committee of Inquiry, Victoria Police Force, (Chair, T. A. Neesham), *Final Report, Volume One*, Ministry for Police and Emergency Services, Melbourne, 1985 (hereafter *Neesham Report*), pp. 10–13; see also Whitrod, 'The accountability of police forces', and *Lusher Report* for evidence of the influence of Denning's comments.

25 Commission of Inquiry (Commissioner G. E. Fitzgerald, Q.C.), *Report*, Government Printer, Brisbane, 1989, p. 278 (hereafter *Fitzgerald Report*).

26 Public Service Management Commission, *Review of the Queensland Police Service*, Government Printer, Brisbane, April 1993, Appendix A reviews current portfolio and accountability arrangements in the various Australian States.

27 NSW Parliament, Joint Select Committee into Police Administration, *Report*, 1993.

28 Public Service Management Commission, *Review of the Queensland Police Service*, p. 39.

29 C. Hughes and B. A. Graham, *A Handbook of Australian Government and Politics 1890–1964*, ANU Press, Canberra, 1968.

30 K. Seggie, 'Aspects of the Role of the Police Force in NSW and its relation to the Government, 1900–1930', PhD thesis, Macquarie University, pp. 185–210; J. Fleming, 'By fair means or foul? The impact of police unionism in Queensland 1915–1932', BA Hons thesis, Griffith University, 1991; Haldane, *People's Force*, pp. 151–161; B. Swanton, *Protecting the protectors*, Australian Institute of Criminology, Canberra, 1982.

31 Confidential memos, 31 March 1909 and 27 April 1909, Commissioner of Police to Under-Secretary, A/36728, Queensland State Archives (QSA).

32 Minute of F. Neitenstein, 29 June 1905, 05/10185. Attorney-General and Justice, NSW State Archives (NSWSA).

33 *Enever v the King*, (1906) 3 *Commomwealth Law Reports*, p. 969.

34 *Ryder v Foley*, (1906) 4 *Commonwealth Law Reports*, p. 422; *Foley v Ryder* (1906) *State Reports Queensland*, 225; Police Department, A/38801, QSA.

35 *Victorian Police Journal*, May 8, 1925

36 See Police Department, A/40860, QSA; also *Brisbane Courier*, 28 Oct. 1920 for Home Secretary supporting differential rates for union and non-union members in public service and police.

37 J. Fleming, 'By fair means or foul?'; Talty stood as Labor candidate in 1928 and a Lang Plan candidate in the 1931 election, B. Costar, 'Controlling the Victims: the Authorities and the Unemployed in Queensland during the Great Depression', *Labour History*, 56, May 1989, p. 13 and information from Jenny Fleming, Griffith University.

38 See Johnston, *Long Blue Line*, pp. 123–5; Seggie, 'Aspects of the role of the Police Force in NSW', p. 187.

39 Industrial Commission of NSW, no 73/474, Report by the President Sir Alexander Beattie on Access to NSW Industrial Tribunals by Public Servants, Teachers in Government Schools and Police, Dec 1974 (Mitchell Library); B. Swanton, *Protecting the Protectors*.

40 Seggie, 'Aspects of the Role of the NSW Police', p. 186.

41 Unionism in the police service, (51/231), 8/2144, Premier's Department, NSWSA.

42 G. Hannigan, 'Industrial relations', in B. Swanton et al (eds), *Police Source Book 2*, p. 291. Swanton, *Protecting the Protectors*, pp. 239ff outlines the protracted development of federation from the 1920s.

43 See below, chapter 8.

44 Haldane, *People's Force*, pp. 290–2; Johnston, *Long Blue Line*, pp. 282–5.

45 See Egger and Findlay, 'Politics of police discretion'; Hogg and Hawker, 'Politics of police independence'.

46 Royal Commission into Aboriginal Deaths in Custody, *National Report, 1991*.

47 I. Freckelton, 'Shooting the Messenger' in *Complaints against the Police: The Trend to External Review*, A. Goldsmith, (ed.), Clarendon Press, Oxford, 1991.

48 Fleming, 'By fair means or foul?', p. 50.

49 K. Inglis, *The Stuart Case*, Melbourne University Press, Melbourne, 1960, p. 315 and see chapter 4 below.

50 Inglis, *Stuart Case*, p. 60.

51 *Fitzgerald Report*, p. 280.

52 See e.g. *Constitution and Police Regulation (Amendment) Act* (NSW), 1964, s. 2.

53 See Sallmann, 'Perspectives on the Police and Criminal Justice Debate'; M. Finnane, 'Police and Politics in Australia — the Case for Historical Revision', *Australian and New Zealand Journal of Criminology*, 23, 4, 1990, pp. 218–229.

3 Conflict, surveillance and control

1 C. Shearing and P. Stenning (eds), *Private Policing*, Sage Publications, Newbury Park, 1987, p. 10.

2 See also M. Finnane, and S. Garton, 'The work of policing — social relations and the criminal justice system in Queensland, 1880-1914, Part 1', *Labour History*, 62, 1992, pp. 52–70.

3 Cf the critical comments of J. Hocking, 'ASIO and the Security State: A Reply to Frank Cain', *Labour History*, 60, 1991, pp. 125–8 in response to F. Cain, 'ASIO and the Australian Labour Movement — An Historical Perspective', *Labour History*, 58, 1990, pp. 1–16.

4 E. Bittner, 'The Function of the Police in Modern Society' (1970), in *Aspects of Police Work*, Northeastern University Press, Boston, 1990, pp. 120ff.

5 R. Reiner, 'Multiple Realities, Divided Worlds: Chief Constables' Perspectives on the Police Complaints System', in *Complaints against the Police*, Goldsmith (ed.), p. 229.

6 Police staff files, A/41013, (Kreutzmann) QSA.

7 Attorney-General and Justice Correspondence, 05/11332, NSWSA.

8 Johnston, *Long Blue Line*, p. 360.

9 Haldane, *People's Force*, pp. 117–8 for evidence of strikers praising behaviour of police.

10 The story is told in R. Evans, *The Red Flag Riots*, UQP, St Lucia, 1988.

11 S. I. Miller, 'New Developments in Police Operational Planning', in *Police in Australia: Development, Functions and Procedures*, K. Milte and T. A. Weber (eds), Butterworths, Sydney, 1977, p. 331.

12 Costar, 'Controlling the Victims'; N. Wheatley 'Meeting them at the door: radicalism, militancy and the Sydney eviction campaign of 1931' in *Twentieth Century Sydney: Studies in Urban and Social History*, J. Roe (ed.), Hale and Iremonger, Sydney, 1980.

13 S. Wilson, 'Police perceptions of protest: the Perth 'Treasury Riot' of March 1991', *Labour History*, 52, 1987, pp. 63–74; R. Walker, 'Violence in industrial conflicts'; but cf. B. York, 'Baiting the tiger: police and protest during the Vietnam war', in *Policing in Australia*, Finnane (ed.).

14 C. Cunneen, et al, *Dynamics of Collective Conflict: Riots at the Bathurst 'Bike Races'* Law Book Company, Sydney, 1989.

15 See e.g. C. Cunneen, *Aboriginal–Police relations in Redfern*, Human Rights and Equal Opportunity Commission, 1990.

16 B. Porter, *Plots and paranoia: a history of political espionage in Britain 1790–1988*, Unwin Hyman, London, 1989, pp. 101–119.

17 R. Evans, *Loyalty and disloyalty: social conflict on the Queensland homefront, 1914–18*, Allen and Unwin, 1987, pp. 109–111; F. Cain, *The origins of political surveillance in Australia*, Angus and Robertson, Sydney, 1983, p. 19.

18 Cain, *Origins of political surveillance*; see also M. Finnane, 'The state versus Chidley' and V. Burgmann, 'The Iron Heel: The Suppression of the IWW during World War I' in *What Rough Beast? The state and social order in Australian history*, Sydney Labour History Group (ed.), George Allen and Unwin, Sydney, 1982.

19 Costar, 'Controlling the victims'; Moore, *Secret Army and the Premier*; Wilson, 'Police perceptions of protest'.

20 Cain, 'ASIO and the Labour Movement'; L. Maher, 'The Lapstone Experiment and the Beginnings of ASIO', *Labour History*, 64, 1993, pp. 103–118.

21 Maher, 'Lapstone Experiment', pp. 108–9.

22 Cain, 'ASIO and the Labour Movement'; R. Hall, *The Secret State*, Cassell, Stanmore, 1978; see also B. Toohey and W. Pinwill, *Oyster: the story of the Australian Secret Intelligence Service*, Mandarin Australia, Melbourne, 1990.

23 A. Ashbolt, 'The great literary witch-hunt of 1952', in *Australia's First Cold War Vol. 1 Society, Communism and Culture*, A. Curthoys and J. Merritt (eds), George Allen and Unwin, Sydney, 1984.

24 M. Findlay, 'The Justice Wood Inquiry: the role of Special branch in the Cameron Conspiracy', in *Travesty! Miscarriages of Justice*, K. Carrington et al (eds), Academics for Justice, Sydney, 1991, p. 42.

25 Mr Justice White, Special Branch Security Records, Initial Report, SA *PP*, 1978.

26 Maher, 'Lapstone experiment', p. 108.

27 Cain, 'ASIO and the Australian Labour Movement'.

28 Cf Hocking, 'ASIO and the Security State'; Findlay, 'The Justice Wood Inquiry'.

29 Findlay, 'The Justice Wood Inquiry', pp. 35–7.

30 Shearing and Stenning, *Private Policing*; L. Johnston, *The rebirth of private policing*, Routledge, London, 1992, pp. 3–23.

31 P. O'Malley, 'Burglary, private policing and victim responsibility', in *Policing Australia*, Moir and Eijkman (eds) p. 299.

32 Johnston, *Long Blue Line*, p. 3.

33 J. B. Castieau, *The Reminiscences of Detective-Inspector Christie*, Geo. Robertson and Co, Melbourne, n.d. [1913].

34 C. Crowe, *The Inquiry Agent*, Melbourne, 1909. A royal commission of 1906 dismissed Crowe's claims about police corruption, casting doubt on his credibility in the light of his record in the Victoria police, 'to which he gained admission by suppressing the important fact that he had been dismissed from the service in New Zealand' (Royal Commission on the Victorian Police Force, *Report*, pp. xix–xx, Victorian *PP*, 1906, vol. 3).

35 See R. Weiss, Jr, 'From "Slugging Detectives" to "Labour Relations": Policing Labor at Ford, 1930–1947', in *Private Policing*, Shearing and Stenning (eds).

36 D. J. Murphy (ed.) *The big strikes: Queensland 1889–1965*, UQP, St Lucia, 1983, pp. 69, 82, 126; S. Svenson, *The shearers' war*, UQP, St Lucia, 1989, pp. 145–7, 207.

37 See e.g. *Police Offences Act* (NSW), 1901, ss. 101–108 and *Police Offences (Amendment) Act* 1908, s.15 (applying to appointment of night watchmen and security guards).

38 Clyne, *Colonial Blue*, p. 170.

39 Select Committee on the Whole Administration of the State Children Relief Act, 1901, Further Progress Report, *NSW Parliamentary Papers*, 1916, v. 2, p. 1011, Evidence, q. 677.

40 *Victorian Police Journal*, 14 Oct. 1927, 8 Nov. 1927.

41 G. Reekie, *Temptations: sex, selling and the department store*, Allen and Unwin, Sydney, 1993, pp. 17, 115; the chief detective was known as the 'House Inspector and Special Constable'.

42 Weiss, 'Policing Labor at Ford', pp. 110–130.

43 P. Cochrane, 'Anatomy of a Steel Works: The Australian Iron and Steel Company, Port Kembla, 1935–1939', *Labour History*, 57, 1989, pp. 61–77.

44 W. Eather, '"Protect the Newcastle Steelworks": BHP, the Trade Unions and National Security, 1939–1940', *Labour History*, 57, 1989, pp. 78–88.

45 Costar, 'Controlling the Victims', p. 11.

46 See e.g. R. Harding, *Police Killings in Australia*, Penguin, Ringwood, 1970, p. 187, cited in 'Crime Prevention and Private Security: Problems of Control and Responsibility', D. G. T. Williams, *The Australian Law Journal*, 48 (8), 1974, p. 383; J. F. Ashby, 'The Private Security Industry' and R. W. Page, 'The Growth and Control of Private Security' in *Policing and Private Security*, A. S. Rees (ed.), Australian Institute of Criminology, Canberra, 1983; C. Corns, 'Privatizing Policing and the Empowerment of Crime Victims', in *Community Issues in Psychiatry, Psychology and the Law*, E. Berah and D. Greig (eds), Proceedings of the 8th Annual Congress of the Australian & New Zealand Association of Psychiatry, Psychology and Law, Melbourne, 1987.

47 Williams, 'Crime Prevention and Private Security', pp. 384–5. Recent legislation is, however, paying more attention to the regulation of the industry personnel, as in 1993 Queensland legislation, *Australian*, 29 July 1993.

48 O'Malley, 'Burglary, private policing and victim responsibility'.

49 Cf. O'Malley, 'Burglary, private policing and victim responsibility'; Corns, 'Privatizing policing'; Shearing and Stenning (eds), *Private Policing*.

50 E.g. Royal Commission into Aboriginal Deaths in Custody, *National Report*, vol. 4, ch. 29.

4 Policing Crime

1 E.g. Clyne, *Colonial Blue*, ch. 2 for South Australian anxiety to prevent the incursion of convicts; and Hill, *Policing the colonial frontier*, Part 2, pp. 565–6, on New Zealand; Sturma, *Vice in a Vicious Society*, on NSW; S. Garton, 'The convict origins debate: historians and the problem of the "criminal class"', ANZ *Journal of Criminology*, 24, 2, 1991, pp. 66–82.

2 Davidson, *Invisible State*, pp. 102 ff and C. McConville, 'From "criminal class" to "underworld"', in G. Davison, D. Dunstan and C. McConville (eds), *The outcasts of Melbourne. Essays in social history*, Allen and Unwin, Sydney, 1985, each detail some of the means and objects of police surveillance of the criminal in the nineteenth century.

3 S. Stevenson, 'The "habitual criminal" in nineteenth-century England: some observation on the figures', *Urban History Yearbook*, Leicester University Press, 1986, pp. 37–60; see D. Dixon, *Detention for questioning in Australia and England*, Hull University Law School, 1992, p. 48 on the continued currency of a NSW police view of the 'criminal classes'.

4 Report of Board of Inquiry into the Management of the Metropolitan Police Force, p. vi, South Australia *PP*, 1872.

5 Johnston, *Long Blue Line*, pp 156–7.

6 Royal Commission on Police, Special Report on the Detective Branch, p. vi, Victoria *PP*, 1883, vol. 2.

7 Report of Board of Inquiry into the Management of the Metropolitan Police Force, p. vi, South Australia *PP*, 1872.

8 E.g. M. O'Sullivan, *Cameos of crime*, Jackson and O'Sullivan, Brisbane, 1947; Castieau, *Reminiscences of Detective-Inspector Christie*; J. Sadleir, *Recollections of a Victorian Police Officer*, Geo. Robertson, Melbourne, 1913; but cf. P. Barnett, *A policeman's progress*, Boolarong Press, Brisbane, 1988.

9 See Emsley, *English Police*, p. 18, on Jonathan Wild, the eighteenth-century thief-taker, who ended up managing and controlling the activities of his objects of attention.

10 Royal Commission on Police, Special Report on the Detective Branch, p. ix.

11 Ibid., passim. See Haldane, *People's Force*, pp. 93–101 for the context and significance of the 1883 Royal Commission, chaired by a parliamentarian, Francis Longmore.

12 Seggie, 'Aspects of the role of the police force in NSW', pp. 215–6.

13 Cf. Haldane, *People's Force*, pp. 99 who follows the Longmore Commission in explaining the system as one which had been suitable to the earlier phase of Victoria's history.

14 See *Australian*, 28 Jan 1993; for early release of prison informers in Victoria see Royal Commission on Police, Special Report on the Detective Branch, pp. ix, xiii.

15 *Australian*, 18 March 1993.

16 See especially Royal Commission on Police, Special Report on the Detective Branch, p. x for nineteenth century exhortations drawing on the authority of Howard Vincent's English *Police Code* as well as the Royal Irish Constabulary Manual; and for police concern about the use of informers in the 1920s, see Seggie, 'Aspects of the role of the police force in NSW', p. 216.

17 T. Wickham, 'Advice to detectives', *Australian Police Journal*, 2,1, Jan-Mar 1948, pp. 34–49.

18 Ibid., pp. 46–7.

19 See M. Brown and P. Wilson, *Justice and nightmares: successes and failures of forensic science in Australia and New Zealand*, NSW University Press, Sydney, 1992; for historical perspective see S. Garton, 'Pursuing incorrigible rogues: patterns of policing in NSW 1870–1930', *Journal of the Royal Australian Historical Society*, 77, 1, 1991, pp. 16–29.

20 Haldane, *People's Force*, p. 130; Johnston, *Long Blue Line*, p. 144.

21 Circular Memo, 1.1.06, A/36277, QSA; see also Clyne, *Colonial Blue*, pp. 226–7; and Johnston, *Long Blue Line*, pp. 143–4

22 D. Garland, 'The criminal and his science', *British Journal of Criminology*, 25 (2) 1985, pp. 109–137; C. Ginzburg, 'Freud, Morelli and Sherlock Holmes', *History Workshop Journal*, 9, 1980, pp. 7–29.

23 O'Brien, *Australian Police Forces*, pp. 124–5; *R v Parker*, (1912) 28 *ALR* 150; Haldane, *People's Force*, p. 130.

24 The conference was first held in 1903, then in 1922 and annually thereafter, except for the years of the Depression (1929–35), Clyne, *Colonial Blue*, p. 226 and Report of the Commissioner of Police, 1935, South Australia *PP*, 1936, vol. 2.

25 Report of the Commissioner of Police, 1945, South Australia *PP*, 1945; Johnston, *Long Blue Line*, pp. 249–50.

26 *First Offenders Probation Act* 1886; M. Finnane, 'Penality and politics: Griffith and law reform in colonial Queensland', *Australian Cultural History*, 8, 1989, pp. 84–97.

27 Johnston, *Long Blue Line*, p. 143.

28 Police Department, *Annual Report*, 1926, p. 2, NSW *PP*, 1927, vol 1.

29 Police Department, *Annual Report*, 1955, p. 6, NSW *PP*, 1956–7, vol. 4.

30 Circular memo, 9.4.35, 12.8.1936, A/36282, QSA; the fingerprints were forwarded to the modus operandi section of the CIB. A direction a month later advised of the necessity to destroy these fingerprints, obtained under s.34, *Vagrants, Gaming and Other Offences Act* if the train-jumper was not convicted. See also Johnston, *Long Blue Line*, p. 144 for early concern of commissioner of police that fingerprinting was being used too readily.

31 Report by Alexander Mitchell Duncan on all aspects of crime investigation..., p. 6, Tasmania *PP*, 1955.

32 *Conference of Commissioners of Police South Pacific Region*, Sydney, 1959 (Mitchell Library).

33 Police Department, *Annual Report*, 1935, p. 8, NSW *PP*, 1935–6; Circular memos, 21.8.33, 12.6.37, A/36282, QSA, for links to Commonwealth Investigation Branch; see also Cain, *Origins of political surveillance*, who nevertheless notes some tensions between State police and Commonwealth intelligence agencies.

34 See G. Sturgess, 'Murphy and the media' and A. R. Blackshield, 'The "Murphy Affair"', in J. Scutt (ed.), *Lionel Murphy. A Radical Judge*, McCulloch Publishing, Carlton, 1987.

35 S. Odgers, 'Experts and evidence', *Current Affairs Bulletin*, March, 1988, pp. 4–11; Brown and Wilson, *Justice and nightmares*, pp. 119–141.

36 Report from the Select Committee on the case of Mr A. L. Robertson, Evidence, q. 805, NSW *PP*, 1918, vol. 5.

37 Report by Alexander Mitchell Duncan on all aspects of crime investigation . . . , Tasmania *PP*, 1955.

38 See Brown and Wilson, *Justice and nightmares*; K. Carrington et al (eds) *Travesty! Miscarriages of Justice*, Academics for Justice, Sydney, 1991; and cf. D. Dixon, 'Legal regulation and policing practice', *Social & Legal Studies*, 1, 1992, pp. 529–31 on the near total absence of a historical knowledge of criminal procedures to enable balanced judgment on current practices.

39 *Argus*, 19 June 1936, p. 11.

40 Haldane, *People's Force*, p. 216.

41 Ibid., p. 217.

42 Royal Commission of Inquiry into certain matters relating to David Edward Studley-Ruxton, *Report*, NSW *PP*, 1954–5, vol. 1.

43 R. R. Kidston, 'Confessions to Police', *Australian Law Journal*, 33, Feb 25, 1960, p. 369.

44 Cf. also the article by R. W. Baker, Dean of the Faculty of Law, University of Tasmania, 'Confessions and Improperly Obtained Evidence', *Australian Law Journal*, 30, June 21, 1956, pp. 59–68, which concentrates on the issue of judicial discretion and decision-making rather than police and prosecution practice in this area.

45 E. Eggleston, *Fear, favour or affection*, ANU Press, Canberra, 1976, p. 31.

46 Inglis, *Stuart Case*. Contrary to the recent account of this in Brown and Wilson, *Justice and Nightmares*, p. 167, the commission emphatically rejected Strehlow's arguments. See Report of the Royal Commission in Regard to Rupert Max Stuart, paras 154–5, South Australia *PP*, 1959, vol. 2.

47 Ibid., p. 25.

48 See D. Brown, D. Farrier, D. Neal, D.Weisbrot, *Criminal Laws*, Federation Press, Sydney, 1990, p. 335.

49 Cf. Baker, 'Confessions', and Kidston, 'Confessions' (notes 46–7 above).

50 F. H. Cleland, 'Questioning of Persons in Custody', *Australian Police Journal*, 3, (1), 1949.

51 Royal Commission into the conviction of Frederick William

McDermott, *Report*, NSW State Archives, 12/1342–5. The Report (by Judge Kinsella) does not appear to have been published.

52 Fitzgerald Report, p. 20.

53 For current discussion of some of the issues in regulating police procedure, see Dixon, *Detention for questioning* and R. Hogg, 'Identifying and Reforming the Problems of the Justice System', in Carrington et al (eds), *Travesty!.*

5 Keeping the peace

1 Queensland Police Department, Larrikinism files, 95M/63, POL/J6.

2 R. Hogg and H. Golder, 'Policing Sydney in the Late Nineteenth Century', in *Policing in Australia*, Finnane (ed.).

3 See M. Finnane, 'Larrikins, delinquents and cops' in *Police and Young People in Australia*, R. White and C. Alder (eds), Cambridge University Press, Melbourne, 1994.

4 W. Chambliss, 'A sociological analysis of the law of vagrancy', *Social Problems*, 12, 1964, pp. 67–77; M. Roberts, 'Public and private in early nineteenth-century London: the Vagrant Act of 1822 and its enforcement', *Social History*, 13, 1988, pp. 273–294.

5 Diary of J. B. Castieau, 23 June 1878, Mss 2218, National Library of Australia; cf. E. Monkonnen, *Police in Urban America, 1860–1920*, Cambridge University Press, Cambridge, 1981, on police in urban America for discussion of role of police in obtaining shelter for homeless.

6 Especially M. Fairburn, 'Vagrants, "folk devils" and nineteenth-century New Zealand as a bondless society', *Historical Studies*, 21 (85), 1985, pp. 495–514.

7 See the duties assiduously documented and costed (in terms of hours) in the Report of the Commissioner of Police, 1935, p. 27, South Australia *PP*, 1935, vol. 2; see Emsley, *English Police*, p. 3, on the suppression of the non-crime functions of police in many police histories and memoirs.

8 Police staff files (AF1143), A/40062, QSA.

9 Sturma, *Vice in a vicious society*, p. 157.

10 Roberts, 'Vagrant Act of 1822', p. 292.

11 S. Garton, ' "Once a drunkard always a drunkard": social reform and the problem of habitual drunkenness in Australia, 1880–1914', *Labour History*, 53, 1987, pp. 38–53.

12 Police staff files, A/38734, QSA; and see Sturma, *Vice in a vicious society*, p. 153 on the significance of drunkenness of crime victims in Sydney in the mid-nineteenth century.

13 Based on data in S. K. Mukherjee et al, *Source Book of Australian Criminal and Social Statistics, 1804–1988*, AIC, Canberra, 1988; see also M. Finnane, and S. Garton, 'The work of policing: social relations and the criminal justice system in Queensland, 1880–1914', *Labour History*, 62, 1992, pp. 52–70 (Part 1) and 63, 1992, pp. 43–64 (Part 2).

14 Report of the Commissioner of Police, Western Australia, 1915, p. 4, WA *PP*, 1915, vol. 2: the move came in the *Traffic Act* 1919.

15 See N. Sanders, 'Private faces in public spaces: The NRMA, 1920–51', in *Australian Communications and the Public Sphere*, H. Wilson (ed.), Macmillan, Sydney, 1989.

16 See F. Brennan, *Too much order with too little law*, University of Queensland Press, Brisbane, 1983.

17 Report of the Commissioner of Police, Western Australia, 1925, p. 6, WA *PP*, 1926, vol. 2.

18 R. Homel, 'Young men in the arms of the law: an Australian perspective on policing and punishing the drinking driver', *Accident Analysis and Prevention*, 15, 6, 1983, pp. 499–500, discussing the work of J. R. Gusfield, *The Culture of Public Problems: Drink-driving and the Symbolic Order*, University of Chicago Press, Chicago and London, 1981.

19 C. Emsley, '"Mother, what *did* policemen do when there weren't any motors?" The law, the police and the regulation of motor traffic in England, 1900–1939', *The Historical Journal*, 36, 2, 1993, pp. 357–381.

20 R. Homel, 'Random breath testing in Australia: getting it to work according to specifications', *Addiction*, 88 (Supplement), 1993, 27S–33S and more generally *Policing the Drinking Driver: Random Breath Testing and the Process of Deterrence*, Macquarie University and the Federal Office of Road Safety, Sydney, 1986.

21 To adapt R. Castel, 'From dangerousness to risk', in *Foucault Effect*, Burchell, Gordon, and Miller (eds).

22 R. Homel, *Policing the Drinking Driver*.

23 Homel, *Policing the Drinking Driver*, p. 65; see also L. Wood, 'A pattern of arrests for drink driving in Hobart, Tasmania', *Australian Geographer*, 20, 2, 1989, pp. 191–194.

24 *Sunday Mail*, 24 August 1986.

25 Homel, *Policing the Drinking Driver*.

26 On 'good' and 'bad' policing from a standard of republican justice, see J. Braithwaite, 'Good and bad policing', in *Policing Australia*, Moir and Eijkman (eds); see also R. Hogg and M. Findlay, 'Police and the Community: Some Issues Raised by Recent Overseas Research', in *Police in our society*, I. Freckelton and H. Selby (eds), Butterworths, Sydney, 1988.

27 On domestic violence see J. Allen, 'The Invention of the Pathological Family: An Historical Study of Family Violence in New South Wales, 1880–1939' in *Family Violence in Australia*, C. O'Donnell and J. Craney (eds), Longmans Cheshire, Melbourne, 1982; K. Saunders, 'The study of domestic violence in colonial Queensland: sources and problems', *Historical Studies*, 82, 1984, pp. 68–84; R. Evans, 'Masculinism and gendered violence', in *Gender Relations in Australia: Domination and Negotiation*, K. Saunders and R. Evans (eds), Harcourt Brace Jovanovich, Marrickville, 1992.

28 *Manual of Police Regulations for the Guidance of the Constabulary of Queensland,* Brisbane, 1876.

29 *Neesham Report,* para. 11.15.3.

30 Attorney-General and Justice Correspondence, 7/5435 (10/2448), NSWSA.

31 Colonial Secretary's Office, COL/A29 (62/1469), QSA.

32 Castieau Diary, 23 Aug. 1877, Mss. 2218, NLA.

33 Sturma, *Vice in a vicious society,* pp. 97, 143.

34 See V. Gatrell, 'Crime, authority and the policeman-state 1990', in *The Cambridge Social history of Britain, 1750–1950,* F. M. L. Thompson (ed.), vol. 3, Cambridge University Press, Cambridge, 1990, p. 277 citing J. Davis.

35 Report of the Commissioner of Police, 1935, p. 7, SA *PP,* 1936, vol. 2; Clyne, *Colonial Blue,* pp. 263–4 on the appointment of the first women police and their early duties.

36 A. Macdonald, 'Women Police in Australia', in *Advance! Australia,* April, 1929, pp. 49–50.

37 Clyne, *Colonial Blue,* p. 264.

38 *Daily Telegraph,* 24 June 1915.

39 *Sun,* 24 June 1915.

40 See Police Department, *Annual Report,* 1965, pp. 17–18, NSW *PP,* 1967–8, vol. 3; *Sydney Morning Herald,* 5 June 1915 for Black's claim re powers of women police; Johnston, *Long Blue Line,* pp. 216–7 on Queensland.

41 Deputation of Women's Progressive Association to NSW Chief Secretary, *Sydney Morning Herald,* 5 June 1915, seeking the appointment of additional women police.

42 See A. Bolger, *Aboriginal Women and Violence,* ANU North Australia Research Unit, Darwin, 1991.

43 J. Allen, 'The Invention of the Pathological Family: An Historical Study of Family Violence in New South Wales, 1880–1939' in *Family Violence in Australia,* C. O'Donnell and J. Craney (eds), Longmans Cheshire, Melbourne, 1982.

44 S. Garton, 'Bad or Mad? Developments in Incarceration in NSW, 1880–1920' in *What Rough Beast? The State and Social Order in Australian History,* Sydney Labour History Group (ed.), Allen and Unwin, Sydney, 1982, and 'The Rise of the Therapeutic State: Psychiatry and the System of Criminal Jurisdiction in New South Wales, 1890–1940', *Australian Journal of Politics and History,* 32, 3, 1986, pp. 378–388.

45 Bolger, *Aboriginal Women and Violence,* pp. 71–9.

46 *Neesham Report,* para. 11.8.5; see also Report of the Queensland Domestic Violence Task Force, *Beyond these walls,* Brisbane, 1988, ch. 6 for a detailed examination of contemporary issues in the policing of domestic violence.

47 Bolger, *Aboriginal Women and Violence*, p. 72.
48 Ibid., p. 78.

6 The government of Aborigines

1 See Hill, *Policing the colonial frontier*, J. Pratt, *Punishment in a perfect society: The New Zealand penal system, 1840–1939*, Victoria University Press, Wellington, 1992, ch. 2.

2 Alan Atkinson, *Camden: farm and village life in early New South Wales*, Oxford University Press, 1988, pp. 21, 229.

3 Lonsdale to Col Sec, 25 Oct 1837, *Historical Records of Victoria*, 2A, p. 246.

4 See *Murrell*, (1836), 1 *Legge* 72. It should be noted that there was minority judicial opinion which differed on this point: see H. Reynolds, *The Law of the Land*, Penguin, Ringwood, 1987, for the variety of legal and political discourses on Aboriginal rights in the nineteenth century.

5 See B. Rosser, *Up rode the troopers: the Black Police in Queensland*, UQP, St Lucia, 1990; M. Fels, *Good Men and True: The Aboriginal Police of the Port Phillip District, 1837–1853*, Melbourne University Press, Melbourne, 1988; H. Reynolds, *With the White People*, Penguin, Ringwood, 1991; Johnston, *Long Blue Line*, pp. 82–102.

6 *Historical Records of Victoria*, 1, 1981, p. 249.

7 Alexander Maconochie to Lord Glenelg, 23 June, 1837, *Historical Records of Victoria*, 1, p. 240.

8 *Historical Records of Victoria*, 1, pp. 237–268; cf. Fels.

9 Police Department, transcript of conversation between Cheeke and Cahill, 25 May 1910, A/38756, QSA.

10 G. Reid, *A Picnic with the Natives: Aboriginal–European Relations in the Northern territory to 1910*, Melbourne University Press, Melbourne, 1990, p. 115 (quoting Sub-Inspector Foelsche) and ch. 8 passim; cf. on Queensland policy, the report by Police Commissioner W. E. Parry-Okeden in 1897, Report on the North Queensland Aborigines and the Native Police, p. 7, Queensland *PP*, 1897, vol. 2.

11 Reid, *Picnic with the Natives*, p. 122.

12 A. Gill, 'Aborigines, Settlers and Police in the Kimberleys, 1887–1905', *Studies in West Australian History*, I, 1977.

13 See R. Evans, ' . . . . "Kings in brass crescents". Defining Aboriginal labour patterns in colonial Queensland.' In *Indentured Labour in the British Empire, 1834–1920*, K. Saunders (ed.), Croom Helm, London, 1984.

14 C. D. Rowley, *The Destruction of Aboriginal Society*, Penguin, Ringwood, 1972; Loos, *Invasion and Resistance*.

15 Royal Commission on the Condition of the Natives, (Commissioner, W. E. Roth), *Report*, pp. 12–13, WA *PP*, 1905, vol. 1.

16 Report on the North Queensland Aborigines and the Native Police, p. 15.

17 See P. Read, *A Hundred Years War*, ANU Press, Canberra, 1988;
    G. Cowlishaw, *Black, white or brindle: race in rural Australia*, Cambridge
    University Press, Cambridge, 1988; N. Parbury, *Survival: A History of
    Aboriginal Life in New South Wales*, Ministry of Aboriginal Affairs,
    Sydney, 1986; and especially Royal Commission into Aboriginal Deaths
    in Custody, *Regional Report of Inquiry in New South Wales, Victoria and
    Tasmania*, AGPS, Canberra, 1991, pp. 201–231.

18 See C. Anderson, 'Queensland Aboriginal Peoples Today', in
    Queensland: A Geographical Interpretation, J. H. Holmes (ed.), Royal
    Geographical Society, Brisbane, 1986 for the effects of removals in
    reconstructing the Aboriginal population.

19 For a compelling account of this life in the 1940s and after, see Ruby
    Langford, *Don't take your love to town*, Penguin Books, Ringwood, 1988.

20 See A. Haebich, *For their own good: Aborigines and Government in
    Western Australia, 1900–1940*, UWA Press, Nedlands, 1988, pp. 304–7;
    Report of the Royal Commissioner appointed to Investigate, Report and
    Advise upon matters in relation to the Condition and Treatment of the
    Aborigines (Commissioner, H. D. Moseley), WA *PP*, 1935, vol. 1 (here-
    after *Moseley Report*).

21 R. Broadhurst, 'Imprisonment of the Aborigine in Western Australia:
    1957–1985', in *Ivory Scales: Black Australians and the Law*, K. Hazelhurst
    (ed.), NSW University Press, Kensington, 1987, pp. 179–181.

22 Eggleston, *Fear, favour or affection*, pp. 327–8.

23 C. Cunneen and T. Robb, *Criminal Justice in North-West New South
    Wales*, NSW Bureau of Crime Statistics and Research, Sydney, 1987,
    pp. 194ff. has data comparing police detention in three NSW towns in
    the 1930s, 1960s and 1980s; see also A. McGrath, 'Colonialism, crime
    and civilisation', *Australian Cultural History*, 12, 1993, pp. 100–114.

24 For some evidence see R. Broadhurst, 'Imprisonment of the Aborigines
    in Western Australia', C. Cunneen and T. Robb, *Criminal Justice in
    North-West New South Wales*, Cowlishaw, *Black, white or brindle*;
    Eggleston, *Fear, favour or affection*.

25 Haebich, *For their own good*, pp. 110ff.

26 Ibid., pp. 116–8; cf. A. McGrath, *Born in the cattle*, Allen and Unwin,
    Sydney, 1987, for similar evidence in the Northern Territory.

27 J. McCorquodale, 'The legal classification of race in Australia', *Aboriginal
    history*, 10, 1, 1986, p. 36.

28 Queensland Police Department, Circular Memorandum, 21 Jan 1925,
    A/36281, QSA. In this respect police were part of a system of govern-
    ment which persistently misused the trust funds, as described by
    R. Kidd, 'Regulating Bodies: Administrations and Aborigines in
    Queensland', PhD in progress, Griffith University.

29 Haebich, *For their own good*, p. 98.

30 Royal Commission into Aboriginal Deaths in Custody, *Regional Report
    Western Australia*, AGPS, Canberra, 1991, pp. 309–314.

31 *Moseley Report*, pp. 18–19, 21.
32 See Johnston, *Long Blue Line*, p. 99; and generally M. Finnane and C. Moore, 'Kanaka slaves or willing workers? Melanesian workers and the Queensland criminal justice system in the 1890s', *Criminal Justice History. An International Annual*, vol. 13, 1992, pp. 141–160.
33 Circular memo, 2 Feb 1932, A/36282, QSA.
34 *Moseley Report*, pp. 22–3.
35 Report of Royal Commission into Aboriginal Deaths in Custody, *Regional report, New South Wales* p. 261, case of Peter Williams.
36 See Royal Commission into Aboriginal Deaths in Custody, *National Report*, vol. 3.
37 See C. Cunneen, 'Policing and Aboriginal Communities: Is the Concept of Over-Policing Useful?', in *Aboriginal Perspectives on Criminal Justice*, C. Cunneen (ed.), The Institute of Criminology, Sydney, 1992, for an overview of the research.
38 Bolger, *Aboriginal women and violence*; J. Atkinson, 'Violence against Aboriginal women: reconstitution of community law—the way forward', *Aboriginal Law Bulletin*, 2, 46, 1990 (October), pp. 9–11.
39 See G. Nettheim, *Victims of the law: Black Queenslanders today*, Allen and Unwin, Sydney, 1981; L. Ryan, 'Aborigines and Torres Strait Islanders' in *Bjelke-Petersen Premiership*, Patience (ed.).
40 See Royal Commission into Aboriginal Deaths in Custody, *Regional Report of Inquiry in New South Wales, Victoria and Tasmania*, pp. 216–217.
41 See Read, *Hundred Years War*, for an account of this process in NSW and Haebich, *For their own good*, for Western Australia.
42 Cunneen and Robb, *Criminal Justice in North-West New South Wales*; Cowlishaw, *Black, white or brindle*; H. Goodall, 'Policing in whose interest?: local government, the TRG and Aborigines in Brewarrina, 1987/8', *Journal for Social Justice Studies*, 3, 1990, pp. 19–34.
43 Royal Commission into Aboriginal Affairs (Laverton), p. v, WA *PP*, 1976.
44 Ibid., p. vi
45 Ibid., p. vii
46 Royal Commission into Aboriginal Deaths in Custody, *Interim Report*, AGPS, Canberra, 1988, p. 51 (recommendation 27).
47 See e.g. Human Rights and Equal Opportunity Commission, *Racist Violence: Report of the National Inquiry into Racist Violence*, 1991, pp. 101–104.
48 See Broadhurst, 'Imprisonment of the Aborigine', for a comprehensive review of the situation in WA.
49 See P. Wilson, *Black Death, White Hands*, Allen & Unwin, Sydney, 1982.
50 See Royal Commission into Aboriginal Deaths in Custody, *Regional Report Western Australia*, pp. 215–236 on Western Australian police attitudes to their work with Aborigines.

51 See e.g. Eggleston, *Fear, favour or affection*, pp. 31–45 for changes in rules regarding procedure in detention and questioning of Aborigines; also J. McCorquodale, 'Judicial racism in Australia?', in *Ivory Scales*, Hazlehurst (ed.).

52 Royal Commission into Aboriginal Deaths in Custody, *National Report*, vols. 3 and 4.

53 *Report of the National Inquiry into Racist Violence*, pp. 79–114; Wootten, J. H. (Royal Commission into Aboriginal Deaths in Custody), *Report of the Inquiry into the Death of David John Gundy*, AGPS, Canberra, 1991.

54 See 1993 struggles over Cairns, with police resisting local government attacks on Aborigines in public spaces in Cairns, *Australian*, 8 April 1993; on Victoria, see D. Palmer, 'Local government and policing public space', *Socio-Legal bulletin*, 5, 1991, pp. 18–19; on NSW, H. Goodall, 'Policing in whose interest?'.

55 See Joint Committee on Foreign Affairs, Defence and Trade, *A Review of Australia's Efforts to Promote and Protect Human Rights*, AGPS, Canberra, 1992, pp. 59–62.

7 Police training

1 See the definition of Egon Bittner, in his 1970 essay 'The functions of police' defining 'the capacity to use force as the core of the police role': *Aspects of police work*, Northeastern University Press, Boston, 1990, pp. 120ff. See also Max Weber on the state as a political association upholding a claim to the monopoly of legitimate use of physical force in the enforcement of its order: *The Theory of Social and Economic Organization*, Free Press, New York, 1964, p. 154.

2 See D. Brown, 'The politics of reform' in *The criminal injustice system*, G. Zdenkowski et al (eds), vol. 2, Pluto Press, Leichhardt, 1987, p. 271.

3 Clyne, *Colonial Blue*, ch. 2.

4 Haldane, *People's Force*, pp. 71–2.

5 These included R. Leane in South Australia (1920–44); G. C. T. Steward (1919–20), J. Gellibrand (1920–22), and T. A. Blamey (1925–37) in Victoria; C. J. Carroll in Queensland (1934–1949); and J. E. C. Lord in Tasmania, though his distinguished war service (1916–19) came in the middle of his three-decade leadership of the police (1906–40).

6 General order 686, Queensland Police Department, in Circular memoranda, 23.10.1896, A/36276, QSA; see also Fitzgerald Report, 211 on these restraints as part of the 'perpetuation of police culture'.

7 For example, see Emsley, *English Police*, ch. 9.

8 Clyne, *Colonial Blue*, pp. 107–8, notes the problems for SA police of attraction of Victorian goldfields in 1851.

9 Haldane, *People's Force*, p. 49.

10 Johnston, *Long Blue Line*, p. 25; Haldane, *People's Force*, pp. 84–5; R. Walker, 'The NSW Police Force, 1862–1900', *Journal of Australian Studies*, 15, 1984, pp. 30–1.

11 Police staff files, A/40173, QSA.

12 See Haldane, *People's Force*, pp. 86–7, in the course of the most sustained discussion of this phenomenon in Australia.

13 R. Reid, *Aspects of Irish Assisted Emigration to New South Wales, 1848–1870*, PhD Thesis, ANU, 1992, pp. 115–119.

14 Police Department *Annual Report* 1926, NSW *PP*, 1926–7, Appendix F; Haldane, *People's Force*, p. 87; cf. Walker, 'NSW Police Force', 1984, p. 30, whose implication that Australian-born were shy of police-work relies on data from a period in which there was still a preponderance of immigrants in the general population.

15 Royal Commission into Aboriginal Deaths in Custody, *Interim Report*, AGPS, Canberra, 1988, p. 44.

16 Cf. Neesham Report, pp. 321, 330 on possible adverse effects on recruitment of ethnic minorities of height and educational requirements in recruiting; also G. Bird, 'Policing Multicultural Australia', in *Policing Australia: Old Issues New Perspectives*, P. Moir and H. Eijkman (eds), Macmillan, Melbourne, 1993, pp. 366–8.

17 *Fitzgerald Report*, pp. 31, 36 and Johnston, *Long Blue Line*, p. 217 for sectarianism earlier in the century.

18 See Clyne, *Colonial Blue*, pp. 22–3 on the recruitment of escaped convicts in South Australia.

19 Police staff files, A/40703, QSA for application form.

20 Actg-Insp. P. Cahion and Sgt. J. A. Wright, 'The police cadet system of NSW', *Australian Police Journal*, 1 (2) Jan. 1947, pp. 100–104.

21 See *Courier-Mail*, Jan. 1993; discussion of the issue in Neesham Report, pp. 317–321, recommending abolition of minimum height standards; Conference of Commissioners of Police, Sydney, 1959 (Mitchell Library), p. 146; Shirley Hotchkiss, 'Policing Promotional Difference: Policewomen in the Queensland Police Service', MA thesis, Griffith University, 1992, p. 47.

22 Haldane, *People's Force*, pp. 86 ff.

23 Circular memoranda, Queensland Police department, 22.9.1909, A/36278.

24 Walker, 'NSW Police Force', p. 33 (NSW); Johnston, *Long Blue Line*, pp. 22 (Qld).

25 Cf. C. D. Shearing, and R. V. Ericson, (1991), 'Culture as figurative action', *British Journal of Sociology*, 42 (4), pp. 481–506 for a recent interpretation of the production of a police culture through such means.

26 Telegram, 22 Oct 1895, Parry-Okeden to Fitzgerald, POL/J1, QSA.

27 Royal Commission on Police, *General Report*, p. xi, Victoria *PP*, 1883, vol. 2.

28 Royal Commission on the Victorian Police, *Report*, p. vii, Victoria *PP*, 1906, vol. 3.

29 Annual Report of the Commissioner of Police, 1915, Western Australia *PP*, 1915, vol. 2.

30 Emsley, *English police*, pp. 151–2, 191–2; B. Weinberger, 'Are the police professionals? An historical account of the British police institution', in *Policing Western Europe*, C. Emsley and B. Weinberger (eds), Greenwood Press, New York, 1991.

31 Bittner, *Aspects of the Police*, p. 5.

32 Royal Commission on Police, 1883, p. xii.

33 Royal Commission on the Victorian Police, 1906, p. ix.

34 Circular memorandum, 19.1.1914, A/36279, QSA.

35 Annual Report of the Commissioner of Police, 1925, p. 4, WA *PP*, 1925, vol. 2.

36 See Haldane, *People's Force*, p. 167, on the inattention of police to training prior to the period of Chief Commissioner Steward (1919–1920).

37 Circular memorandum, 28.3.1935 and 18.11.37, A/36282, QSA.

38 Annual Report of the Commissioner of Police, 1915, p. 4, Western Australia *PP*, 1915, vol. 2; 1925, p. 4, Western Australia *PP*, 1926, vol. 2.

39 Police Department *Annual report*, 1935, p. 2, South Australia *PP*, 1936, vol. 2.

40 Sgt Instr E. C. S. Meldrum, 'The Police Training System of South Australia', *Australian Police Journal*, 1 (2), 1947, pp. 264–271.

41 Cahion and Wright, 'Police cadet system', pp. 100–104.

42 Ibid., p. 104.

43 J. A. Vogelsang and R. W. Whitrod (1949), 'Wartime crime in South Australia', *Australian Police Journal*, 3 (3) 1949, pp. 205–213; for Whitrod's role in the formation of the Australian Police College, see *Conference of Commissioners of Police South Pacific Region*, Sydney, 1959 (Mitchell Library).

44 Det. Insp. C. E. North, 'The Police College at Ryton-on-Dunsmore, Warwickshire', *Australian Police Journal*, 5 (1) 1951, pp. 7–15.

45 R. W. Whitrod, 'Thoughts on the introduction of a police administrative grade', *Public Administration*, 19, 1959–60, p. 122.

46 Ibid., p. 127.

47 Ibid., p. 129.

48 See R. L. Russell, *From Nightingale to Now: Nursing Education in Australia*, Harcourt Brace Jovanovich, Sydney, 1990, esp. chs. 9–11; J. Cattoni, 'Death of a Nightingale: Nursing—a Practice in Search of a Theory', BA Hons. thesis, Griffith University, 1990.

49 Seggie, 'Aspects of the role of police', p. 202 on the indifference of the NSW Police Association to questions of 'qualifications and expertise'.

50 Det Sgt J Pestell (England), 'The professional status of police', *Australian Police Journal*, 5 (4), 1951, p. 302.

51 See chapter 2 above and D. Bradley (1992), 'Escaping Plato's Cave: the Possible Future of Police Education', in *Policing Australia Old Issues New Perspectives*, Moir and Eijkman (eds), Macmillan, Melbourne, 1992, pp. 141–2.

52 *Fitzgerald Report*, p. 211.

53 Finnane, 'Police rules and the organisation of policing', and chapter 8 below.

54 *Fitzgerald Report*, p. 248.

55 Ibid., p. 249.

56 J. Avery, *Police: Force or Service?*, Butterworths, Sydney, 1981.

57 D. Sullivan, 'Educating Police for Effective Job Performance', in *Police Source Book 2*, Swanton et al (eds), p. 635.

58 *Neesham Report*, p. 345.

59 *Fitzgerald Report*, p. 250.

60 *Fitzgerald Report*, p. 250. With the establishment of the Unified National System in tertiary education, the distinction between Colleges of Advanced Education and Universities disappeared as CAEs were amalgamated with or became Universities.

61 Swanton et al (eds), *Police Source Book 2*, pp. 190–217 for summary. Exceptions included Western Australia, Northern Territory and the Australian Capital Territory.

62 Ibid., pp. 218–9.

63 See *Courier Mail*, Mar. 25 1993.

8 Rules and discipline

1 Cf. Sub-Inspect. Foelsche in the Northern Territory in the 1870s: 'no doubt you will say why don't you go this time, my reply is that there are too many tale-tellers in the party; but my official excuse is that it would have delayed the party at least four days', cited in Reid, *Picnic with the Natives*, p. 67.

2 Haldane, *People's Force*, pp. 30–32, 51–52; Hill, *Policing the Colonial Frontier* pp. 572–6 on influence of the Victorian rules on the Otago police; Johnston, *Long Blue Line*, p. 11 for its influence in Queensland.

3 Clyne, *Colonial Blue*, p. 83.

4 E.g. Circular memorandum, 18 May 1905, General Order 735, enforcing compliance with general orders 'which are in many cases disregarded in practice and others treated with scant attention', A/36277, QSA.

5 See D. Dixon, A. K. Bottomley, C. A. Coleman, M. Gill and D. Wall, 'Reality and rules in the construction and regulation of police suspicion', *International Journal of the Sociology of Law*, 17 (1989), pp. 185–206; S. Walker, 'Controlling the Cops: A Legislative Approach To Police Rulemaking', *University of Detroit Law Review* 63(3), 1986, pp. 361–391.

6 Cf. Dalby magistrate's report, April 1862 (62/1447), COL/A29, QSA.

7 Historically, Walker says, American police manuals have suffered from two serious defects. Firstly, they were ignored by superiors and by rank and file; secondly, the manuals grew increasingly technical, concerned with the internal discipline of the police and ignoring discussion of the more difficult policy decisions of everyday policing. Walker, 'Controlling the Cops', p. 368.

8 Finnane, 'Police rules', is the basis for this and the subsequent discussion.

9 See Royal Commission on the Victorian Police Force, *Report*, p. xii.

10 Royal Commission on the Organisation and Administration of the Police Force, Tasmania, 1906, p. 5, Tasmania *PP*, 1906, vol. 55.

11 Report of the Royal Commission . . . into . . . the Criminal Investigation Branch . . . , p. xxviii, Queensland *PP*, 1899, vol. 4.

12 Royal Commission into the Police of Victoria, 1883, p. ix.

13 Summary memorandum, 17 February 1909, COL 203, QSA.

14 See *R. v. Many Many*, 1895 *Queensland Law Journal*, p. 224 (Harding J.) and *R. v. Crown*, 1896 *Queensland Law Journal*, p. 283 (Griffith C.J.). Cf. Circular memoranda, 30 Aug 1906, A/36277, QSA: General order 762, 'Interrogating or conversing with prisoners' drawing police attention to cl. 22 of the *Police Manual* warning against obtaining a confession from a prisoner. This instruction was possibly prompted by an impending Supreme Court appeal against the admission of confessional evidence, see *McNamara v. Edwards, ex parte Edwards*, [1907] *St. R. Qd., 9.*

15 Memorandum 28 Apr. 1909, A/44815, QSA and see Finnane, 'Politics of police powers', pp. 107–8 in *Policing in Australia*, Finnane (ed.).

16 On circumstantial evidence, one of the Kenniff brothers was hanged on conviction for murder; see R. B. Joyce, *Samuel Walker Griffith*, University of Queensland Press, St Lucia, 1984, pp. 228–232.

17 See *Lee Fan v. Dempsey* [1907] *C.L.R.* 5, 310.

18 Home Office correspondence, 1916/10424, HOM/J2185, QSA.

19 RCIADIC, vol. 3, pp. 34–38; cf. D. Dixon, *Detention for questioning in Australia & England*, Hull University Law School, 1992, pp. 36–9 showing the way in which police rules or 'Instructions' interpret judicial dicta in ways which preserve police criteria of factors such as 'reasonableness'.

20 *Fitzgerald Report*, pp. 238–9.

21 Dixon, *Detention for questioning*, p. 50.

22 See Qld Act 1860s; Palmer, 'Making of the Victorian colonial police', p. 73 for Victorian *Police Act* of 1853 giving local magistrates power to discipline police in locality, 16 Vic 24, s. 12 (Victoria); and see Queensland, *Rules for the General Government and Discipline of the Police Force of Queensland*, 1869, rule 96 on powers of Police Magistrates.

23 Clyne, *Colonial Blue*, pp. 150–1.

24 Finnane, 'Governing the police' in F. B. Smith (ed.), *Ireland, England and Australia: 'Essays in honour of Oliver Mac Donagh*, ANU Press, Canberra, 1990.

25 Palmer, *Police and protest*, p. 350; see also Haldane, *People's Force*, pp. 49–50; Sturma, *Vice in a Vicious Society*, pp. 164–5; Finnane, 'Governing the Police'; Emsley, *English Police*, p. 59; H, Boritch, 'Conflict, Compromise and Administrative Convenience: the Police Organization in Nineteenth-Century Toronto', *Canadian Journal of Law and Society*, 3, 1988, pp. 141–174.

26 M. Punch, 'Researching police deviance: a personal encounter with the limitations and liabilities of field-work', *British Journal of Sociology*, 40 (2), pp. 182, 204.

27 Police staff files, A/40113, QSA.

28 Police staff files, A/ 40563, QSA.

29 Clyne, *Colonial Blue*, p. 199.

30 Police staff files, (AF1143), A/40062, QSA.

31 *Police Regulation Act* (Vic) 1946, s.22, amending 1928 Act, ss. 60–65; see also *Police Regulation Act* 1938, s. 12, removing imprisonment as a disciplinary option; Haldane, p. 233 for 1946 changes.

32 Circular memoranda, 4.5.1906, 19.2.1910, A/36277-8, QSA.

33 Finnane, 'Governing the police'.

34 Neesham, pp. 13ff; in 1993 a new commissioner sought to recover the power lost in 1946, *Australian*, 28 April 1993.

35 Annual Reports, NSW Police Department and see Walker, 'NSW Police Force', p. 32.

36 See C. Procter, 'The Police', in *Bjelke-Petersen Premiership*, Patience (ed.).

37 Haldane, *People's Force*, pp. 290–292.

38 Police staff files, A/40313 (Mathers) — inspector demoted; A/40223 (Bowen) — sergeant demoted; A/40293 (Kindregan) — senior constable demoted; A/40343 (Twaddle) — senior constable demoted: A/40554 (Bradburn) — senior constable, QSA; Tasmania: demotion of Superintendent to Inspector in wake of a 1954–5 inquiry into the CIB, Report of the Commissioner of Police, 1955, p. 2, Tasmania *PP*, 1955, vol. 153.

39 Haldane, *People's Force*, p. 124.

40 Johnston, *Long Blue Line*, p. 22.

41 M. O'Sullivan, *Cameos of crime*, Brisbane, 1947; pp. 15–16

42 Police staff file, A/40582 (Keane), QSA.

43 Cf. H. Boritch, 'Conflict, Compromise and Administrative Convenience: The Police Organization in Nineteenth-Century Toronto', *Canadian Journal of Law and Society*, vol. 3, 1988, p. 155 for a similar view of the functions of disciplinary mechanisms in the Toronto police; cf. Emsley, *English Police*, pp. 219–220 who suggests that the 'severity of punishments' declined in English police forces particularly early in the twentieth century, but notes also that in inter-war years this correlated with a decline in the number of defaulters charged with neglect of duty or other minor breaches.

44 T. Wickham, 'The Psychology of Discipline as applied to Criminology', *Australian Police Journal*, 1 (1) 1946, pp. 57–64.

45 Seggie, 'Aspects of the role of the police force', p. 346.

46 See chapter 4 above.

47 Report of the Royal Commission... relating to David Edward Studley-Ruxton, NSW *PP*, 1954–5, vol. 1.

48 G. F. Godfrey, 'The Police and the Press', *Australian Police Journal*, 11(4) 1957, pp. 308–9.
49 M. Goode, 'Complaints about the Police in Australia', in A. Goldsmith, *Complaints against the police: the trend to external review*, Clarendon Press, Oxford, 1991, pp. 143–8.

9 Corruption and reform
1 William Lonsdale to Colonial Secretary, 5 August 1838, Port Phillip, *Historical records of Victoria*, Vol. 1, pp. 193–4.
2 *Fitzgerald Report*, pp. 206ff.
3 E.g. in A. McCoy, *Drug Traffic: narcotics and organized crime in Australia*, Harper and Row, Sydney, 1980.
4 The following discussion draws on material in Police staff files, A/41013 and A/40610, QSA.
5 W. G. Cahill, *The policeman's manual*, Brisbane, 1913, p. 2.
6   Ibid., p. 7.
7 See T. Wickham, 'Advice to detectives' *Australian Police Journal*, 2 (1), 1948, pp. 34–49.
8 Circular memorandum, 20.10.1904, A/36277, QSA.
9 Circular memorandum, 22.12.1909, A/36278, QSA.
10 Sly grog files, 149SG—case of Sun Lee, POL O10, QSA.
11 Police staff files, A/38726, QSA.
12 McCoy, *Drug traffic*, pp. 178–9 for Healey and pp. 104–6 for Victorian police.
13 C. Fox, 'Bookies and coppers: policing starting price betting', in *Workers & Intellectuals*, R. Nile and B. York (eds), Edward Blackwood, London, 1992.
14 *Fitzgerald Report*, p. 65.
15 Allen, *Sex and Secrets*, pp. 73–7 and 90–6 and 'Policing since 1880: some questions of sex'; S. Davies, 'Working their way to respectability: women, vagrancy and reform in late nineteenth century Melbourne', *Lilith*, 6, 1989, pp. 50–63.
16 J. Weeks, *Sex, Politics and Society*, Longmans Cheshire, London, 1981, Ch. 5.
17 J. Allen, 'The making of a prostitute proletariat', in *So Much Hard Work: Women and Prostitution in Australian History*, K. Daniels (ed.), Fontana, Sydney, 1984. See also chapters by R. Evans (for Queensland) and R. Davidson (for Western Australia) in the same volume.
18 Daniels (ed.), *So Much Hard Work*; K. Thomas, 'The double standard', *Journal of the History of Ideas*, vol. 20, No. 2, 1959, pp. 195–216.
19 See J. Allen, 'Rose Scott', feminism and sexuality, 1880–1925', *Australian Feminist Studies*, No. 7–8, 1988, pp. 65–91.
20 Finnane, 'Politics of police powers', p. 101.
21 J. Allen, 'Policing since 1880: some questions of sex', in *Policing in Australia*, Finnane (ed.).

22 J. O'Hara, *A Mug's Game: A History of Gaming and Betting in Australia*, NSW University Press, Kensington, 1988, pp. 171–6; W. Selby, *Motherhood in Labor's Queensland*, PhD thesis, Griffith University, 1992.

23 See Johnston, *Long blue line*, pp. 64–5, 161–5 for a detailed account of Queensland policing of sly grog and McCoy, *Drug traffic*, pp. 167–76 for corruption in such policing in NSW.

24 Circular memo, 27 July 1910, A/36278, QSA.

25 Hill, *Policing the Colonial Frontier*, Part 2, pp. 557–8.

26 Fox, 'Bookies and coppers'; O'Hara, *A mug's game*.

27 Royal Commission Investigating Certain Charges of Corruption, *Report*, p. xvi, WA *PP*, 1937, vol. 1.

28 Ibid., p. xvii.

29 Cf. McCoy, *Drug traffic,* and G. Wardlaw, 'Drug control policies and organised crime', in *Understanding crime and criminal justice*, M. Findlay and R. Hogg (eds), Law Book Co., Sydney, 1988.

30 O'Hara, *A mug's game*, pp. 188–194.

31 Ibid., p. 192.

Conclusion

1 *Australian*, 22 July 1993.

2 *Australian*, 27 January 1993.

Further reading and research

The history of policing in Australia is a subject of growing interest to professional historians and, evidently, to police themselves. Regrettably the subject does not appear to have seized the imagination of many post-graduate students, though this situation seems likely to change in the current climate of public debate over policing. Police departments over the last decade have tended to facilitate greater access to their records and encouraged the writing of their history. The New South Wales Police Department remains an undistinguished exception to this tendency, having in fact increased restrictions on access to its records a decade ago.

Three States now have substantial published histories of their police forces, all of them verging on the genre of 'official history', to the extent that two were written by serving police officers and the third was a commissioned history. R. Haldane, *The People's Force: A History of the Victoria Police* (Melbourne University Press, Carlton, 1986)and W. R. Johnston, *The Long Blue Line: A History of the Queensland Police* (Boolarong Press, Bowen Hills, 1992) are more comprehensive than R. Clyne, *Colonial Blue* (Wakefield Press, Netley, 1987) which covers the South Australia police only to the First World War. Other States await their historians of policing, although useful introductions may be obtained in G. M. O'Brien, *The Australian Police Forces* (Oxford University Press, Melbourne, 1960) and the relevant brief histories of individual forces in B. Swanton et al (eds), *Police Source Book 2*, (Australian Institute of Criminology, Canberra, 1986). A valuable treatment of Tasmania police history is available in A. K. Jackman, 'Development of Police Administration in Tasmania 1804–1960', Dip. Public Admin. thesis, University of Tasmania, 1966.

For New South Wales, R. Walker 'The New South Wales Police Force, 1862–1900' in *Journal of Australian Studies*, 15, 1984, pp. 25–38, may be complemented by the unpublished thesis of K. Seggie, 'Aspects of the Role of the Police Force in New South Wales and its relation to the Government, 1900–1930', PhD thesis, Macquarie University, 1988 valuable especially for the period 1900–1940. The early history of New South Wales policing has been examined in a number of publications, especially the invaluable early work of H. King, 'Some aspects of police administration in New South Wales 1825–1851', *Journal of the Royal Australian Historical Society*, 42, pt. 5, 1956, pp. 205–230. M. Sturma, *Vice in a vicious society* (University of Queensland Press, St. Lucia, 1983) explores the policing of crime and public order in early New South Wales, while two recent works have added immeasurably to the small body of work in Australia which analyses policing as part of a history of legal regulation and criminal justice: D. Neal, *The rule of law in a penal colony: law and power in early New South Wales* (Cambridge University Press, Melbourne, 1991), including a chapter on policing in early New South Wales and H. Golder, *High & Responsible Office: a history of the New South Wales magistracy* (Oxford University Press/Sydney University Press, Melbourne, 1991), which touches on police history at numerous points. Such a context is also addressed in A. Davidson, *The invisible state* (Cambridge University Press, Melbourne, 1991). P. J. Byrne, *Criminal law and colonial subject New South Wales 1810–1830* (Cambridge University Press, Melbourne, 1993) is a richly sourced treatment of its subject with a lengthy treatment of policing, not confined to a history of public police, in the early colony. A special issue of the *Royal New South Wales Historical Society Journal* (vol. 77, part 3, December 1991) with articles by Sturma, Garton and Golder provides a convenient recent overview of many of the themes addressed in their more detailed historical work.

For more specialised work, the reader or scholar must engage in some detective work of their own. Two kinds of records are basic to the historian's trade: the published official records, including Parliamentary debates, official inquiries and annual reports, and the public archives. A guide to many of the former on a state by state basis for the twentieth century (to the mid–1970s) is available in S. White and A. Edwards, *Criminological Materials in the Parliamentary Papers of Australia & New Zealand* (Australian National University, Canberra, 1977) and in the various guides and 'checklists' to published reports of official inquiries, edited for all the States and Commonwealth for the nineteenth and twentieth centuries by D. Borchhardt.

Archival sources are best sought through the respective archives authorities for each jurisdiction. A useful guide to the types of material available is H. D. Harris and G. Presland, *Cops and Robbers: A Guide to Researching 19th Century Police and Criminal Records in Victoria, Australia* (Harriland Press, Nunawading, 1990; see also R. Fosteret al, *South Australian Police Historical Society*, Australian Legal Record Inventory, Working Paper No. 2, Adelaide, 1989). Generally there are a number of categories of records which are indispensable to understanding policing through departmental archives. They include police watch-house books, police court or petty sessions books, police diaries and station records, and general administrative correspondence between the commissioner's office and various levels of the police organisation. All have been used in different ways in various chapters in this book. Comprehensive guides to police records in Australia await publication, although the official Guides to the archives of Victoria and New South Wales provide detailed holdings of records specific to those states.

Using these types of records, considerable advances in understanding the history of specialised functions of police have been made in recent years. Much work could and should be done on policing local communities. Some examples include S. Wilson,

'Police Work: The Role of the Police in the Kalgoorlie Community, 1897–1898' in *Journal of Australian Studies,* No. 11, November, 1982, pp. 9–20 and M. O'Connor, 'Policing in a Country Town, the 1860s and Today' in R. Tomasic and R. Lucas (eds), *Power, Regulation and Resistance, Studies in the Sociology of Law* (Canberra College of Advanced Education, Canberra, 1986), pp. 150–160. There is little work on the policing of urban locales, but see H. Golder and R.Hogg, 'Policing Sydney in the late nineteenth century' in M. Finnane (ed.), *Policing in Australia: historical perspectives* (New South Wales University Press, Kensington, NSW, 1987) pp. 59–73, C. McConville, 'From criminal class to underworld' in G. Davison et al (eds.), *The Outcasts of Melbourne. Essays in Social History* (Allen and Unwin, Sydney, London, 1985) pp. 69–90 and D. Palmer, 'The making of the Victorian colonial police: from colonisation to the new police', MA (Criminological Studies) thesis, LaTrobe University, 1990.

More attention has been paid in recent years to the history of policing in relation to Aborigines. This is in fact rapidly becoming one of the best known fields of policing history, though much detailed local statistical and case study work might be done in the future. The native police in various guises and jurisdictions have attracted significant attention. The best study is M. H. Fels, *Good Men and True. The Aboriginal Police of the Port Phillip District, 1837–1853* (Melbourne University Press, Carlton, 1988), but it is confined to a study of Port Phillip and to a short period during what was arguably a more favourable context for meliorative Aboriginal policy than later. H. Reynolds, *With the White People* (Penguin, Ringwood, 1991) reviews the history of the native police more generally, while B. Rosser, *Up Rode the Troopers: the black police in Queensland* (University of Queensland Press, St. Lucia, Qld., 1990), paints a considerably less favourable picture of the Queensland police. N. Loos, *Invasion and Resistance. Aboriginal–European relations on the north Queensland frontier, 1861–1897* (Australian National University Press, Canberra, Miami, 1982) and G. Reid, *A Picnic with the Natives. Aboriginal–European relations in the Northern Territory to 1910* (Melbourne University Press, Carlton, Vic., 1990) provide a great deal of material on the policing of Aborigines generally in the later nineteenth century in north Queensland and the Northern Territory respectively. For the general context of dispossession in Tasmania in the early nineteenth century, see L. Ryan *The Aboriginal Tasmanians* (University of Queensland Press, St Lucia, 1981) and L. Robson, *A History of Tasmania,* Vol. 1 (Oxford University Press, Melbourne, 1983) and for Western Australia, A. Gill, 'Aborigines, Settlers and Police in the Kimberleys, 1887–1905' in *Studies in Western Australian History,* No. 1, 1977, is valuable on the late nineteenth century.

Detailed work on the history of the policing of Aborigines in the twentieth century is less available. Inevitably histories of Aborigines in the era of Protection touch on the contexts of policing, as in A. Haebich, *For their own good. Aborigines and government in the southwest of Western Australia, 1900–1940* (University of Western Australia Press, Nedlands, 1988) on Western Australia and, on the Northern Territory, A. McGrath, *Born in the cattle. Aborigines in cattle country* (Allen and Unwin, Sydney, 1987). Important works with a historical dimension on Aborigines, police and the criminal justice system include E. Eggleston, *Fear, favour and affection,* (Australian National University Press, Canberra, 1976), C. Cunneen and T. Robb, *Criminal justice in north-west New*

South Wales, (NSW Bureau of Crime Statistics and Research, Sydney, 1987) and G. Cowlishaw, *Black, white or brindle: race in rural Australia* (Cambridge University Press, Melbourne, 1988). An important perspective on the behaviour and attitudes of police towards Aborigines in the 1950s is provided in K. S. Inglis, *The Stuart Case,* (Melbourne University Press, Parkville, 1961). The many reports of the Royal Commission into Aboriginal Deaths in Custody (1987–91), including those on individuals as well as regional reports and the final Report, published in 1991 provide invaluable evidence for understanding the relations between police and Aborigines in the late twentieth century. A recent overview of the history of Aborigines and the criminal justice system is provided by A. McGrath, 'Colonialism, crime and civilisation', *Australian Cultural History*, 12, 1993, pp. 100–114.

From being an area which was criticised as neglected and invisible a decade ago, the history of policing as it affects women, as victims, offenders and police officers, has begun to receive significant attention. The key reference for Australia is J. Allen, *Sex and Secrets: crimes involving Australian women since 1880* (Oxford University Press, Melbourne, 1990) and the many articles of the same author. Regrettably little further work appears to have been carried out on the history of the policing of domestic violence to build on a key article by Allen, 'The Invention of the Pathological Family: An Historical Study of Family Violence in New South Wales, 1880–1939' in C. O'Donnell and J. Craney (eds), *Family Violence in Australia* (Longmans Cheshire, Melbourne, 1982). Prostitution has been examined in various States in the collection edited by K. Daniels, *So much hard work* (Fontana Collins, Sydney, 1984). Other dimensions of women's experience of policing are discussed in S. Davies, 'Working their way to respectability: women, vagrancy and reform in late nineteenth century Melbourne', *Lilith*, 6, 1989, pp. 50–63. Contemporary attention to issues involving women and crime has included the edited volume of contributions, S. Mukherjee and J. Scutt (eds.), *Women and Crime*, (George Allen and Unwin in association with Australian Institute of Criminology, Sydney, 1981) and the official inquiries into violence which have been held in the last few years, including *Beyond these walls*, Report of the Queensland Domestic Violence Task Force, Brisbane, 1988, and the results of a national inquiry, *Violence: directions for Australia* (National Committee on Violence, Australian Institute of Criminology, Canberra, 1990). The history of women police is unwritten, except for the biography of one of the first two New South Wales women police, in V. Kelly, *Rugged angel: the amazing career of policewoman Lillian Armfield* (Angus and Robertson, Sydney, 1961).

The range of general functions of police, including the policing of public order as well as crime control and prosecution, is yet to receive major historical treatment in Australia. An overview of some of the relevant debates and themes is in M. Finnane and S. Garton, 'The work of policing: social relations and the criminal justice system in Queensland, 1880–1914', in *Labour History*, No. 62, 1992, pp. 52–70 (Part 1) and No. 63, 1992, pp. 43–64 (Part 2). A range of diverse subjects including the policing of bushranging, lunacy, political dissent, crime, and public order is dealt with in M. Finnane (ed.), *Policing in Australia Historical Perspectives* (New South Wales University Press, Kensington, 1987). D. Moore, 'Origins of the Police Mandate: The Australian Case Reconsidered', *Police Studies*, 14, 1991, pp. 107–120 brings together a historical perspective and an understanding of contemporary policing to provide an important overview of its subject.

The policing and prosecution of specific crimes has received some attention in recent years. P. Grabosky, *Sydney in ferment* (Australian National University Press, Canberra, 1977) dealing with 'crime and official reaction', covers both nineteenth and twentieth centuries and is valuable for an overview of trends in policing and punishment. It has not been repeated for any other cities or States in Australia. A criminological study of official crime statistics is outlined in S. K. Mukherjee, *Crime Trends in Twentieth Century Australia* (Allen and Unwin, Sydney, 1980), to be compared with Allen, *Sex and Secrets*, in respect of crimes involving women, as victims and offenders . J. Braithwaite, 'The political economy of punishment' in E. Wheelwright and K. Buckley (eds), *The political economy of capitalism*, vol. 4 (ANZ Books, Sydney, 1980) interprets crime and punishment from a neo-marxist perspective, while S. Garton, 'The state and labour markets: a critique' in M. Findlay and R. Hogg (eds), *Understanding Crime and Criminal Justice* (Law Book Co., Sydney, 1988) reviews such perspectives historically.

Homicide has been the subject of little work apart from that of Allen, but is addressed from the perspective of the prosecution of Aborigines, in S. Davies, 'Aborigines, murder and the criminal law in early Port Phillip' in *Historical Studies*, vol. 22, No. 88, April 1987, pp. 313–335. Rape has been examined in a number of articles including D. Philips, 'Sex, Race, Violence and the Criminal Law in Victoria: Anatomy of a Rape Case in 1888', *Labour History*, No. 52, May 1987, pp. 30–49, G. Reekie, 'Writing about rape in 1888' in *Australia 1888 Bulletin*, No. 42, November 1983, pp. 31–39, and A. M. Collins, 'Testimonies of sex: rape in Queensland, 1880–1919' in *Journal of Australian Studies*, No. 29, June 1991, pp. 50–63. Other crimes and their policing which have been examined historically in Australia include the colonial phenomenon of bushranging, in R. Walker, 'Bushranging in Fact and Legend' in *Historical Studies*, vol. 11, No. 42, April 1964, pp. 206–221, J. Hirst, *The birth of colonial democracy, New South Wales 1848–1884* (Allen and Unwin, Sydney, 1988) and J. McQuilton, *The Kelly outbreak, 1878 –1880: the geographical dimension of social banditry* (Melbourne University Press, Carlton, 1979).

Few other distinct categories of crime have been the subject of historical investigation. A major exception is the work of A. McCoy, *Drug Traffic: Narcotics and organised Crime in Australia* (Harper and Row, Sydney, 1980). Other aspects of the history of organised crime are examined in D. Hickie, *The Prince and the Premier* (Angus and Robertson, North Ryde, 1985). Some perspectives on the work of police in crime investigation are available in a chapter by A. Castles, 'Detective work', in B. Gammage and P. Spearritt (eds), *Australians 1938* (Fairfax, Syme and Weldon Associates, Broadway, 1987) pp. 319 – 325, dealing with crime work in 1930s Melbourne, and M. Brown and P. Wilson, *Justice and nightmares* (New South Wales University Press, Sydney, 1992), dealing with forensic science successes and failures.

Work on political policing in Australia has been growing. There is a major history of the pre-ASIO period in F. Cain, *The Origins of Political Surveillance in Australia* (Angus and Robertson, Sydney 1983). Other sources include R. Hall, *The Secret State:*

Australia's spy industry (Cassell Australia, Stanmore, 1978) and B. Toohey and W. Pinwheel *Oyster: the story of the Australian Secret Intelligence Service* (W. Heinemann, Port Melbourne, 1989). The ill-defined boundary between public police and right-wing political activism in the inter-war period is the subject of A. Moore, *The Secret Army and the Premier: conservative paramilitary organisations in New South Wales 1930–32* (NSW University Press, Kensington, 1989). The State special branches await extended treatment but see A. Moore, 'A secret policeman's lot: the working life of Fred Longbottom of the New South Wales Police Special Branch', in J. Shields (ed.), *All our labours: oral histories of working life in 20th century Sydney*, (NSW University Press, Kensington, 1992) pp. 193–226 and M. Findlay, 'The Justice Wood Inquiry: the role of Special branch in the Cameron Conspiracy', in K. Carrington et al (ed.), *Travesty! Miscarriages of Justice*, (Pluto Press Australia in association with Academics for Justice, Leichhardt, 1991) pp. 27–43. Indispensable on the relations between ASIO and the special branches is the report of Mr Justice White on Special Branch Security Records, in South Australia *Parliamentary Papers*, 1978.

The policing of other particular populations is a matter of increasing attention. The subject of the policing of migrants has received little attention, but see M. Finnane, 'The Irish and crime in the late nineteenth century: a statistical inquiry', in O. MacDonagh and W. Mandle (eds), *Irish–Australian Studies, Papers delievered at the Fifth Irish–Australian Conference* (Australian National University Press, Canberra, 1989) pp. 77–98 and M. Finnane and C. Moore, 'Kanaka slaves or willing workers? Melanesian workers and the Queensland criminal justice system in the 1890s', *Criminal Justice History An International Annual*, vol. 13, 1992, pp. 141–160. The policing of children's welfare receives attention in R. van Krieken, *Children and the state: social control and the formation of child welfare* (Allen and Unwin, North Ryde, 1992) and is addressed also in D. Walker, 'Youth on trial: the Mt. Rennie case' *Labour History*, No. 50, 1986, pp. 28–41 and M. Finnane, 'Larrikins, delinquents and cops' in C. Alder and R. White (eds), *Police and Youth in Australia* (Cambridge University Press, Melbourne, 1994). The policing of labour is a subject for R. Walker, 'Violence in industrial conflicts in New South Wales in the later nineteenth century', *Historical Studies*, No. 86, 1986, pp. 54–70 and more generally in M. Finnane and S. Garton, 'The work of policing—social relations and the criminal justice system in Queensland, 1880–1914', cited above. The potential of close historical scrutiny of the police record to throw light on a more general social history is evident in G. Wotherspoon, ' "The Greatest Menace Facing Australia": Homosexuality and the State in NSW during the Cold War', *Labour History*, No. 56, 1989, pp. 15–28. The journal *Labour History* has become probably the chief Australian location for the social history of policing.

Regrettably there are as yet no major biographies of police commissioners, if one excepts Blamey of Victoria, the subject of one by J. Hetherington, *Blamey: the biography of Field-Marshall Sir Thomas Blamey* (Cheshire, Melbourne, 1954). B. Swanton, 'Commissioner James Mitchell: a biographical sketch', *Journal of the Royal Historical Society*, vol. 70, No. 4, April 1985, pp. 280–287, is a rare journal treatment of one of the NSW police commissioners, and there are short journal biographies of other NSW police commissioners by the same author. Many of the major figures have however been the subject of entries in the *Australian Dictionary of Biography*. Other police have occasionally written memoirs, often worth reading for the colour they add to the dry police annual reports, but they need to be read beside the archival record as well. Oral history is likely to be another fruitful source of police histories in the future and has been put to good use by A. Moore in the article on Fred Longbottom, cited above.

Contemporary writing on Australian policing is growing in volume. There are few monographs but many edited collections. P. O'Malley, *Law, capitalism and democracy: a sociology of Australian legal order* (George Allen and Unwin, Sydney, 1983), includes one of the few attempts to establish an argument about the historical sociology of policing in Australia, while C. Corns, 'Policing and social change', *Australian and New Zealand Journal of Sociology*, vol. 24, No. 1, March 1988, pp. 32–46, reviews some recent trends. D. Chappell and P. Wilson, *The Police and the Public in Australia and New Zealand* (University of Queensland Press, St Lucia, 1969), was the first study of its subject in Australia. Some of its results may be compared with the surveys conducted for the Neesham Inquiry in Victoria, *Committee of Inquiry, Victoria Police Force, Final Report*, Volume Two (Ministry for Police and Emergency Services, Melbourne, 1985). A number of collections have been published in the last two decades, including K. Milte with T. Weber (eds), *Police in Australia: development, functions and procedures* (Butterworth, Sydney, 1977), successive editions of D. Chappell and P. Wilson (eds), *The Australian Criminal Justice System* (Butterworths, Sydney, 1977 and 1986), M. Findlay and R. Hogg (eds.), *Understanding Crime and Criminal Justice* (Law Book Co., North Ryde, 1988), M. Findlay, S. Egger and J. Sutton (eds) *Issues in Criminal Justice Administration* (George Allen and Unwin, London, 1983), I. Freckelton and H. Selby (eds), *Police in our society* (Butterworth, North Ryde, NSW, 1988), D. Chappell and P. Wilson (eds), *Australian Policing: Contemporary Issues* (Butterworth, Sydney, 1989) and P. Moir and H. Eijkman (eds), *Policing Australia: Old Issues New Perspectives* (Macmillan and Co., Melbourne, 1992). The recent development of tertiary education for police is likely to see an increase in both research and publishing on Australian policing, as evident in a current set of introductory texts by K. Bryett et al, *Introduction to Policing Series* (Butterworths, Sydney, 1993, 4 vols. in press.)

Finally, a number of comments in this book have emphasised the importance of a comparative perspective. The international publications on policing are extensive. Recent texts which are helpful for contextualising historical and contemporary developments in policing include M. Tonry and N. Morris (eds), *Modern Policing* (University of Chicago Press, Chicago and London, 1992), especially valuable for its overview of current perspectives in North America and Britain including three historical essays. C. Emsley, *The English Police: a political and social history* (St. Martins Press, New York, 1991), R. Reiner, *The Politics of the Police* (Harvester Wheatsheaf, New York, 1985) and M. Brogden, T. Jefferson and S. Walklate, *Introducing policework* (Unwin Hyman, London, 1988) are all important recent contributions to the new history of policing in England and Wales, for which there are an increasing number of specialist studies. S. H. Palmer, *Police and Protest in England and Ireland 1780–1850* (Cambridge, University Press, Cambridge, 1988) is a major study of the development of police in Ireland and England. For international comparative perspectives, see D. Bayley, *Patterns of policing: a comparative international analysis* (Rutgers University Press, New Brunswick, New Jersey, 1985) and C. Emsley, *Policing and its context,*

1750–1870 (Macmillan, London, 1984). Policing in the British empire has been the subject of attention in two recent volumes edited by D. Killingray and D. Anderson, *Policing the empire: government, authority and control, 1830–1940* and *Policing and decolonisation: nationalism, politics and the police, 1917–1965* (both published by Manchester University Press, Manchester, 1991) and is the subject of an influential article by M. Brogden, 'An Act to Colonise the Internal Lands of the Island: Empire and the Origins of the Professional Police', *International Journal of the Sociology of Law,* 15, 1987, pp. 179–208.

R. Hill, *Policing the colonial frontier: the theory and practice of coercive social and racial control in New Zealand, 1767–1867* (Vol.1, Parts 1 and 2) (V. R. Ward, Wellington, New Zealand, 1986) is a massively detailed and informative history of policing in New Zealand, supplemented by the same author's *The Colonial Frontier Tamed New Zealand Policing in Transition, 1867–1886* (Historical Branch, Dept of Internal Affairs, GP Books, Wellington, 1989) and soon to be supplemented by a volume on the twentieth century by G. Dunstall. Canada, another important imperial comparison, is less well served, but see R. C. Macleod, *The NWMP and law enforcement, 1873–1905* (University of Toronto Press, Toronto, 1973), N. Rogers, 'Serving Toronto the Good: the Development of the City Police Force 1834–1880', in V. Russell (ed.), *Forging a Consensus: Historical Essays on Toronto* (University of Toronto Press, Toronto, 1984), H. Boritch and J. Hagan, 'Crime and the changing forms of class control: Policing Public Order in "Toronto the Good", 1859–1955', *Social Forces,* vol. 66, No. 2, 1987, pp. 307–335 and H. Boritch, 'Conflict, Compromise and Administrative Convenience: the Police Organization in Nineteenth-Century Toronto', *Canadian Journal of Law and Society,* 3, 1988, pp. 141–174. Historical and contemporary perspectives on Canadian policing and Aboriginal peoples are reviewed in a major government inquiry, contemporaneous with the Royal Commission into Aboriginal Deaths in Custody, *Report of the Aboriginal Justice Inquiry of Manitoba,* 1991, 2 vols.

Index